The Holy Drama

IRANIAN STUDIES SERIES

The *Iranian Studies Series* publishes high-quality scholarship on various aspects of Iranian civilisation, covering both contemporary and classical cultures of the Persian cultural area. The contemporary Persian-speaking area includes Iran, Afghanistan, Tajikistan, and Central Asia, while classical societies using Persian as a literary and cultural language were located in Anatolia, the Caucasus, Central Asia and the Indo-Pakistani subcontinent. The objective of the series is to foster studies of the literary, historical, religious and linguistic products in Iranian languages. In addition to research monographs and reference works, the series publishes English-Persian critical text-editions of important texts. The series intends to publish resources and original research and make them accessible to a wide audience.

THE HOLY DRAMA

PERSIAN PASSION PLAY IN MODERN IRAN

Mahnia A. Nematollahi Mahani

Leiden University Press

Cover design: Tarek Atrissi Design
Lay out: Hanneke Kossen, Amsterdam and De Typesetter, Haren

ISBN 978 90 8728 115 1
e-ISBN 978 94 0060 034 8
NUR 630

In loving memory of my parents,
who inspired me to move forward in my life

Contents

Preface

From my childhood I remember the beginning of the month of Muharram, when my mother wore black to honour the martyrdom of Imām Ḥuseyn. People in my city, Kerman, as in other cities, held mourning rites during the ten days from the first to the tenth of Muharram, the first month of the Islamic calendar, to commemorate the death of Imām Ḥuseyn. Their houses were thrown open to the public. The city was decorated with black cloths and banners. Many people dressed in black to show their commitment to Shiism and their fidelity to Imām Ḥuseyn. Others would make vows to distribute sweets and sherbet among the poor or to the people on the streets, and believed that they received God's grace for doing so. Sheep were sacrificed and the meat distributed among the needy, people cooked food and gave it to those who came to their door. Those who received the food treated it as a sanctified gift.

Finally, the tenth of Muḥarram dawns. People gather on the streets and in the bazaars through which the many processions to mourn the martyrdom of Imām Ḥuseyn will pass. The sounds of drums, cymbal and clarinet announce that the first procession is coming. As a child, on hearing the music, I would hurry outside, curious to watch the procession. At the head of each procession are several men carrying banners. They are followed by the musicians, and then the procession itself. The *ta'ziya* director walks along with the procession and reads elegies for the martyrs of Karbalā. He carries a copy (*nuskha*) of the script to read. He both directs the procession and stimulates the audience to lamentation and mourning. There is a harmony between the musicians, the procession, and the people who stand on both sides of the street or bazaar, crying and beating their chests and heads.

The procession carries various flags and banners in black or green, on which the names of Imām Ḥuseyn and his family are sewn. There are some cross-shaped banners, called *'alam*. They are large and very heavy and are decorated with specific signs: green and coloured cloths, bronze pigeons and bronze hands. A young man rests the 'alam in a holster on his belt, and others help him. When he arrives at an open space in the middle of the bazaar, the tone of the music changes and he begins whirling slowly. The people step back to give him more space to whirl. It is very important that the *ʿalam* does not fall. That would be a bad omen.

Alongside each procession walks a youth carrying rose water, which he sprinkles on the spectators. Another youth carries water or sherbet and distributes it among the people. It may take hours for all the processions to pass through the bazaar. The procession group may eventually arrive at a large house, or an open space prepared as a theatre, where they perform the *taʿziya*, but in my childhood in Kerman and other large cities this was rare. At noon the members of the procession go to the houses to which they have been invited, taking blessings and honouring the landlord.

I also have a memory of a *taʿziya* play being performed in Mahan, a small district in Kerman province. Close to the tomb of the master of the Nematollahi order, Shāh Nematollāh Vali, a crowd gathers. They stand in a circle and from either side the antagonists and protagonists ride in on their horses, swords in hand. The protagonists recite the elegies of Imām Ḥuseyn, and the antagonists answer them. Then they fight, and those representing Imām Ḥuseyn and his companions are killed. At that moment, a man wearing a lion dress enters the arena, pouring dust and straw on his head. He is followed by several camels bearing litters, and young boys seated in each. As they enter, the people lament loudly, for they represent Imām Ḥuseyn's family being carried into captivity.

Acknowledgements

I would like to take this opportunity to express my gratitude to those who have helped me: to Dr. Ali Asghar Seyed-Gohrab for his supervision, advice, and guidance from the very early stages of this research. He has encouraged and supported me in various ways. I am indebted to him more than he knows. Words fail me to express my deepest appreciation to my husband Mahyar Kavoosi, whose support and love for me have taken a load off my shoulders. I am indebted to him for being unselfishly beside me.

I am very much indebted to the Netherlands Organisation for Scientific Research (NWO) for the opportunity to write my PhD dissertation as part of the project *Of Poetry and Politics: Classical Poetic Concepts in New Politics of Twentieth-Century Iran*, and to finish this book. I would also like to thank Sen McGlinn for his careful editing of the text, and J.G.J. ter Haar for his invaluable comments and suggestions. I am also grateful to anonymous reviewers who offered me valuable suggestions to improve the contents of the book. Any inconsistency to be found in this book is my responsiblity.

Studies on Persian Passion Play

Despite the fundamental importance of passion play (*ta'ziya*) in Iranian cultural patterns, studies on the topic have been limited. More research on the topic is necessary to fully explicate how deeply *ta'ziya* has influenced Iranians' senses and thought.

Scholarly research on passion play commenced with the publishing of Peter J. Chelkowski's 1971 article 'Dramatic and Literary Aspects of Ta'ziya-khāni-Iranian Passion Play'. Notably, this piece offers a general and clear overview of various aspects of *ta'ziya* performance, such as its historical development, players, place of performance and its decorations, and its embedded narrative and mystical elements.[1] Ṣādiq Humāyūni published another study on *ta'ziya* in 1975 entitled *Ta'ziya va ta'ziya-khāni*. Aside from addressing the historical roots of passion play, this book examines the text, instruments and characteristics of the players. Also of significance, it contains the following *ta'ziyas*, in addition to several medieval manuscripts of *ta'ziya* texts: *ta'ziya* of *Qāsem*, *ta'ziya* of *'Abbās*, *ta'ziya* of *Imâm Reẓā* and *ta'ziya ḥaẓrat-e Ma'ṣūma*.[2] The first two illustrate the tragic events that happened in Karbalā.

Another scholar, Mahmoud Ayoub, explores how *ta'ziya* performance and the conceptualization of Ḥuseyn's death have been derived from the traditions later attributable to the Prophet in his work *Redemptive Suffering in Islam* (1978). Such Prophetic traditions are used to show that the angels informed the Prophet about Ḥuseyn's cruel death in order to promote a sense of legitimate leadership amongst the audience. Ayoub further elaborates the latent effects of *ta'ziya* on the Shiite Iranians. For instance, Shiites actively participate in *ta'ziya* to receive heavenly rewards. Their act guarantees their eternal life in Paradise. Ayoub also examines the growth and expansion of *ta'ziya* performance in various periods. He describes the places, instruments and their symbolic meanings, and the audience's reactions. The importance of lamentation poetry (*marāṯi*) and its development in regards to the motives related to Ḥuseyn's death is another subject that is dealt with in his book. Ayoub shows how the Shiite Muslims treat Ḥuseyn's tomb as a sacred sanctuary (*ḥaram*).[3]

In 1979, an invaluable collection of articles on the topic under the title of *Ta'ziyeh: Ritual and Drama in Iran*, edited by Chelkowski, was published. As the outcome of a symposium organized by the Shiraz Festive of Arts in the summer of 1976, the book deals with yet another aspect of *ta'ziya*: its origin, method of performance and symbolic meaning of the instruments, cultural dimensions, and its roots among Iranians before Islam. The literary and musical progression of *ta'ziya*, as well as its philosophy, are studied. Several articles are dedicated to addressing the extent to which Western-style theatre is influenced by *ta'ziya*.

Moreover, Chelkowski published an article in 1984 titled 'Islam in Modern Drama and Theater,' in which he illustrates various theatrical plays in Iran such as *naqqāli*, *rūhowzi*, *kheyma šab-bāzi* and *rowza-khāni*. Chelkowski enriches this study with analysis of the development of written drama in Iran and the Middle East in conjunction with the social changes surrounding theatre. He goes on to explain various aspects of several rare *ta'ziyas*; namely, *Dhekr-e Muṣibat-e bar dār kardan-e Manṣūr-e Ḥallāj raḥmatullāh aleyh* (a remembrance of the tragedy of Ḥallāj on the gallows 'God blesses him').[4] In 1985, the journal *Drama Review* published yet another article on *ta'ziya* by Chelkowski entitled 'Shia Muslim Processional Performances.' In it, he sketches the development of *ta'ziya* performance from its Buyid dynastic beginnings (352/963), to the victory of the Islamic Revolution (1357/1979). Chelkowski also discusses various paraphernalia, such as *nakhl* or horses, prepared for performances, as well as places where *ta'ziya* has been performed, including open and enclosed areas, streets, and *tekkiya*.[5] In 1986, Chelkowski published two articles in *al-Ṣerāt* magazine. In the first, entitled 'Popular Shī'ī Mourning Ritual,' he discusses ritual performance in the Middle East in Arab, Persian, Turkish and South Asian Muslim communities.[6] In the second, 'From Maqātil Literature to Drama,' Chelkowski illustrates how Ḥuseyn's death is depicted in *ta'ziya* texts written by Arab composers. At the end of this article the author offers a translation from a *ta'ziya* entitled The Martyrdom of the Luminous Leader of the Bani Hāšem, Ḥaẓrat-e Abū 'l-Faẓl al-Abbās.[7]

Michael M.J. Fischer's *Iran: From Religious Dispute to Revolution* (1980) sheds light on the political conflict over passion play performance between several Iranian intellectuals and modern Shiite *'ulamā* such as Khomeini and Aḥmad Kasravi.[8] The author mentions that in the city of Yazd, several objects, such as a mirrored *nakhl*, are carried as symbols of Ḥuseyn's martyrdom and the captivity of his family. In three small villages outside of the city, parades represent Ḥuseyn's martyrdom. He further draws a comparison between the biblical story of Joseph and his brothers, and the Qur'ānic story and *ta'ziya* texts, with the intention of showing that, for the Shiites, the concepts of sacrifice and suffering have a deep meaning. Fischer additionally discusses *'Āšūrā* from historical and ethnographical perspectives in order to demonstrate how these events and their consequences have evolved into a remedy for social problems.[9]

A scholarly article written by Mary Hegland titled 'Two Images of Ḥuseyn: Accommodation and Revolution in an Iranian Village' (1983) is also worth mentioning. Poignantly, she stresses the influence of Ḥuseyn's martyrdom on the formation and victory of the Islamic Revolution. She assesses that the Shiites of Iran believe in Ḥuseyn's intercession on the Day of Judgement. According to Hegland, Ḥuseyn's death at Karbalā becomes a focal point during the Islamic Revolution and, moreover, Ḥuseyn became the archetype of protest against the tyrannical Umayyad caliph Yazid, which Iranians sought to emulate. Furthermore, the author describes how the passive concept of hope for intercession shifted to active protest against the Pahlavi regime. In other words, every one aspired to the ideal, inspired by Ḥuseyn, of bravely standing up to a totalitarian regime.[10]

Moreover, Ṣādiq Humāyūni published a scholarly work in 1989 titled *Ta'ziya dar Iran* (*Ta'ziya* in Iran). He discusses a wide range of topics including, but not limited to, the history *of ta'ziya* and its roots, how *ta'ziya* developed in Iran and how it declined. The writer asserts that aristocracy is the main reason for the destruction of *ta'ziya*. He gives valuable information about different types of *ta'ziya*, the composers, and how both Iranians and foreigners discussed *ta'ziya*. Humāyūni writes about the instruments that are used in *ta'ziya*, the copies, and the order of reciting *ta'ziya* during performance, and the famous *ta'ziya* reciters (*ta'ziya-khān*) and the place of *ta'ziya* performance. The book contains a large number of *ta'ziyas*, such as *ta'ziya* of *Abbās*, *ta'ziya* of *Imām Reẓā*, *ta'ziya* of *'Ali Akber*, *ta'ziya* of *Qāniqā-e shāh-e farang* (Qāniqā the king of a foreign country). The book is illustrated with a considerable number of photographs and manuscripts.[11] Another commendable body of research has been produced by David Pinault. In his study *The Shiites: Ritual and Popular Piety in a Muslim Community* (1992), he hones in on a particular aspect of Shiism within the context of the *ta'ziya* ritual in India.[12] One of Pinault's articles entitled 'Zaynab bint 'Ali and the place of the Women of the Households of the First Imāms in Shiite Devotional Literature,' published in 1998, is another attempt to get a handle on the topic, in which he asserts Zeynab's protest in the court of Yazid after the battle of Karbalā provided a model of activism for Iranian women during the Revolution. He goes on to explain how Fāṭima, the Prophet's daughter and Ḥuseyn's mother, has become a role model for Iranian women.[13]

In 1993, Johan G.J. ter Haar published an invaluable article on passion play performance in Iran under the heading 'Ta'ziyeh: Ritual Theater from Shi'ite Iran.'[14] Lāla Taqiyān additionally provides the reader with general information about Iranian *ta'ziya* and theatre in her 1995 book *Dar bāra-ye ta'ziya va te' ātr dar Iran* (*About Ta'ziya and Theatre in Iran*). In 1998, Ṣādiq Humāyūni published a brief survey on the historical origins and development of *ta'ziya* in Iran called *Širāz khāstgāh-e ta'ziya* (*Shiraz, the Original Home of Ta'ziya*).[15]

The Administrative and Social History of the Qajar Period [*The Story of My Life*] (1997) by Abdullāh Mostowfi is an autobiographical chronicle of *ta'ziya* performance during the Qājār period. Mostowfi conveys how Nāṣer al-Din Shah changed the commemoration of Ḥuseyn's martyrdom into a rationale based on pleasure and ostentatious luxury throughout the course of his reign. The author mentions that *ta'ziya* composers put in a great deal of effort, more to mobilize their audience than develop the plot. He describes the appearance of protagonists and antagonists, the role of *Mu'in al-Bukā'in* ('coordinator of weeping'), the stage, and the parade of more than 200 camels before Nāṣer al-Din Shah. Mostofi also provides an account of a *ta'ziya* that was performed in the house of Ezzat al-Dowle, the sister of Nāṣer al-Din Shah.[16] Significantly, it demonstrates that the religious aspects of *ta'ziya* performance were not of great importance to the Shah.

Kamran Scot Aghaie published a scholarly work in 2004 entitled *Martyrs of Karbalā: Shi'i Symbols and Rituals in Modern Iran*, in which he illustrates how what occurred in Karbalā has transformed from a historical event into a symbolic paradigm and has been used in various time periods in the form of *ta'ziya* ritual to legitimize the state. The Pahlavi dynasty (1925-1979) is an exception in this regard, as it tried to suppress *ta'ziya* performance in order to restrict its political influence. Importantly, Aghaie discusses how *ta'ziya* served the political purpose of the Qājārs, who ruled between 1796 and 1925, and the 1979 Islamic Republic of Iran. In particular, the Qājār elites participated in *ta'ziya* performance, which essentially represented their integration with the indigenous people. In other words, *ta'ziya* served as a social bond, one that connected them to society. Conversely, the Islamic Republic created a religious identity from the *ta'ziya* rituals to motivate the common people to overthrow the secular Pahlavi regime; later, the same rituals were used to mobilize youth to fight in the war against Iraq between 1980 and 1988.[17]

A collection of articles about passion plays was recently published in *The Drama Review Journal* (2005). As an introduction, Rebecca Ansary Petty offers a translation of a *ta'ziya* titled 'The martyrdom of Hussein Ta'ziyeh dar Khour.'[18] The rest of the articles in this volume cover a wide range of topics: Ṣādiq Humāyuni's article 'A View from the Inside, the Anatomy of the Persian Ta'ziyeh Plays' deals with the poetry, music, place and performance of *ta'ziya*.[19] 'Acting Styles and Actor Training in Ta'ziyeh' by William O. Beeman and Mohammad B. Ghaffari examines the artistic skills required from *ta'ziya* players. For instance, a player is expected to know how to fight, run, and perform other athletic movements while singing. Additionally, they consider the influence of *ta'ziya* on modern media such as Hollywood films.[20] Peter Chelkowski, in his article 'From the Sun-Scorched Desert of Iran to the Beaches of Trinidad: Ta'ziyeh's Journey from Asia to the Caribbean,' studies how *ta'ziya* performance migrated from Iran to India. More specifically, he concentrates on explaining *nakhl*: meaning its production process, and the symbolic meanings of objects associated with it. Chelkowski shows various developments of *ta'ziya* from India to the Caribbean, where *ta'ziya* has become both a symbol of pan-Indian unity and the community of Indians.[21]

Another informative contemporary text on *ta'ziya* is Negar Mottahedeh's 'Karbalā Drag Kings and Queens.' Here, she observes the role of gender in *ta'ziya* performance, which, in turn, leads to an important discourse on national identity. Mottahedeh claims *ta'ziya* performance differs amongst Iranian Twelver Shiite in Iran and its neighbouring countries, and that through studying *ta'ziya*, one may understand the concept of Otherness in respect to Iranians.[22]

Another collection of articles (2005) is *The Women of Karbalā: Ritual Performance and Symbolic Discourses in Modern Shi'i Islam* edited by Kamran Scot Aghaie. The book is illustrated and divided into two parts. In the first part, the articles focus on Iran. The second part deals with the Arab world, South Asia, and the United States of America. In her article '*Ta'ziyeh*: A Twist of History in Everyday Life,' Negar Mottahedeh argues how the gender dynamics of *ta'ziya* developed during the Qājār period. She holds that women were engaged in organizing the ritual.[23] 'The Gender Dynamics of Moharram Symbols and Rituals in the Latter Years of Qajar Rule' by Kamran Scot Aghaie examines social, psychological and spiritual functions of Shiite symbols and rituals in Iranian women's life in the Qājār period. He discusses how women played in *ta'ziya* rituals in both public and private rituals.[24] Ingvild Flaskerud's 'Oh, My Heart Is Sad. It Is Moharram, the Month of Zaynab: The Role of Aesthetics and Women's Mourning Ceremonies in Shiraz,' examines the signs and symbols, places and the iconography of the images in modern Shiraz and the fact that women actively participate in *ta'ziya* rituals to achieve salvation in the physical world and the other world.[25] In her article 'The Daughters of Karbalā: Images of Women in Popular Shi'i Culture in Iran,' Faegheh Shirazi explains the representation of female characters in religious eulogies and chants in modern Iran. She argues that the representations are used to support the Islamic Republic of Iran.[26] 'Iconography of the Women of Karbalā: Tiles, Murals, Stamps, and Posters,' by Peter J. Chelkowski examines the images of female characters in Shiite religious drama. The writer illustrates how these female characters serve as a model for chastity, purity, and self-sacrifice through which the leaders of the Islamic Republic represented their ideals.[27] In the second part of the book one reads the following articles: 'Sakineh, The Narrator of Karbalā: An Ethnographic Description of a Women's *Majāles* Rituals in Pakistan,' by Shemeem Burney Abbas. She analyses how the narrative voice of Sakina presents gendered themes in mourning rituals in Pakistan.[28] In his article 'Sayyedeh Zaynab: The Conqueror of Damascus and Beyond,' Syed Akbar Heyder studies how Zaynab is presented in modern Urdu poems and pious elegies.[29] 'Gender and Moharram Rituals in an Isma'ili Sect of South Asian Muslims' by Reyhana Ghadially examines how women in the Isma'ili community of Bohra in India tend to be more active in private rituals than public ones. She finds that the women play a major part in universalistic Shiite Ideals.[30] Mary Elaine Hegland's 'Women of Karbalā Moving to America: Shi'i Rituals in Iran, Pakistan, and California' draws a comparison between two Shiite communities that have migrated to the United States. She illustrates the distinction between them and holds that South Asian women are more active in religious rituals than Iranian women.[31] 'Women's Religious Rituals in Iraq' by Elizabeth Warnock Fernea and Basima Q. Bezirgan illustrates that both men and women are active in public religious rituals. They show the supportive role of women in men's rituals and men's supportive role in women's private rituals.[32] The last article of this book is 'From Mourning to Activism: Seyyedeh Zaynab, Lebanese Shi'i Woman, and the Transformation of Ashura' by Lara Z. Deeb. She focuses on Shiite Lebananse rituals and their recent changes under the influence of urbanization, modernization and political Shiite parties: Amal and Hezbollāh.[33]

A valuable work on the subject is *Ta'ziya-khāni ḥadiṯ-e maṣā'ebe qudsi dar namāyeš-e ā'ini* (*Performing Ta'ziya: Holy Tradition of Tragedy in Ritual*

Play) by 'Ali Bulūkbāši (2006). This study illustrates historical aspects of *ta'ziya* and its effective influence on Iranians as a holy religious ritual.[34]

In 2010, Ḥuseyn Ismā'ili published a collection of *ta'ziya* texts entitled *Tešna dar miqāt, matn va matnšenāsi-ye ta'ziya*. This collection, published in 1928 by the German diplomat Wilhelm Litten, is the first *ta'ziya* collection to be published in Persian in the nineteenth century, according to Ismā'ili. The book contains 15 gatherings or *majles* of *ta'ziya* and begins with mourning for the sacrifice of Ismael (*ta'ziya-ye qurbani kardan-e Ismā'il*) and ends with mourning for Amir Teymūr (*ta'ziya Amir Teymūr*). At the beginning of each *majles*, Ismā'ili has added an introduction (*darāmad*) that consists of an explanation about the gathering afterwards. Under the heading of the origin of *majles* (*khāstgāh-e majles*), he notes the Shiite sources from which the main theme of the *majles* is derived; then, in the copies of *majles* (*nuskha-hā-ye majles*), Ḥuseyn Ismā'ili refers to the collections in which the *majles* is mentioned. This work contains manuscripts of several *majles-e ta'ziyas*.[35]

In 2011, William O. Beeman published an invaluable book entitled *Iranian Performance Tradition*. In it, he explains Iranian behaviour and norms in order to offer a deeper understanding of Iranian culture to the reader. He observes theatre, both comedy and tragedy, and holds that they have their roots in Iranian tradition. Beeman illustrates the connection between performance activity and daily life in Iran. In other words, ceremonies reflect real life and the ideals of the Iranian community are illustrated. This book covers a wide range of subjects about Iranian life, behaviours, folk culture, religious rituals, Rūhowzi comedy and media and the Revolution (1979).[36]

Another scholarly work published in 2011 is *Gender, Sainthood, & Everyday Practice in South Asian Shi'ism* by Karen G. Ruffle. In her work, the writer observes how the battle of Karbalā is commemorated by the Indian Shi'i community. She illustrates how deeply Indians are influenced by *ta'ziya*. For this study, she relies on hagiographical texts to show how Imām Ḥuseyn, his family and his companions are illustrated in these texts. On the importance of hagiography, Ruffle asserts that it 'reflects local cultural values, variations in religious practice, political ideology, language and gender norms.' In this study, the role of the saints (i.e. the twelve Shiite Imams) in the Indian Shiite community and the historical role of Iranian Shiites in developing and cultivating Shiite Islam are depicted.[37]

Citing another, yet older, source of literature on passion plays, *ta'ziya* processions are vividly portrayed in European travel accounts written during the sixteenth and seventeenth centuries. They provide valuable descriptions of the objects used in *ta'ziya* performance, in addition to the scenes and players. A detailed description of the events at Karbalā is preserved in the works of the European traveller Pietro Della Valle. Significantly, he documents the 1618 Muḥarram ceremonies in Isfahan. Cornelis de Bruyn, a Dutchman, describes a *ta'ziya* scene in his work *Travels into Muscovy and Part of the East-Indies*. Likewise, William Franklin, in his *Observations Made on a Tour from Bengal to Persia*, reports on a *ta'ziya* procession, consequently revealing the rapid development of *ta'ziya* in the second half of the seventeenth century.[38] Morier's travel account titled *Second Journey through Persia, Armenia, and Asia Minor between the Years 1810-1816*, written in 1818, observes a form of *ta'ziya* performed before the king and his courtiers. The author illustrates how the objects used in the performance symbolically represented Ḥuseyn's death at Karbalā. Morier also divulges in detail various other aspects of the performance, even decorating his work with several illustrations.[39]

James Bassett is another traveller-observer of Muḥarram *ta'ziyas*. In his 1887 work *Persia the Land of the Imams: A Narration of Travel and Residence 1871-1885*, he explains the theatrical features of these ceremonies and the ostensibly pathetic stories that are read during the performance. According to Bassett, on the tenth day of the Muḥarram, members of the procession donned white clothing resembling shrouds, while walking with bare heads and feet. Later, they wounded their heads with sharp blades.[40]

There is yet another vivid portrayal of *ta'ziya* performance in *A Narrative Journey into Persia and Residence at Tehran* by J.M. Tancoigne. He not only describes the procession of mourners, but also illustrates how the events of Karbalā and Ḥuseyn's martyrdom are expressed in the nineteenth century.[41]

Passion play processions and various forms of flagellation are also explained in travel accounts by Europeans. From a European perspective, these acts are important because they indicate that the mourning procession has theatrical features. Jean Chardin offers a vivid description of *sinazani* (beating one's breast) that he witnessed in 1667.[42] The *ta'ziya* procession is also described by Pierre Ponafiedine in his travel account entitled *Life in the Moslem East* (1910). He describes the procession of the mourners. For instance, they not only inflicted wounds on their bodies, but also hung padlocks, daggers and horseshoes on their backs, arms and breasts. The mourners wounded their foreheads and shaved their heads, motivated by the belief that they would receive a reward. The author further mentions that throughout the first ten days of the month of Muḥarram, both non-

Qur'ānic and Qur'ānic stories were used to show the sufferings of Imām Ḥuseyn and his family.[43]

The Shia World (1910) by Muḥammad Ḥuseyn Khān Esfahāni provides a short but vivid description of a *ta'ziya* procession in the city of Yazd. In this travel account, Esfahāni illustrates how the procession was characterized by several theatrical features symbolically depicting the events of Karbalā. Like Morier, he uses an illustration, though, in this case, to visually demonstrate what the procession leaders looked like.[44]

Translations in European languages

Moreover, several translations of passion play performance also exist. Thirty-seven *majles* of *ta'ziya* have been translated into English by Lewis Pelly. It was during his journey to India and Iran that Pelly became intrigued by the *ta'ziya* performance. He dedicated two volumes of his 1879 work *The Miracle Play: Ḥasan and Husain* to this iḥnvaluable task. The first volume starts with the *ta'ziya* of 'Joseph and his Brethren' and then proceeds to sketch the events leading up to 'the death of 'Ali Akbar,' who was Ḥuseyn's son. The second volume begins with the death of Qāsim, the Bridegroom, and culminates in the scene of the Resurrection. Also of note, Pelly writes a short introduction at the beginning of each *majles*.[45]

Edward G. Browne, in *A Literary History of Persia,* (1924), offers an English translation of *ta'ziya* martyrdom of Muslim ibn al-'Aqil (*ta'ziya-ye šahādat-e Muslim ibn 'Aqil*).[46] Two *ta'ziya* episodes have been translated into French by Louis Massignon and Parwiz Mamnoun, '*Le Majlis de Mansur-e Hallaj, de Shams-e Tabrezi et du Molld de Roum*,' in *Revue des Etudes Islamiques* (1955), and Parwiz Mamnoun *Ta'ziya: Schi'itisch-Persisches Passionsspiel* (Vienna, 1967), respectively.

In this book, I illustrate the major role of *ta'ziya* performance among Shiites of Iran. It analyses the role of the Prophet's granddaughter in modern twentieth-century Iran and, more specifically, how Iranian women perceived her as the archetype of resistance and protest against the tyrannical Pahlavi monarch during the Islamic Revolution of 1979. In this study, the religious prohibitions and restrictions infused in *ta'ziya* performance are examined. It further shows how devotional themes such as predestination, salvation, intercession, free will and martyrdom are used in *ta'ziya* texts.

Notes

1 P.J. Chelkowski, 'Dramatic and Literary Aspects of Ta'zieh-khani-Iranian Passion Play,' *Review of National Literature*, eds. A. Paolucci & J. Haidari, vol. II, No. 1, spring 1971; for further information on the mourning rites (*'azādāri*) see J. Calmard, in *Encyclopaedia Iranica*, under 'Azādārī; for mourning procession see P.J. Chelkowski, in *Encyclopaedia Iranica*, under Dasta.

2 Ṣ. Humāyūni, *Ta'ziya va ta'ziya-khāni*, Tehran: čāpkhāna-ye bist-o panjom-e šahrivar, 1354/1975.

3 M. Ayoub, *Redemptive Suffering in Islam: A Study of the Devotional Aspects of 'Āshūrā in Twelver Shi'ism*, The Hague: Mouton Publishers, 1978.

4 P.J. Chelkowski, 'Islam in Modern Drama and Theater,' in *Die Welt des Islams*, New Series, Bd., 23/24 (1984), pp. 45-69.

5 P.J. Chelkowski, 'Shia Muslim Performance,' in *The Drama Review*, vol. 29, No. 3, Processional Performance (Autumn, 1985), pp. 18-30. *Nakhl* 'is a big, tall bier (coffin) to which are attached daggers swords, luxurious fabrics, and mirrors. On the day of 'Āšūrā, it is carried as if it was the coffin of Imām Ḥuseyn. Some times the *nakhl* is so colossal and heavy that it requires several hundred strong men to lift and carry it.' See P.J. Chelkowski, 'Art for Twenty-Four Hours,' in *Islamic Art in the 19th Century: Tradition, Innovation, and Eclecticicism*, eds. D. Behrens-Abouseif & S. Vernoit, Leiden: Koninklijke Brill NV, 2006, p. 410.

6 P.J. Chelkowski, 'Popular Shī'ī Mourning Ritual,' in *al-Ṣerāt*, vol. XII, Paper from Imam Husein Conference London: Routledge & Kegan Paul plc, 1986.

7 Ibid.

8 M.M.J. Fischer, *Iran: From Religious Dispute to Revolution*, Cambridge: Harvard University Press, 1980, pp. 133-4.

9 Ibid. pp. 170-7.

10 M.E. Hegland, 'Two Images of Husein: Accommodation and Revolution in an Iranian Village,' in *Religion and Politics in Iran: Shi'ism from Quietism to Revolution*, ed. N.R. Keddie, New Haven & London, Yale University Press, 1983, pp. 218-35.

11 Ṣ. Humāyūni, *Ta'ziya dar Iran*, Tehran: Navid, 1368/1989.

12 D. Pinault, *The Shiites: Ritual and Popular Piety in a Muslim Community*, London: I.B. Tauris & Co Ltd Publishers, 1992.

13 D. Pinault, 'Zaynab bint 'Ali and the Place of the Women of the Households of the First Imāms in Shiite Devotional Literature,' in *Women in the Medieval Islamic World Power, Patronage and Piety*, ed. G.R.G. Hambly, New York: St. Martin's Press, 1998.

14 J.G.J. ter Haar, 'Ta'ziye: Ritual Theater from Shiite Iran,' in *Theatre Intercontinental: Forms, Functions, Correspondences*, eds. C.C. Barfoot & C. Bordewijk, Amsterdam: Rodopi, 1993.

15 Ṣ. Humāyūni, *Shirāz khāstgāh-e ta'ziya*, Shirāz: Bunyād-e Fārs-šenāsi, 1377/1998.

16 A. Mostowfi, *The Administrative and Social History of the Qajar Period* [*The Story of My Life*], vol. 1, From Agha Muhammad khān to Nāṣer ed-Din Shah (1794-1896), trans. by Nayer Mostofi Glenn, Costa Messa Californa: Mazda Publishers, 1997, pp. 163-170.
17 K.S. Aghaie, *Martyrs of Karbalā: Shi'i Symbols and Rituals in Modern Iran*, Seattle: The University of Washington Press, 2004.
18 R. Ansary Petty, 'The Ta'ziyeh of the Martyrdom of Hussein,' in *The Drama Review*, vol. 49, no. 4 (T118), Winter 2005, pp. 28-41.
19 Ṣ. Humāyūni, 'A View from the Inside, the Anatomy of the Persian Ta'ziyeh Plays,' in *The Drama Review*, vol. 49, no. 4 (T118), Winter 2005, pp. 68-72.
20 W.O. Beeman, & M.B. Ghaffari, 'Acting Styles and Actor Training in Ta'ziyeh' in *The Drama Review,* vol. 49, no. 4 (T118), Winter 2005, pp. 48-60.
21 P.J. Chelkowski, 'From the Sun-Scorched Desert of Iran to the Beaches of Trinidad: Ta'zieh's Journey from Asia to the Caribbean,' in *The Drama Review*, vol. 49, no. 4 (T118), Winter 2005, pp. 156-170.
22 N. Mottahedeh, 'Karbalā Drag Kings and Queens,' in *The Drama Review*, vol. 49, no. 4 (T118), Winter 2005, pp. 73-85.
23 N. Mottahedeh, '*Ta'ziyeh*: A Twist of History in Everyday Life,' in *The Women of Karbalā: Ritual Performance and Symbolic Discourses in Modern Shi'i Islam*, ed. K.S. Aghaie, Austin: The University of Texas Press, 2005, pp. 25-43.
24 K.S. Aghaie, 'The Gender Dynamics of Moharram Symbols and Rituals in the Latter Years of Qajar Rule,' in *The Women of Karbalā: Ritual Performance and Symbolic Discourses in Modern Shi'i Islam*, ed. K.S. Aghaie, Austin: The University of Texas Press, 2005, pp. 45-63.
25 I. Flaskerud, 'Oh, My Heart is Sad. It is Moharram, the Month of Zeynab: The Role of Aesthetics and Women's Mourning in Ceremonies in Shiraz,' in *The Women of Karbalā*, ed. K.S. Aghaie, Austin: The University of Texas Press, 2005, pp. 65-91.
26 F. Shirazi, 'The Daughters of Karbalā: Images of Women in Popular Shi'i Culture in Iran,' in *The Women of Karbalā*, ed. K.S. Aghaie, Austin: The University of Texas Press, 2005, pp. 93-118.
27 P. J. Chelkowski, 'Iconography of the Women of Karbalā: Tiles, Murals, Stamps, and Posters,' in *The Women of Karbalā*, ed. K.S. Aghaie, Austin: The University of Texas Press, 2005, pp. 119-160.
28 Sh. Burney Abbas, 'Sakineh, The Narrator of Karbalā: An Ethnographic Description of a Women's *Majles* Rituals in Pakistan,' in *The Women of Karbalā: Ritual Performance and Symbolic Discourses in Modern Shi'i Islam,* ed. K.S. Aghaie, Austin: The University of Texas Press, 2005, pp. 141-160.
29 S.A. Heyder, 'Sayyedeh Zaynab: The Conqueror of Damascus and Beyond,' in *The Women of Karbalā: Ritual Performance and Symbolic Discourses in Modern Shi'i Islam,* ed. K.S. Aghaie, Austin: The University of Texas Press, 2005, pp. 161-181.

30 R. Ghadially, 'Gender and Moharram Rituals in an Isma'ili Sect of South Asian Muslims,' in *The Women of Karbalā*, ed. K.S. Aghaie, Austin: The University of Texas Press, 2005, pp. 183-198.

31 M.E. Hegland, 'Women of Karbalā Moving to America: Shi'i Rituals in Iran, Pakistan, and California,' in *The Women of Karbalā*, ed. K.S. Aghaie, Austin: The University of Texas Press, 2005, pp. 199-227.

32 E. Warnock Fernea & B.Q. Bezirgan, 'Women's Religious Rituals in Iraq,' in *The Women of Karbalā*, ed. K.S. Aghaie, Austin: The University of Texas Press, 2005, pp. 229-230.

33 L.Z. Deeb, 'From Mourning to Activism: Seyyedeh Zaynab, Lebanese Shi'i Woman, and the Transformation of Ashura,' in *The Women of Karbalā*, ed. K.S. Aghaie, Austin: The University of Texas Press, 2005, pp. 231-266.

34 A. Bulūkbāši, *Ta'ziya-khāni: ḥadiṯ-e qudsi-ye maṣā'eb dar namayeš-e ā'inī*, Tehran: Amir Kabir, 1383/2004.

35 *Tešna dar miqātgah, matn va matnšenāsi-ye ta'ziya, (majmū'a leiten), tasḥiḥ va taḥlil az Ḥuseyn Ismā'ili*, Tehran: Našr-e mo'in, 1389/2010.

36 W.O. Beeman, *Iranian Performance Tradition*, California: Mazda Publications, 2011. Rūhowzi or 'over the pool' 'is typically performed on a board placed over the pool commonly found in the yard of a Persian home. Rūhowzi usually involves several players engaging in comic dance, music dance, and song.' See E.L. Daniel & A.A. Mahdi, *Culture and Customs of Iran*, Westport, CT: Greenwood Press, 2006, p. 93.

37 K.G. Ruffle, *Gender, Sainthood, & Everyday Practice in South Asian Shi'ism*, North Carolina: The University of North Carolina Press, 2011.

38 See J.G.J. ter Haar, 'Ta'ziye: Ritual Theater from Shiite Iran,' pp. 163-5.

39 J. Morier, *Second Journey through Persia, Armenia, and Asia Minor between the Years 1810-1816*, London: Longman & et al., 1818, pp. 176-184.

40 J. Bassett, *Persia the Land of the Imams: A Narration of Travel and Residence 1871-1885*, London: Black & Son, 1887, p. 306.

41 See M. Momen, *An Introduction to Shi'i Islam, the History of Doctrines of Twelver Shi'ism*, Oxford: George Ronald, 1985, pp. 241-2.

42 J.G.J. ter Haar, 'Ta'ziye: Ritual Theater from Shiite Iran,' p. 163.

43 P. Ponafidine, *Life in the Moslem East*, E. Cochran Ponafidine, London: Hodder and Stoughton, 1911, pp. 341-47.

44 M.H. Esfahāni, *The Glory of the Shia World: The Tale of a Pilgrimage*, trans. by Major P.M. Sykes, London: Macmillan & Co., 1910, pp. 191-201.

45 L. Pelly, *The Miracle Play: Hasan and Husain*, vol. I&II, London: W.M.H. Allen and Co., 1879.

46 E.G. Browne, *A Literary History of Persia (1500-1924)*, vol. iv., Cambridge: The University Press, 1924, pp. 190-193.

Introduction

The development of technology has overwhelmed the traditions of many Eastern countries. For them, following the Western pattern of life has become more attractive than preserving their own traditions and transmitting them to the following generations. Iran too has been affected by the wave of modernity. Iranians have discarded some of their traditions in favour of the attractions of modernity. *Taʿziya*, an Iranian form of 'passion play' commemorating suffering and martyrdom, has been one of the victims of this process. It has been banished from the large cities to more remote villages; but, despite the limitations imposed on it, a trace of the past glory of *taʿziya* has survived. Through *taʿziya* performances, an audience learns about the life of the Shiite Imāms[1] the afflictions that they suffered, the laws of religion, the social virtues, and historical events.

This study focuses on the character of Zeynab, Imām Ḥuseyn's sister, the third Shiite Imām. The way she demonstrated exceptional behaviour in standing up to the Umayyad caliph Yazid (d.63/683)[2] during and after the battle of Karbalā is a crucial issue for Shiites. She protested against the tyrannies and oppressions that were inflicted upon Imām Ḥuseyn's family. After analysing Zeynab's behaviour during the battle and during her subsequent imprisonment, I will focus on how modern Iranian women have received Zeynab, especially during the Iran-Iraq war in the 1980s.

A Short History of *Taʿziya*

Taʿziya is an Arabic word, literally meaning 'condolence,' and referring to mourning for the dead, or enjoining patience. The Iranian *taʿziya* play is a form of religious drama, analogous to the Middle-English passion plays. It has its historical roots in pre-Islamic Persia, where Persians performed the tragedy of Mitrā (*maṣā'b-e mitrā*). During these rites, the worshippers wore masks and mimicked the afflictions that Mitrā had suffered, acting them out on a platform.[3] Mitrā is an Indo-Persian name meaning contract, agreement, treaty, alliance and promise. The name is associated with the sun (*mehr*). The god Mitrā punishes people who break their contract: he takes the strength from their feet and the light out of their eyes. He is a warrior who drives a chariot and carries a weapon. On the other hand, he rewards the faithful by bringing rain and making the plants grow, and he brings rugs, cattle herds and other rewards to the one who faithfully worships him.[4]

It is reported that two other mourning rituals were performed in Iran. The first commemorated the tragedy of Zarir, the brother of King Vištāsp, who converted to the religion of Zoroaster. The story comes from the Sasanian period (224-651), when Middle Persian was spoken, and originated in Parthian history. Briefly, the story is that a neighbouring king, Arjāsb, objected to King Vištāsp's conversion and attacked Vištāsp with a huge army. In spite of the odds, Zarir goes to the battlefield where he is murdered by Bidarafš, the brother of king Arjāsb.[5] Zarir, like Imām Ḥuseyn, is the archetype of one who is murdered for his faith.

The other pre-Islamic tragedy commemorated the death of Siyāvuš, the son of Keykāwūs, Iran's mythical king. Siyāvuš was brought up by Rustam, the Iranian hero of Sistān. When Siyāvuš returns to the palace of his father, he is falsely accused by Sūdāba, his father's wife, who has made several attempts to seduce him. Siyāvuš proves his innocence in a trial by fire, but is forced to leave the country. He goes with his companions to Tūrān where initially the king, Afrāsiyāb, honours him. Siyāvuš even marries Afrāsiyāb's daughter, but jealous courtiers induce Afrāsiyāb to murder Siyāvuš, and his head is cut off. The main source for this account is the history of Bukhāra by Naršakhi, who says that in his own era, each year, 'The people of Bukhāra sing songs about the killing of Siyāvuš. The singers (*qawwālān*) call the songs the weeping of the Zoroastrians (*geristan-e mughān*)'.[6]

The Movements after 'Āšūrā and the Development of Ta'ziya[7]

Contemporary Iranian *ta'ziya* is performed mainly to commemorate the death of Imām Ḥuseyn, the grandson of the Prophet Muḥammad (d.11/632), and the other events of 'Āšūrā.[8] Imām Ḥuseyn was killed on the plain of Karbalā in 61/680.[9] The people of Kūfa had invited him to come to lead their community, but he never reached Kūfa. On the plain of Karbalā, on the first day of the month of Muḥarram in 60/680, he and his household were surrounded by the army of Yazid, the successor of the Umayyad caliph

Mu'āwiya. Imām Ḥuseyn preferred death to swearing allegiance to Yazid as the caliph of the Muslim community. After nine days of negotiations, during which the Imām and his followers were deprived of food and water, the battle started on the tenth of Muḥarram (*'Āšūrā*). It lasted one day. Imām Ḥuseyn and his companions were killed and the surviving members of his household were arrested and taken to Yazid's palace in Damascus, along with the heads of the dead mounted on lances.

After the martyrdom of Imām Ḥuseyn, the Shiites of Kūfa repented their failure to prevent his martyrdom and decided to kill his murderers or sacrifice their own lives. They felt ashamed before the Prophet and worried about the Day of Judgement when they would have to confess their shortcomings to God. They called themselves the Penitents (*Tawwābūn).* The penitents believed that 'Ali Ibn al-Ḥuseyn (later named Imām Zeyn al-'Ābedin) was Imām Ḥuseyn's legitimate successor because he was related to Fāṭima, the Prophet's daughter. They put more emphasis on his relationship to the Prophet through Fāṭima than through 'Ali (the cousin of the Prophet). The *Tawwābūn* gathered Shiites from Kūfa and the neighbouring cities, encouraging them to fight against the Umayyad army. But before going into battle they went to Karbalā, to the grave of Imām Ḥuseyn, and lamented for him. In 65/684 they fought with Syrian forces in the siege of 'Ayn al-Wardā, where they were defeated. Most were killed; the remainder fled to Qarqisiya, where their movement was eclipsed.

In 66/865 another movement was begun, by Al-Mukhtār Ibn Abi 'Ubayda al-Thaqafi.[10] The movement also sought to revenge Imām Ḥuseyn's blood, and supported the succession of Muḥammad Ibn al-Ḥananfiyya, 'Ali's third son from a Hanafi woman. Since he was not from the bloodline of the Prophet, the two movements did not unite. The movement of 'Ubayda ath-Thaqafi was also defeated by the Umayyad army.[11]

Almost three centuries after the *Tawwābūn* movement, the impulse of penitent commemoration developed into processions commemorating the martyrdom of Imām Ḥuseyn. On the tenth of Muḥarram 963, by order of the Buyid rulers (945-1055), the martyrdom of Imām Ḥuseyn was officially commemorated for the first time by mourning processions that passed through the streets and markets. In the following year, the commemoration was supplemented with the recitation of elegies, beating on the head and face and begging for water in imitation of Imām Ḥuseyn, who had asked for water for his infant, 'Ali Asġar, on the plain of Karbalā.[12] The combination of processions and dramatic recitations gives us the elements of the late Medieval *ta'ziya*. Such rites continued during the Buyid era.[13]

Late Medieval and Modern Ta'ziya

The mourning performance developed until it reached a high point during the Ṣafavid period (1501-1722). The emergence of the Ṣafavids had a lasting effect on the history of Iran. It was during their rule that the mass of the population converted to Shiite Islam. Many theatrical features were added to *ta'ziya*, which helped the director to make a vivid portrayal of the events of Karbalā.

Shah Ṭahmāsb (1525-1576), the second king of the Ṣafavid dynasty, ordered poets 'to devote their time to writing eulogies of Imāms.'[14] He favoured devotional subjects so much that other literary forms such as lyrics and storytelling (*dāstān-sarā'i*) declined. However, the poets of this period responded by using and adapting poetic forms for religious subjects. Muḥtašam from Kāšān (d.996/1587-8) wrote the famous *dawāzdah-band* ('the twelve-stanza poem'),[15] an elegy on the martyrdom of Imām Ḥuseyn and a milestone in the development of Persian poetry. Hātef from Isfahān (d.1198/1783)[16] followed Muhtašam in composing elegies, and later Qā'āni (1808-54) imitated Muḥtašam.[17] Waqār from Shiraz (d.1298/1881) wrote his *haft-band* (seven stanza poem) in imitation of the *dawāzdah-band* of Muhtašam from Kāšān.[18]

Another important book of elegies for the Imāms in the Ṣafavid period is the *Rawẓat al-šuhadā* (*the Garden of Martyrs*) by Ḥuseyn Wa'eẓ Kāšefi (d.1504-5). This book relates the deaths of the Shiite Imāms, particularly the martyrdom of Imām Ḥuseyn. *Rawẓat al-šuhadā* had a major effect on the *ta'ziya* texts. It provided a broader perspective for *ta'ziya* composers. The recitation of *Rawzat al-šuhadā* and other books with similar religious subjects led to the practice of *rawza-khāni*, the animated reading of the passion of Imām Ḥuseyn, the singing of elegies and a sermon. *Ta'ziya* as a dramatic form and devotional practice has developed from the *rawza-khwāni*. There are brief mentions of 'Āšūrā mourning processions with dramatic re-enactments in accounts by Pietro Della Valle in 1618, and Cornelis de Bruyn in 1704.[19]

During the Afshāriya period there was a sharp decline in *ta'ziya* performances. Nāder Shah Afshār (r.1147-60/1736-47), the founder of the Afshāriya dynasty, was a Sunnite Muslim and did not wish to commemorate the martyrdom of Imām Ḥuseyn.

With the advent of the Zand dynasty (1751-1796), the popularity of *ta'ziya* was restored, and it reached a peak during the Qājār dynasty (1796-1925). Something about the development of *ta'ziya* performances at the time can be deduced from an account written by William Francklin around 1786-87:

> [...] Among the most affecting representations is the marriage of young Casim, the son of Hussun and nephew of Hossein, with his daughter; but this was never consummated as Casim was killed in a skirmish on the Banks of the Euphrate, on the 7th of Muḥarram. On this occasion, a boy represents the bride, decorated in her wedding garment, and attended by the females of the family chanting a mournful elegy, in which is related the circumstance of her betrothed husband being cut off by infidels – (for such is the term by which sheias speak of Sunnies). The parting between her and her husband is also represented when on his going to the field she takes an affectionate leave of him, and on his quitting her presents her with a burial vest, which she puts around his neck.[20]

Nāṣer al-Din Shah (r.1848-96) was very fond of *taʿziya*. During his long reign, *taʿziya* was greatly developed and became popular among different classes of society. From this period, *taʿziya* was performed in an enclosed area. The places used for *taʿziya* performances were named *tekiya*s. The most famous in the Qājār period was the *tekiya-dawlat* (the Royal Tekiya), a circular building modelled on the Royal Albert Hall in London, which Nāṣer al-Din Shah had built on his return from London in 1873.[21] It was used for *taʿziya* performances for the royal family.[22] It was destroyed in 1948.

From 1925, as Reẓā Shah Pahlavi (r.1925-1941) initiated a process of modernization in Iran, the entertainment offered by radio, cinema, and later television supplanted *taʿziya* performances, which went into a gradual decline. After World War Two, *taʿziya* performances were largely limited to small towns and remote villages.[23]

The Shiite Muslims later divided into several branches. Among these are the Zaydiyya, the Imāmiyya or 'twelver' Shiites, and the Ismāʿiliyya. The Imāmiyya, the majority Shiite sect in Iran today, believe that the twelfth Imām, a child, was supernaturally concealed after the death of the eleventh Imām: he is still alive today and is expected to return before the end of the world.[24] One of the fundamental doctrines of the Imāmiyya is that the Imām is protected (*maʿṣūm*) from sin and error. If the Imām fears for his own safety or for that of his community, he has to practice dissimulation (*taqqiya*).[25]

The Devotional Contents of *Ta'ziya*

Ta'ziya is the most important popular devotional ritual in Iran. Every year, from the first day to the tenth day of the month of Muharram, Iranian Shiites commemorate the martyrdom of Imām Ḥuseyn. They perform *ta'ziya* to keep alive the memory of the events of Karbalā and the tyranny that the family of the Prophet suffered. There are separate *ta'ziya* for each of the main events of Karbalā, and its aftermath. For instance, the *ta'ziya* called 'the bazaar in Damascus' (*ta'ziya-ye bāzār-e Šām*) describes the conditions of the prisoners after 'Āšūrā. There is a *ta'ziya* on the martyrdom of two of Zeynab's sons, a *ta'ziya* on the survivors' 'entrance to Medina' (*ta'ziya-ye vurūd-e be Medina*), on the death of Zeynab (*ta'ziya-ye vafāt-e ḥaẓrat-e Zeynab*), and on the death of the two sons of Muslim Ibn al-'Aqil, an uncle of Ḥuseyn. Muslim Ibn 'al-Aqil was martyred as well. There is also a conversion tale known as the *ta'ziya* on the Monastery of Širin.

There are also *ta'ziya*s for other events not directly related to Karbalā, such as the death of the Prophet (*ta'ziya-ye vafāt-e payġambar*) and the martyrdom of Imām 'Ali (*ta'ziya-ye šahādat-e haẓrat-e 'Ali*). Another *ta'ziya* centres on the martyrdom of Qāsem, the son of Imām Ḥasan, the second Shiite Imām. But these are less frequently performed than the *ta'ziya*s on the martyrdom of Ḥuseyn. There are also *ta'ziya* on biblical figures.

Ta'ziya is a medium that teaches and reinforces Shiite beliefs and piety. In commemorating Imām Ḥuseyn's martyrdom and other devotional events, the audience is dramatically confronted with Shiite doctrines such as fate, predestination and free will. Several of the written sources that have transmitted *ta'ziya* texts to us show Imām Ḥuseyn sacrificing himself for the salvation of the Shiites. Here, the concept of free will (*ekhtiyār*) is highlighted.

The language of the *ta'ziya* texts is simple and understandable for all kinds of Persian audiences: even illiterate people can appreciate the text. Its leaders and performers require no formal religious training, and no knowledge of Arabic. *Ta'ziya* was (and is) composed in verse form, to be read aloud and preferably performed.

Oral Tradition in *Ta'ziya* Texts

Although the performers and director of a *ta'ziya* have texts, *ta'ziya* has many of the characteristics of oral literature. An oral text is composed for audiences and is based on their needs. It is composed for memorization and recitation.[26] Ruth Finnegan states that an oral text is composed in performance;[27] at least, it is not separate from recitation or performance. The composer thinks about the time of performance and the expectations of his audience. The message of the *ta'ziya* text is what the audience understands when they see it and hear it being performed.

As oral literature, the *ta'ziya* text is not memorized word for word. If a player forgets a part, he improvises. The text is written, as an aid to memory, but it cannot be checked against one written version that is correct.[28] In oral literature, every version is correct.[29] In *ta'ziya*, each copy (*nuskha*) is treated as correct: the composers, performers and spectators do not seek an authoritative version.

Another characteristic of an oral text is that it is made up of formulaic thoughts and expressions that are memorized.[30] The next is repetition, an important device in oral literature, and drama, because the listeners cannot go back to refresh their memories. Repetition fills the gaps when the speaker does not remember the next subject, but it also reinforces the thought in the mind of the audience, particularly through the repetition of motifs.[31] Another characteristic of oral literature is the use of antithetical terms and balanced patterns, which again serve to make the message more understandable for the spectators.[32] Finally, in oral literature, physical violence is vividly described.[33] Examples of these four characteristics of orality in *ta'ziya* will be given below.

Firstly, some formulaic thoughts and expressions, drawn from everyday speech that one would not normally find in Persian written literature. To 'give one's heart to credit, and be quit of cash' (*be nesiya del bedahad naqd rā rahā bekunad*) (9)[34] means to live in a fool's paradise, believing promises. 'My house will be destroyed' (*khāna kharāb būdan*) (9) is the state of a person losing all hope. 'To see the brand-mark (portent of death) of one's child is intolerable' (*dāġ-e farzand didan āsān nist*) (14) is self-explanatory. 'Light of the eye' (*nūr-e češm*) (23) is a clichéd expression said to a person whom one loves, for instance by parents to their child. 'The black dust is on my head' (*šud khāk-e siyāh bar sar-e man*) (47) refers to an irretrievable calamity such as the death of a loved one or having an incurable disease. 'He was raised with the salt of my father' (*namak parvarda-ye bābam*) (63) refers to a person who has grown up in a family or is indebted to them. The proverb shows that the recipient is inferior to the speaker. To 'cry with one's face to a wall' (*rūy be divār geristan*) (157) represents a condition in which there is no hope of assistance or improvement. Another cliché, used to encourage the audience to give alms, is 'give alms because it repels calamity' (*ṣadaqa deh ṣadaqa daf'-e balāst)* (180). The above examples are repeated in the *ta'ziya* text.

Another characteristic of oral literature is repetition. Participants may insert this to fill gaps, and there is also simple repetition of words in a single passage for rhythmic effect. The examples below show the repetition of motifs, whether as images or concepts, in words that may seem different but convey the same sense to the audience. For instance, the thirst of Imām Ḥuseyn, and his men and family, is a very common theme in *ta'ziya*. For those who have seen *ta'ziya*, the first association of the Imām Ḥuseyn's name is that he was killed while suffering from thirst. This motif is repeatedly associated with the name of Imām Ḥuseyn, as an epithet. For instance, he is called the thirst king (*Shah-e tešna kām*) (41), the king whose lips are athirst (*Shah-e tešna lab)* (49), and the king whose liver thirsts (*Shah-e tešna jegar)* (51). The motif is more fully developed in particular episodes. In one, the sons of Imām Ḥuseyn's sister Zeynab go to the battlefield, and are defeated. When Šemr is about to kill them he gives them some water but they do not drink it, so both are killed while suffering from thirst (18). Also, on the day of 'Āšūrā, Imām Ḥuseyn writes a letter to one of his Shiite followers and asks him to bring some water for the thirst ([...] *gar mitavāni barā-ye tešnegān ābi resāni*) (73). In another episode a European messenger has come to the court of Yazid. He intercedes on behalf of Imām Ḥuseyn's son, Imām Zeyn al-'Ābedin, who is about to be killed. Yazid orders the executioner to kill the European. He asks for a sip of water but then does not drink it: he says,

ābat nanūšam ḥāšā-vo kallā
lab tešna bāšand owlād-e Zahrā (132).

I will never drink water,
While the lips of Zahrā's children are dry[35] (132).

In another passage, Zeynab tells the audience that when Imām Ḥuseyn fell from his horse he tried to say something, but his lips were stuck together because of thirst (*būd labhāš be ham časbida*) (147). Then, she says, 'he wanted water: dust be on my head!' (*āb mikhāst ke khākam bar sar)* (147).

Another motif in the *ta'ziya* texts is *ġurbat*, meaning exile and alienation, but also wretchedness. The term is used in poetry to describe the condition of looking back, in nostalgic memory, at the place that was home. In classical poetry, Nāṣer Khosrow (1004-1088) did in fact travel widely. He was for many years away from home, but the persona of the wandering poet in exile is used widely, even by poets who were geographically less adventurous. Poets speaking in this voice call on their past memories to sustain them: exile and memory are two parts of one motif.[36] In the *ta'ziya* texts, the *ġurbat* motif shows that Imām Ḥuseyn and his family are far from their homeland and that they bewail the loss of their glorious past. Part of the pain of exile is not being in control of one's fate. In the struggle between Imām Ḥuseyn and Yazid, Imām Ḥuseyn is represented as one who is bound in exile: he has no choice but to fight Yazid's army.

Two terms, *ġurbat* and *ġarib*, are repeated in many episodes. The former is the abstract noun for the condition of living away from one's homeland, and the latter refers to a person living in another land. Both terms are used in relation to the martyrdom of Imām Ḥuseyn and his followers on the plain of Karbalā. The *ġurbat* motif highlights their alienation, hopelessness and helplessness in the face of the enemy's army. The term appears in all of the *ta'ziya* stories, underlining that Imām Ḥuseyn was killed in another land, far from his Shiite followers. For example:

Imām Ḥuseyn says to Zeynab:

> In exile, I only have you
> (*dar ġaribi hamin tu rā dāram*) (14).

Zeynab says to Šemr:

> We are strangers, and have no protector
> (*ġaribim-o kasi bar sar nadārim*) (25).

Šahrbānū says to Zeynab:[37]

> What can I do, I am an exile, and in my exile you are my Friend
> (*če kunam ke man ġaribam be ġaribiyam tu yāri*) (43).

Imām Ḥuseyn says to the Heavens (*rūzgār*):

> See our condition: we are strangers, alone and far from our family
> (*mā rā ġarib-o bi kas-o bi aqrabā bebin*) (61).

Ruqiya says to Zeynab:

O! God I am a stranger, despised and afflicted
(*khudāvandā ġarib-o khār-o zāram*) (138).

Dorra Ṣadaf is a warrior who attacks Yazid's army when she hears that the household of Imām Ḥuseyn has been taken captive. When Muštari, one of her companions, hears that Imām Ḥuseyn has been killed, she says,

ġarib-e vādiy-e karb-o balā Ḥuseynam vāy
šahid-e khanjar-e Šemr-e daġā Ḥuseynam vāy (100).

Alas, for my Ḥuseyn, the stranger of the plain of Karb-o balā,[38]
Martyred by the dagger of deceitful Šemr, alas! (100).

In the *ta'ziya* on the martyrdom of 'Abdullāh Ibn al-'Afif,' Ibn al-Ziyād threatens Zeynab with death. There is no one to rescue her, but Sakina intercedes on behalf of her aunt and says,

bejuz in 'amma mā yāvar nadārim
dar in ġurbat kasi bar sar nadārim (84).

We have no helper but this aunt,
In this our exile (*ġurbat*), we have no protector (84).

In a passage relating to the imprisonment period, Zeynab looks back on the time, in Medina when she was respected and protected. She tells Yazid's wife Hendeh, who was previously Zeynab's maid, 'in Medina, the parasol of royalty was over my head' (*man dar madina čatr-e Shahi bar saram būd*) (146). Other members of Imām Ḥuseyn's family also talk about their glorious past when they lived in Medina, when the martyrs of Karbalā were alive. Imām Ḥuseyn's daughter, Sakina, says, 'How fine the day, when my father was alive' (*khuš ān rūzi ke bar sar būd bābā*) (76).

The term orphan (*yatim*) often appears in the *ta'ziya* texts. A *yatim* is a child whose father and mother are dead; the concept complements the concept of *ġaribi* and makes a full image of the tragic situation of Imām Ḥuseyn's children after the battle. It points to both the cruel behaviour of Yazid's commanders and the unfair behaviour of the people of Kūfa. Both protagonists and antagonists use the term, reminding the audience that Imām Ḥuseyn's children are orphaned. For example:

Come beside me, sister, for we are both orphans (*biyā khāhar ke mā har du yatimim)* (23).

He (Šemr) is the cause of the deaths of orphans (*ke gardad bā'eṯ-e marg-e yatimān*) (25).

I am orphaned, I am orphaned, I am orphaned (*man yatimam, yatimam, yatimam*) (51).

Another example is:

az yatimi du česmam pur āb ast
bar yatimān taraḥum ṯavāb ast (53).

My eyes are full of tears, because I am an orphan,
Compassion for orphans is requited (53).[39]

Much more could be said about the terms that are repeated in the *ta'ziya* texts, but we will suffice here with a brief review of some other terms that are repeated often. 'Infidel' (*kāfar*) (18, 40) is frequently used in reference to the antagonists. Its connotation is of infidelity rather than heresy. The enemies of Imām Ḥuseyn are infidels because they fight against him. 'Damned' or 'cursed' (*la'in*) (24, 30, 33, 53, 76, 77) refers to those to whom God will show no mercy. 'Imprisonment' (*asir, zendāni*) (26, 40, 43, 51, 54, 72) refers to the period when Imām Ḥuseyn's family are at the court of Yazid in Damascus. They are taken there, passing from town to town (*šahr-o bāzār burdan*)[40] (74, 76), with their heads kept bare (77, 81), and are then held in chains (*zanjir, rismān).*

Another feature of the *ta'ziya* text as oral literature is the heavy reliance on antithetical terms. The antagonists are unbelievers (*kāfar*), lacking faith (*bi-imān*), shameless (*biḥayā*), faithless and oppressive (*bivafā, jafākār*), rebellious (*'ašrār*), tyrants and oppressors (*ẓālem va setamkār*). The protagonists are full of faith (*bi-imān, musalmān*), fidelity (*bā vafā*), pious (*'abrār*), innocent and oppressed (*bigonāh va maẓlūm*).

Physical violence is presented vividly in *ta'ziya*: the audience is encouraged to imagine themselves present in the battlefield. The antagonists' cruel behaviour is described in detail, and the antagonists themselves explain their tyranny. The purpose is to increase the spectators' hatred. In the *ta'ziya* on 'entering the place of execution' *(ta'ziya vurūd-e be qatlgāh)* (21-

22), there is an episode in which Yazid's commander, Ibn-e Sa'd, orders the army to plunder and burn the tents. Then they take the prisoners to the plain of Karbalā where the headless bodies of their loved ones are lying. The prisoners recognize them from their clothes. In another episode in the same *ta'ziya*, Ibn al-Sa'd and his companion Būkhaliq go to the battlefield to count the wounds of the dead (28-31). They talk about each of them and describe how cruelly they killed the companions of Imām Ḥuseyn. They regret that they killed Imām Ḥuseyn, because he was a good servant of God. Another example is the description of the death scene of Imām Ḥuseyn and his infant 'Ali Asġar (115-117). Šemr describes how violently he treated the corpse of Imām Ḥuseyn, and says that Yazid's army did not allow a sip of water for 'Ali Asġar or the other family of Imām Ḥuseyn. Instead, they kill the child with an arrow, and Šemr kicks the wounded body of Imām Ḥuseyn.

The physical violence of the antagonists is described in formulae such as 'the shameless people tear you in pieces' *(ze bas in qowm bi šarm-o ḥayāyand šumā rā pāra pāra minamāyand*) (12), 'I whip the prisoners' *(mizanam bā tāziyāna*) (24), while their victims suffer a 'wounded side' *(pahlū-ye čāk-khurda)* (26) and 'broken chest' (*sina-ye šekasta*) (26). Imām Zeyn al-'Ābedin wails, 'my father's body is cut into pieces in the dust' (*qat'a qat'a na'š-e bābam bar zamin*) (31). The exiles suffer from 'wandering door to door' or 'homeless' *(dar be dar būdan)* (137), living in a ruined place *(dar kharāba tu rā gašta maskan)* (139). Ruqaya says, 'My face is bruised blue by Šemr's slaps' *(rūyam kabūd gašta az ẓarb-e sili-ye Šemr)* (139).

Both the depiction of violence and the antitheses are very much reinforced by patterns of repetition. Repetition could be described as the most influential stylistic feature of the *ta'ziya* texts.

Ta'ziya Players and Devices

The *ta'ziya* players are all men. They are divided into two main groups, protagonists and antagonists. The former perform the roles of the Imāms, their families and their followers. The latter play the role of the enemies of Imām Ḥuseyn's family. The director and the audience also participate in the performance.

In the *ta'ziya* performance, the director uses specific devices to distinguish the protagonists from antagonists. Antagonists are ugly, with harsh voices and rude behaviour. They wear red and yellow. Antagonists are cruel to the protagonists, or they act the buffoon and appear ridiculous.[41] They motivate the audience to hate them. Protagonists are handsome with soft voices. They chant when they speak, behave reasonably and are kind to their enemies. They wear white and green, colours that reflect their virtues. In the Qur'ān, the face of the blessed on the Doomsday is said to be white,[42] while green is the colour of the Prophet. In Islamic tradition, the archangel Gabriel has two green wings and the well-Preserved Tablet (*lawḥ-e maḥfūz*, see below, *Zeynab and Imām Ḥuseyn*) is made of green emerald.[43] The good and bad behaviour of the two groups is used to instruct the spectators in the laws of religion. For instance, the antagonists are shown drinking wine, which is forbidden in Islam.

There is a repertoire of stylized gestures and props that allude to the historical setting. For instance, a player will raise his hand as a shade over his eyes, to indicate a hot, sunny day. Circling the stage several times is used to represent the distance between two places, and thus a change of scene, for instance from the plain of Karbalā to Damascus.

A bowl of water symbolizes the Euphrates, which the Umayyad troops prevent Imām Ḥuseyn and his family from reaching to drink water. A shroud (*kafan*) is the symbol of death: when a player wears it, the audience knows that he will soon die as a martyr. When the shroud is spotted with red, the player is wounded. The audience is familiar with the symbolic meanings of the objects. They help the audience to transcend the borders of time and space and feel like real observers of the events of Karbalā.

Audience Participation in the *Ta'ziya*

The role of the spectators is also important. The spectators freely show their anger and hatred towards the antagonists by shouting at them and cursing them, and they show sympathy for the protagonists. They follow the director's actions, indicating when the audience members should beat their chests or heads. The audience's role begins with literally setting the scene before the performance. For instance, if the *ta'ziya* is to be performed in a closed place such as the courtyard of a house or in a *tekiya*, the audience will decorate the walls or carpet the ground. If the *ta'ziya* is to be performed in an open area, the audience will help the director to erect a temporary *tekiya*. Some people may donate props for the performance, others will undertake to distribute sweets or sherbet among the spectators.

The *ta'ziya* spectator has a complex symbolic role. He is both mourner for Imām Ḥuseyn, and his enemy. On the one hand, he is mourning and wailing for his Imām, but at the same time the spectators surround the players in a circular form, like Yazid's army around Imām Ḥuseyn and his followers on the plain of Karbalā. The background knowledge of the spectators helps them to form a perfect mental image of the events of Karbalā.

By actively participating in the *ta'ziya*, the audience bridge the emotional gap that separates them from the real events of Karbalā.[44] They react like real observers near the battlefield, who cannot help Imām Ḥuseyn and his family. They curse Šemr and Ibn al-Sa'd. They mourn, lament, and beat their heads and chests, showing their frustration at not being able to intervene. Chest beating (*sina-zani)* is a form of physical audience participation that heightens the identification of the audience with the *ta'ziya*. First, the director beats his chest, then the procession of mourners (or players) follows him, and then the audience imitates them. There is a harmonic interplay between the director, the players in the procession and the audience. Beating one's hands over one's head operates similarly: the director sits and initiates this, the procession of mourners and the audiences follow his actions. It could be said that the audience takes part in the *ta'ziya* performance as amateur players.

The active participation of the audience in the *ta'ziya* is not limited to the performance itself. As previously mentioned, before the performance, people help the director to arrange the space, decorating the walls or spreading carpets on the ground, or helping the director to erect a temporary *tekiya*. They also bring objects to be used during the performance; through these contributions they become participants. Every object related to *ta'ziya* is acceptable.[45] During the first ten days of the month of Muḥarram, some people make vows to God to distribute sweets and sherbet among the spectators. The audience's eating can be seen as a symbolic re-enactment of the family of Imām Ḥuseyn, eating their last remaining food during the siege and imprisonment. Those who participate in the *ta'ziya* in these ways can hope for Imām Ḥuseyn's intercession on Judgement Day, and to receive God's reward in the Hereafter.

Whether the *ta'ziya* is performed in an enclosed place such as the yard of a private house or in an open area such as a bazaar or street, the audience stands in a circle around the *ta'ziya* players. Standing in this way, they represent the enemies of Imām Ḥuseyn who surrounded him,[46] while also representing the supporters of Imām Ḥuseyn who wished to be present and help him, but are unable to intervene. They show their emotions while remaining completely aware that the situation is non-realistic. They draw on their background knowledge to enrich the image of the battle of Karbalā. They are reminded of, or learn about, religious prohibitions, beliefs and moral virtues, and see vices embodied in the antagonists.

Zeynab in *Ta'ziya*

The main focus of this study is the presentation of Zeynab, Imām Ḥuseyn's sister. She was present at the battle of Karbalā, as part of the household of Imām Ḥuseyn. After the battle, the survivors were taken to Damascus, to the court of the Umayyad ruler Yazid. Along the way, when the captives arrived in Kūfa, Zeynab preached a sermon and called the people of Kūfa 'infidels' because they had invited Imām Ḥuseyn to come, but then did not assist him in Karbalā. Zeynab preached another sermon at the court of Yazid, when the ruler boasted of his ancestors and claimed that this war was revenge for the death of his ancestors, killed by the Prophet Muḥammad and his companions. Here, Zeynab criticized Yazid as being of the same rank as his pagan ancestors.

Zeynab's character traits deserve a profound study, but a general outline of her character, beliefs and behaviour can be derived from several examples of *ta'ziya* texts compiled by Ḥasan Ṣālehi Rād Darbandsari, in his *Majālis-e ta'ziya*. This is the collection used in this study. It is recent (2001), and attracted my attention because it is a complete collection of the main copies (*sar-nuskha*) used by the directors. In the various episodes in the *Majālis-e ta'ziya*, Zeynab is seen playing an effective part before and after the battle of Karbalā, so it is an appropriate example to take for this study.

In this collection, Zeynab appears as the archetype of Shiite women and as a mirror reflecting a constellation of Shiite beliefs. For instance, she submits herself to fate and God's decree. She talks to God in different tones in various situations. Sometimes she complains about Yazid and his commanders and asks desperately for justice, at other times she describes the situation and patiently waits for God's decision. A Shiite learns from Zeynab that belief in predestination and submission to God's decision is fundamental, but she also shows the concept of free will. Like other members of Imām Ḥuseyn's family, Zeynab receives inspiration (*elhām*) from the divine source. She is aware of her fate and accepts her destiny without trying to change it. Zeynab is the archetype of sacrificial behaviour. She sacrifices her children to serve justice. She is also the archetype of a leader. She teaches her community how to protest against the tyrannies of the Umayyad caliph.

Zeynab's role as a woman is emphasized by a crowd of women in the audience, who identify themselves with her.

The effect of Zeynab's curses is emphasized in several episodes. For instance, after the tenth day (*'Āšūrā*), Šemr takes the earring of Fāṭima, Imām Ḥuseyn's daughter, against her will. She cries and Zeynab curses Šemr, asking the earth to take him. In a moment, Šemr is paralyzed, until Zeynab asks God to forgive him. Zeynab's spiritual power is emphasized repeatedly. For instance, when Ibn al-Ziyād orders his soldiers to trample the bodies of the martyrs, Zeynab sends her servant, Feẓẓa, to bring a lion to protect the bodies.

As an archetype of Shiite virtue, Zeynab is portrayed as a generous person. When she and her family, who are treated as prisoners of war, return to Medina, Zeynab gives her anklet to Bašir, a man who helped them during the journey. Imām Zeyn al-'Ābedin follows Zeynab's example and gives his turban, while Sakina, the daughter of Imām Ḥuseyn, gives her necklace to Bašir (184).

A prominent feature of Zeynab is her role as the preserver of precious objects that are believed to exempt the Shiites from punishment on the Day of Judgement. These objects are two teeth of the Prophet, the bloody turban of Imām 'Ali, the torn liver of Imām Ḥasan, and the bloody robe of Imām Ḥuseyn. These objects are described as trusts (*amānāt*), given to Zeynab who, on her deathbed, gives them to her sister 'Umm al-Kulṯūm. These objects symbolize the Shiite devotional tradition, reminding Shiites of injustices done by Sunnite Muslims. For instance, the bloody turban of Imām 'Ali reminds a Shiite Muslim of the murder of 'Ali.

In the *ta'ziya* texts, Zeynab is the saviour of the line of Shiite Imāms. After the battle of Karbalā, Imām Ḥuseyn's son, Imām Zeyn al-'Ābedin, was the last surviving member of the Prophet's bloodline. When the prisoners were taken to the court, and Yazid saw Zeyn al-'Ābedin, he ordered him to be killed. Zeynab rescued her nephew, by telling Yazid that if he wished to kill him, he would have to kill her as well. Yazid released Zeyn al-'Ābedin and he returned to Medina with the other survivors from Imām Ḥuseyn's household.

In what follows, I have focused on Zeynab's relationship with several members of the family of the Prophet, beginning with her brother Imām Ḥuseyn. In the *ta'ziya* texts, their relationship is portrayed in connection with the events at Karbalā. Imām Ḥuseyn is so extremely dear to Zeynab that she offers her two sons to him. There is always a parallel between Imām Ḥuseyn and his sister Zeynab. For instance, both of them were aware of their fates at Karbalā: one fragment of text describes how they share the events of Karbalā between themselves. Imām Ḥuseyn says that he has accepted his fate, and that he knows what is going to happen to his family, informing Zeynab about the bodies of the martyrs, the dagger wounds, and the shameless Yazid's attack on the holy household. Zeynab tells Ḥuseyn about the events that were to follow the battle, elaborating on the enemy's assault on the tents and her responsibility to take care of the household. In addition to a theological dimension concerning fate, these conversations rouse the audience to sympathize with Imām Ḥuseyn and Zeynab.

There is a splendid portrayal of the relation between Zeynab and Sakina, the daughter of Imām Ḥuseyn. Zeynab behaves like a mother, a supporter and a protector of Sakina. Zeynab sacrifices herself to protect Sakina from Yazid's tyrannies. Another person who is portrayed in the *ta'ziya* texts in relation to Zeynab is the mother of Qāsem, the wife of Imām Ḥasan. Her son was killed in the battlefield. The close relation between her and Zeynab is described briefly, but sufficiently, to show that Zeynab is a leader whose words are accepted by Qāsem's mother.

Zeynab's protest against the antagonists is also described. The Umayyad caliph Yazid and his commanders Šemr, Ibn al-Ziyād and Ibn al-Sa'd are the most notorious enemies of the Prophet's family. Šemr killed Imām Ḥuseyn while he was suffering from thirst, and beat on his severed head in the presence of Zeynab and other prisoners. After the battle, Yazid ordered his army to arrest the women and children and take them through a bazaar and to his court, without allowing them to cover their heads with veils. The issue of unveiling is a crucial one in Iranian history. Reẓā Shah (1925-1941), the founder of Pahlavi dynasty (1925-1979), outlawed the veil (*ḥejāb*) in public in 1936, as part of a modernization plan for Iran.[47] Zeynab does not fear Yazid's commanders, talking to them in loud voice, cursing them, and reminding them of God's justice.

The *ta'ziya* composers have transformed several historical facts. For instance, Sakina, the four-year-old daughter of Imām Ḥuseyn, died during the imprisonment, but in the *ta'ziya* she appears as a mature girl who is Zeynab's companion. In the last part, we see how the events of Karbalā are influenced by Persian concepts. For instance, Imām Ḥuseyn has eponyms such as 'the headless king' (*Shah-e bi-sar*) and 'the king of Karbalā' (*Shah-e karbalā*). The term for kingship, and the ethic of kingship alluded to, draws on the Persian monarchial tradition. In the *ta'ziya* of 'the Damascus bazaar,' Ḥuseyn is referred to as *ān Shah-e bā farr* – that glorious king (130), but the 'glory' (*farr*) is a specific divinely-given quality associated only with ancient Persian kings.

Zeynab plays an important role in modern Iranian culture. After their conversion to Shiite Islam, Iranians elaborated on the role of Zeynab in the context of Imām Ḥuseyn's martyrdom, taking her as a religious and social example. Beliefs and virtues are represented in her behaviour. Thus, many women follow her character as the archetype of an ideal woman. Zeynab is particularly present in Shiite Iran during the first ten days of the month of Muḥarram. Sometimes, she is remembered during the devotional rituals; at other times, preachers recite an elegy for the oppressions that she suffered. For instance, she is honoured in connection with the commemoration of the martyrdom of Imām 'Ali. She is present in everyday life and in the hearts of Iranians. Every year, many Iranians travel to Syria to visit Zeynab's shrine.

Notes

1 The term Imām refers to the leadership of the Shiite community after the death of the Prophet. See 'The Concept of Imāma in Shiite Tradition' in the present study.

2 The first date is in the Islamic lunar calendar, followed by the Western calendar, i.e. A.H. /A.D.

3 A. Bulūkbāši, *Ta'ziya-khāni, hadiṭ-e qudsi-ye maṣā'eb dar namāyeš-e ā'inī*, Tehran: Amir kabir, 1383/2006. p. 42.

4 H.P. Schmidt, in *Encyclopaedia Iranica*, under Mithra, I. Mitra in Old Indian and Mithra in Old Iranian; W. Sundermann, in *Encyclopaedia Iranica*, under Mithra, III. in Manicheism.

5 E. Yarshater, 'Ta'ziyeh and Pre-Islamic Mourning Rites in Iran', in *Ta'ziyeh: Ritual and Drama in Iran*, ed. P.J. Chelkowski, New York: New York University Press & Soroush Press, 1979, p. 89.

6 Ibid., p. 90; J.G.J. ter Haar, 'Ta'ziye: Ritual Theater from Shiite Iran,' pp. 160-161. For further information on mourning rites for Siyāvuš and their connection to death see E. Yarshater, 'Iranian National History', in *The Cambridge History of Iran, the Seleucid, Parthian and Sasanian Periods*, vol. 3 (1), ed. E. Yarshater, Cambridge: Cambridge University Press, 1983, pp. 450-1.

7 For further information on *'Āšūrā* see M. Ayoub, in *Encyclopaedia Iranica*, under 'Āšūrā. For information about the 40th day (*arba'in*) after the death of Imām Ḥuseyn see M. Ayoub, in *Encyclopaedia Iranica*, under Arba'īn. Ṣāleḥi Najafābādi in his *Šahid-e jāvid* (The Eternal Martyr) discusses how Imām Ḥuseyn protested and how his martyrdom at the plain of Karbalā was a political act. Najafābādi observes the roots of the battle in the historical conflicts between the Umayyad dynasty (661-750) and the Prophet's family. See N.Ṣ. Najafābādi,

Šahid-e jāvid (The Eternal Martyr), Tehran: *mu'assesa-ye khadamāt-e farhangi-ye Rasā*, 1361/1982.

8 The term 'Āšūrā is derived from the Arabic number *'ašar*, meaning ten.

9 According to Shiites, Imām Ḥuseyn was martyred (*šahid*) in the battle of Karbalā. The term *šahid* means 'being witness' and 'testifying witness.' The term *šahāda* refers to the formula used to profess faith in Islam: 'there is no God but God and Muhammad is the messenger of God'. See D. Gimaret, in *The Encyclopaedia of Islam* (second edition), under *Shahāda*. E. Kohlberg, in *The Encyclopaedia of Islam* (second edition), under *Shahīd*. See also A.A. Seyed-Gohrab, *Martelaren: Van mystieke weg tot oorlogspad*, Amsterdam: KNAW Press, 2009.

10 For information on the Al-Mukhtār's movement see 'Abd al-Husain Zarrinkūb, 'The Arab Conquest of Iran and its Aftermath', in *The Cambridge History of Iran*, vol. 4, ed. R.N. Frye, Cambridge: Cambridge University Press, 1975, pp. 33-38.

11 S. Husain M. Jafri, *Origins and Early Development of Shi'a Islam*, Tehran: Ansariyan Publications, 1989, pp. 222-233.

12 For further information on 'Ali Asġar see J. Calmard, in *Encyclopaedia Iranica*, under 'Ali Asġar.

13 J.G.J. ter Haar, 'Ta'ziye: Ritual Theater from Shiite Iran,' p. 159.

14 R.M. Savory & C.E. Bosworth, in *The Encyclopaedia of Islam* (second edition), under *Tahmāsp* (*Tahmāsb*).

15 See J.T.P. de Bruijn, in *The Encyclopaedia of Islam* (second edition), under *Muḥtas̲h̲am-i Kāshānī*.

16 See Zabih Allāh Ṣafā and EIr, in *Encyclopaedia Iranica*, under *Ḥātef, Sayyed Aḥmad Eṣfahanī*.

17 See M. Shaki, in *The Encyclopaedia of Islam* (second edition), under *Ḳā'* ānī.

18 Ṣ. Humāyūni, *Ta'ziya va ta'ziya-khāni* [Tehran]: čāpkhāna *bist-o panjom* šahrivar, [1354/1975], pp. 34-35; P.E. Losensky, in *Encyclopaedia of Islam*, under Waḳār.

19 J.G.J. ter Haar, 'Ta'ziye: Ritual Theater from Shiite Iran,' pp. 161-162; M. Bektash, 'Ta'ziyeh and its Philosophy', in *Ta'ziyeh: Ritual and Drama in Iran*, ed. P.J. Chelkowski, New York: New York University Press and Soroush Press, 1979, pp. 101-102.

20 As cited by J.G.J. ter Haar, 'Ta'ziye: Ritual Theater from Shiite Iran,' pp. 164-165.

21 Ibid., pp. 165-167.

22 Ibid., pp. 173-174.

23 Humāyūni, *Ta'ziya va ta'ziya-khāni*, p. 22.

24 Ibid., for more information on the Mahdi see Colin Turner, *Islam without Allah? The Rise of Religious Externalism in Safarid Islam*, Richmond: Curzon, 2002, pp. 187-230.

25 Ibid.

26 R. Narasimahan, 'Literacy: Its Characterization and Implications', in *Literacy and Orality*, ed. D.R. Olson and N. Torrance, Cambridge: Cambridge University Press, 1991, p. 178.

27 R. Finnegan, *Literacy and Orality Studies in the Technology of Communication*, Oxford: Opus, 1988, pp. 88-89.
28 Ibid., p. 69.
29 Ibid., p. 89.
30 W.J. Ong, *Orality and Literacy the Technologizing of the World*, London & New York: Methuen, 1982, pp. 23-26.
31 Ibid., pp. 39-41.
32 Ibid., p. 38.
33 Ibid., p. 44.
34 References in parentheses are pages numbers in H. Ṣāleḥi Rād Darbandsari, *Majālis-e ta'ziya*, vol. 2, Tehran: Suroush, 1380/2001.
35 Zahrā is a title of Fāṭima, the Prophet's daughter.
36 S. Sharma, *Persian Poetry at Indian Frontier: Mas'ud Sa'd Salman of Lahore*, Oxford: Permanent Black, 2000, pp. 47-48.
37 Šahrbānū is the daughter of Yazdgerd III, the last Sasanian king of Iran. She is the wife of Imām Ḥuseyn. See M. Boyce, *Zoroastrians their Religious Beliefs and Practices*, London: Routledge & Kegan Paul Ltd, 1979, p. 151.
38 Karbalā here is called Karb-o balā, meaning 'affliction and calamity.'
39 For more examples see H. Ṣāleḥi Rād Darbandsari, *Majālis-e ta'ziya*, pp. 54, 55, 62, 74, 75, 76.
40 '*šahr-o bāzār burdan*', refers to showing slaves in the bazaar to be sold.
41 A. Shahidi, 'Literary and Musical Developments in the Ta'ziyeh', in *Ta'ziyeh: Ritual and Drama in Iran*, ed. P.J. Chelkowski, New York: New York University Press and Soroush Press, 1979, p. 42.
42 A. Schimmel, in *The Encyclopaedia Iranica*, under *Colour*.
43 A. Morabia, in *The Encyclopaedia of Islam* (second edition), under *Lawn*.
44 W.O. Beeman, 'Cultural Dimensions of Performance Conventions in Iranian Ta'ziyeh' in *Ta'ziyeh: Ritual and Drama in Iran*, ed. P.J. Chelkowski, New York: New York University Press and Soroush Press, 1979, p. 28.
45 P.J. Chelkowski, 'Ta'ziyeh: Indigenous Avant-Garde Theatre of Iran', in *Ta'ziyeh: Ritual and Drama in Iran*, ed. P. J. Chelkowski, New York: New York University Press and Soroush Press, 1979, p. 8.
46 W.O. Beeman, 'Cultural Dimensions of Performance Conventions in Iranian Ta'ziyeh', in *Ta'ziyeh: Ritual and Drama*, pp. 26-30.
47 H. Afra, in *Encyclopaedia Britannica*, under *Reza Shah Pahlavi*.

'Āšūrā, the Martyrdom of Imām Ḥuseyn

A Crisis of Succession

After the death of the Prophet Muḥammad (13/632) Muslims faced a major problem in relation to leadership of their community. The Sunnis, who are today the majority group, trace their tradition to those who denied the importance of a blood relationship between the elected Imām and the Prophet. They believed that the Imām, in the sense of the leader of the Muslims, could be chosen by consensus (*ejmā'*) or acknowledged by the community. The Shiites trace their tradition to those who believed that the Prophet had chosen 'Ali Ibn Abi Ṭālib[1] as his successor, at Ġadir Khumm,[2] and that 'Ali also had a superior claim, being the cousin of the Prophet and the husband of his daughter, Fāṭima.

Those of the first group, who had majority support among the powerful men of the Muslim community, appointed Abū Bakr. He was one of the first companions of the Prophet to be called the 'Vicar of the Messenger of God' (*khalifa rasūl Allāh*). After Abū Bakr two other companions of the Prophet, 'Umar and 'Uthmān, were selected to lead the Muslim community. Only after them did 'Ali assume the leadership, as the fourth caliph. He led the Muslim community for just five years. When he was murdered (in 41/661), the Sunnite community accepted the leadership of Mu'āwiya, even though he was not among the first companions of the Prophet. He was accepted for the sake of unity. Mu'āwiya died in 680 but, before his death, he took the oath of allegiance from several tribes to choose his son Yazid as the caliph. Few refused to give the oath of allegiance to Yazid. According to the Shiites, Yazid drank wine and behaved immorally. Sunnites make a distinction between the first four caliphs, known as the rightly guided caliphs (*rāšidūn*), who completely followed the Sunna, and whose just acts and decisions have guided the community ever since, and the later caliphs such as Mu'āwiya and Yazid who are considered mere worldly rulers. Obedience to them is justified by the importance of maintaining the internal peace of the Muslim community.

The Shiites, however, believed in the leadership of the Muslim community by the descendents of Imām ʿAli. After his death, his two sons, first Ḥasan and then Ḥuseyn, were the Shiite Imāms, and the Imāmate was then handed down from father to son. The elder son Hasan was deprived of the caliphate by Muʿāwiya and seems to have been politically inactive. It is the life and tragic death of the second son, and third Imām, Ḥuseyn, which is the subject of *taʿziya*.

The Martyrdom of Imām Ḥuseyn

After the death of Muʿāwiya in Damascus, the Shiites of Kūfa wrote several letters to Imām Ḥuseyn, inviting him to their city to lead them. Imām Ḥuseyn sent his uncle Muslim Ibn al-ʿAqil Ibn Abi Ṭālib to investigate the situation in Kūfa. Muslim Ibn al-ʿAqil took the oath of allegiance from the people of Kūfa. Then he sent a letter to Imām Ḥuseyn confirming what the Kufians had written. When Ibn Ziyād, the governor of Kūfa, found out about the revolt of the people of Kūfa, he arrested Muslim Ibn-e ʿAqil and executed him. When Imām Ḥuseyn received Muslim Ibn al-ʿAqil's letter (almost 17 days after his death), he set out from Medina to Kūfa with a small group of followers and his household, but he never reached Kūfa. The army of Yazid surrounded them on the plain of Karbalā near the Euphrates, but blocked their access to water. ʿUmar Ibn al-Saʿd, ʿUbaydullah's commander, offered two options to Imām Ḥuseyn: to give an oath of allegiance to Yazid, or to fight Yazid's army. The negotiation between Imām Ḥuseyn and the Yazid's commanders lasted nine days, during which Ḥuseyn and his followers suffered from thirst and hunger. Abu al-Faẕl al-ʿAbbās, the half brother of Imām Ḥuseyn, could not tolerate the crying of the children, and galloped to the Euphrates several times to bring some water for them, but he was killed.[3] On the tenth day of the month of Muḥarram in 60/680, the battle started: it lasted one day. Imām Ḥuseyn and his men were killed while suffering from thirst and hunger. In *taʿziya* performances, the thirst of Ḥuseyn and his family is elaborated to fan the audience's emotions. To give one example, ʿAli Asġar was Ḥuseyn's six-month old child, who died of thirst. When Imām Ḥuseyn asked for a sip of water for him, a man from the tribe of Banū ʾAsad shot an arrow at the throat of the infant and killed him.

During the war, several warriors from Yazid's army joined Imām Ḥuseyn and fought to the death. One famous *ta'ziya* episode is the story of Hurr Ibn al-Riyāhi, who was Ibn al-Ziyād's commander. He joined Imām Ḥuseyn during the fight.

During the battle of Karbalā, all the men were killed except 'Ali Ibn al-Ḥuseyn, later called Imām Zeyn al-'Ābedin. It is said that he was extremely ill and could not join the fight, or that he had to live in order to guarantee the line of the Shiite Imāms. After the battle, the survivors from Imām Ḥuseyn's household were arrested and taken to Yazid's court in Damascus (a distance of some 180 kilometres), along with the severed heads of the martyrs mounted on lances. According to the Shiites, Yazid treated the prisoners harshly, not even sparing the severed heads. He humiliated the prisoners and even struck the lips of the severed head of Imām Ḥuseyn with his staff. Zeynab protested and saved the life of Zeyn al-'Ābedin. After several days, during which the four-year-old daughter of Imām Ḥuseyn died, the prisoners were released and returned to Medina.

The Concept of Imāma in Shiite Tradition

Imāmi theologians taught that there must always be an Imām, designated by the Prophet (in the case of 'Ali) or the previous Imām. Under the leadership of Imām Ja'far al-Ṣādiq (d.148/765), the Shiite doctrine of the Imāmate crystallized. The Imām's station was raised almost to the level of prophethood, except that the Imām did not have a Holy Book.[4]

The Shiite Muslims later divided into several branches. Among these are the Zaydiyya, the Imāmiyya or 'twelver' Shiites, and the Ismā'iliyya. The Imāmiyya, the majority Shiite sect in Iran today, believe that the twelfth Imām, a child, was supernaturally concealed after the death of the eleventh Imām: he is still alive today and is expected to return before the end of the world.[5] One of the fundamental doctrines of the Imāmiyya is that the Imām is protected from sin and error (*ma'ṣūm*). If the Imām fears for his own safety or for that of his community, he has to practice dissimulation (*taqqiya*).[6]

According to Shiite readings, the Qur'ān addresses the Imām as 'the light of God,' and his 'witness' (*šāhed*) among mankind. The Imāms are the 'vicegerents' (*khulafā'*) of God on earth. They have the knowledge of the Qur'ān, and of the past and present. Indeed, their knowledge is the same as the knowledge of the Prophet. The Imāms are inspired by angels, although unlike the Prophet they cannot see the angels. For the community, disobeying the Imām is equal to disobeying the prophet.[7]

In the *ta'ziya* texts, the Imām Ḥuseyn has the same characteristics as the Prophet. He advises Šemr, Yazid's commander, that it would be better for him to join Imām Ḥuseyn. He claims to be one who reveals the secrets of the Torah to Jewish priests; who showed Moses the path, because he sees the manifestation of the light. Then he warns Šemr of the punishment (*'azāb*) that he will receive in the grave (*gūr*) and on the day of Resurrection (10). In the above episode, Imām Ḥuseyn shows that his knowledge is equal to the knowledge of the prophets. In the *ta'ziya* texts, even Imām Ḥuseyn's enemies regret his death. For instance, Šemr says that they have shot with an arrow a person whose heart derives inspiration from the divine source (*ṣandūq-e 'elm-e vahi-ye khudā*) (171).

Several other characteristics are attributed to Imām Ḥuseyn. For instance, he is the locus of the lights of divine guidance (*maẓhar-e anvār-e hedāyat*) (200), an intermediary between God and the people, and he guides Shiite Muslims. Similarly, in some passages, Zeynab (25) and Batūl (the title of Fāṭima) (16, 34, 241) are shown as able to intercede on behalf of the Shiite Muslims on the Day of Judgement. In the following examples we see that Imām Ḥuseyn sacrificed himself for the salvation of the Shiites. In other words, he accepted that he would see his family and followers killed and would himself be drowned in blood, for the sake of the Shiite community. Šemr, the archetype of a heartless enemy and the murderer of Imām Ḥuseyn, reports that when he was about to kill Imām Ḥuseyn, the Imām prayed to God that he would forgive the sins of the Muslims. Šemr says,

> *be ẓulmhā ke be jānam resid khursandam*
> *be piš-e dida buridand sar ze farzandam*
> *reẓā šudam ke be khūn ġūtavar šavad qaddam*
> *be šarṭ-e ān ke bebakhši be 'ummat-e jaddam* (174).

> The tyranny I have suffered, I accept:
> They severed the heads of my children before my eyes.
> I am content, that my body should be drowned in blood,
> On condition, that you forgive the followers of my grandfather (Muḥammad) (174).

In the *ta'ziya* texts, the Imām is respected by the angels. For instance, Imām Ḥuseyn in his childhood had such dignity that the angels around the throne of God salute him (79). In the scene set in the Damascus bazaar, the young Imām Zeyn al-'Ābedin boasts about the dignity of his family before Yazid. He says that a carpet spread in their portico is the most exalted throne, that all who breathe (lit., all who eat) are their guests, that natural forces such as clouds, rain and wind obey their orders. He is the heir of the King of Religion [Imām Ḥuseyn] (127).

During her imprisonment in the ruins in Damascus, Zeynab says:

jalāl-o raf'at-e mā rā khudā-ye'ālamiyān
nemūda yād be 'ezzat be sūra-ye Qur'ān (144).

For honour's sake, the Lord of the Worlds,
Has recalled our glory and dignity in a chapter in the Qur'ān (144).

In the *ta'ziya*, Yazid too calls Imām Ḥuseyn the beloved of the Lord of the two worlds (*'aziz-e khāṣ-e rabb-o al-'ālameyn*) (162).

Another important feature relating to the Shiite concept of leadership (*Imāma*) is that Shiites have to obey their Imām. When the Imām Ḥuseyn's family are freed, they return to Medina. Bašir is the leader of their caravan. When they arrive near Medina, Bašir says to Imām Zeyn al-'Ābedin,

dardhā-ye hama darmān az tu
ḥukm ḥukm-e tu-vo farmān az tu (182).

You are the cure for all people's pains,
It is yours to judge, and yours to give orders (182).

Such passages remind the audience that they have to obey the Imām, and turn to him because he heals their grief.

Martyrdom (*Šahādat*)

The term martyr (*šahid*) literally means 'a witness,' referring to a person who is slain in the path of God. *Šahid* is a Qur'ānic term and a divine name. Several verses, such as 3/140 and 4/69, emphasize the rank and dignity of martyrs in the eyes of God. According to the Qur'ānic statements, the *šuhadā* are alive (*aḥyā*). The term *šahādat* (the station of a martyr) summons images of the rewards that a *šahid* receives in paradise. For instance, he is among the blessed, his intercession for 70 members of his family will be accepted, and he does not suffer the torments of the grave.[8]

According to both Sunnite and Shiite traditions, the body of a *šahid* does not have to be ritually washed (*ġusl*) before burial, because his martyrdom itself has cleansed the ritual impurity of dead things. He is buried in his own clothes, because the blood on them is a testimony to his martyrdom.[9] Death in battle against infidels guarantees forgiveness and rewards from God in the Hereafter. The martyr has sacrificed his life, but receives a higher rank after death. In the early Islamic period, mothers whose children had been martyred in the battlefield did not mourn and did not organize a mourning service for them. This was also practised during the Islamic Revolution of 1979 and during the war between Iran and Iraq (1980-88).[10]

Imām Ḥuseyn is called the master of the martyrs (*seyed al-šuhadā'*): he was killed in the battle of Karbalā, fighting to preserve the religion of God. In paradise, he is the host for the other martyrs, who are called his guests. A person who fights in the path of God hopes to see his master after death. In the *ta'ziya* texts, when Zeynab sends her two sons to the battlefield, she states: 'So that you may both be the guests of my Ḥuseyn (*ke hastid har du mehmān-e Ḥuseynam*)' (24).

In the *ta'ziya* texts, the concept of martyrdom is central, and is vividly depicted. The darkness of death is turned into the bright start of a new life beside the blessed saints in paradise. Death in the path of God is a medium through which the martyr receives grace (*fayẓ*) emanating from God. After the death of her brother, Zeynab tells Ibn-e Ziyād that God has given an emanation of His grace to Ḥuseyn through the cup of martyrdom (*fayẓ az jām-e šahādat be Ḥuseyn dād khudā*) (84). Martyrdom is likened to a cup of wine: by drinking it the martyr imbibes an effusion (*fayẓ*) of grace from God.

The eminent medieval mystic Šihāb al-Din Suhrawardi (d.587/1191) presents a descending hierarchy of emanation from God, in which each entity receives the emanation from its superior entity, which is created by God. The lower entities are subordinate to the higher ones. The first medium of grace is universal intellect and the lowest is man. Love connects the entities together and it is love for the Creator that motives man to seek union with God, who is the origin of emanation.[11] The Most Holy Emanation (*al-fayẓ al-aqdas*) is a reference to those entities that were in the presence of God before they entered the world. The Holy Emanation (*al-fayẓ al-muqaddas*) is the manifestation of divine qualities in the world, in the form of a creature.[12] These creatures act as a medium between God and mankind; they receive the emanation of grace from God and bestow it to other creatures. However, death in the path of God allows the martyr to receive the grace emanating from God directly.

In the *ta'ziya* texts there is an episode in which 'Abd al-Allāh Ibn al-'Afif, a follower of Imām 'Ali who had lost his eyes in the battles of Jamal and Seffin, protests against Ibn al-Ziyād. 'Abd al-Allāh is present at the court of Ibn al-Ziyād when the survivors of Imām Ḥuseyn's household are brought in. When Ibn al-Ziyād strikes the lips and teeth of Imām Ḥuseyn's severed head, 'Abd al-Allāh condemns him and Ibn al-Ziyād orders the executioner to kill him.[13] 'Abd al-Allāh is happy and says, 'Why should I be frightened, because I am to be a martyr in the path of God' (*če tarsi bāšadam zirā šahid-e rāh-e ḥaqq gardam*) (92). 'Abd al-Allāh prays to God: 'Martyrdom is to be my part, at the hand of the worst enemy' (*šahādat šud naṣib-e man be dast-e badtarin dušman*) (92). Belief in the concept of martyrdom eliminates the fear of death, and one killed by the enemy of religion will be rewarded in the Hereafter.

Another image, one which covers the fear of death with an attractive worldly desire, is the comparison of the martyr to a bridegroom. Marriage is associated with joy. The 'marriage' of a martyr will be on the Day of Judgement when he receives his reward. In the *ta'ziya*, when Zeynab sends her sons (Muḥammad and 'Awn) to the battlefield to help her brother, she says to Muḥammad, 'I wish I could see your wedding' (*delam mikhāst tā gardi tu dāmād*) (17). He answers, 'My wedding will be on the Day of Judgement' (*'arūsiyam buvad dar rūz-e maḥšar*) (17). When Zeynab asks her son what she should say to his father about their impending martyrdom, Muḥammad says, 'Tell him that they were married at Karbalā' (*begū dar Karbalā gaštand dāmād*) (18). Another example is the death of Qāsem, a young bridegroom who never consummated his marriage, and who is referred to as the martyr-groom. During the tragic events of Karbalā he married Fāṭima, the daughter of Imām Ḥuseyn, at the latter's suggestion. After the battle, Zeynab goes to the battlefield, and when she recognizes Qāsem's dead body, she says, 'May his marriage be blessed' (*buvad dāmādi-ye Qāsem mubārak*) (22). Imām Zeyn al-'Ābedin responds, 'May his festive clothes be blessed' (*lebās-e šādiy-e Qāsem mubārak*) (22), likening his bloodstained shroud to the fine clothes put on for a festive occasion. Qāsem's wife, Fāṭima, in her loneliness and helplessness, talks with her husband as a bridegroom just married (*tāza dāmād*): 'I greet you, my sorrowful new groom, O! I greet you' (*as-salām ey tāza-dāmād-e ġaminam as-salām*) (103).

The shroud (*kafan*) is compared to the groom's wedding clothes (*lebās-e dāmādi*). When Zeynab sends her two sons to the battlefield, she first prepares their shrouds, saying:

kafan az bahr-e ṭeflānam buridam
vali rakht-e 'arūsi būd inhā
kafan rakht-e 'arūsi gašt ḥālā (15).

I am making shrouds for my children,
but these were to be their wedding clothes:
Now the shroud is a wedding dress (15).

Another image of the martyr is as a 'rose all in petals' (*gul-e parpar*), referring to a rose that has been torn apart, petal by petal. When Zeynab recognizes her brother in the battlefield among the dead bodies, she says, 'I guess this scattered rose is Ḥuseyn' (*gamānam in gul-e par par Ḥuseyn ast*) (22). The metaphor of a rose whose petals are torn apart is a fitting image, emphasizing how the bodies of Ḥuseyn and his followers were cut to pieces. The image was widely used for soldiers killed in the Iran-Iraq war (1980-88). For instance, this exclamation was used, 'From where is this torn rose coming? / It is returning from Karb-o-bala' (*in gul-e par par ze kujā āmada/ az safar-e karb-o balā āmada*). War cemeteries were named the flower gardens of the martyrs (*gulzār-e šuhadā*).

Notes

1 E. Kohlberg & I.K. Poonawala, in *Encyclopaedia Iranica*, under *'Ali b. Abi* Ṭāleb.
2 When the Prophet Muḥammad returned from his farewell pilgrimage *(ḥajat al-vedā')* he stopped at Ġadīr Khumm and said to his companions, 'He for whom I am the *mawlā* (the patron), for him 'Alī is also the *mawlā* (*man kuntu mawlāhu fa-'Alī mawlāhu*)'. For further information see L. Veccia Valieri, in *The Encyclopaedia of Islam* (second edition), under *Ghadīr Khumm*.
3 For information on Abu al-Fazl al-'Abbās see J. Calmard, in *Encyclopaedia Iranica*, under *Abbas ibn B. 'Ali ibn Abū Ṭāleb*.
4 W. Madelung, in *The Encyclopaedia of Islam* (second edition), under *Imāma*. For contemporary doctrines on twelver Shiite see C. Turner, *Islam without Allah? The Rise of Religious Externalism in Safavid Iran*, Richmond: Curzon, 2002, pp. 72-138.

5 Ibid. For more information on the Mahdi see C. Turner, *Islam without Allah...*, pp. 187-230.
6 Ibid.
7 Ibid.
8 E. Kohlberg, in *The Encyclopaedia of Islam* (second edition), under *Shahīd.*
9 Ibid.
10 Ibid.
11 R.C. Solomon & K.M. Higgins, *From Africa to Zen: An Invitation to World Philosophy*, Rowman & Littlefield, 2003.
12 S. Murata, *The Tao of Islam: A Sourcebook on Gender Relationships in Islamic Thought*, Albany, N.Y.: State University of New York Press, 1992, pp. 98-99.
13 H. Ṣāleḥi Rād Darbandsari, *Majālis-e ta'ziya*, p. 73.

Eschatology

Islamic Eschatology

The events that precede the Last Day (*yawm al-ākher*) are an important theme in the Qur'ān. The Last Day is indicated with terms such as 'the day of resurrection' (*yawm al-qiyāma*) and 'the day of judgement' (*yawm al-din*).[1] Several verses warn people of the day of resurrection: a day that is already specified but is not known to men, including the Prophet. God is the only one who knows it. However, the Qur'ān refers to several natural apocalyptic signs as preludes of the Last Day. For example:

> When the sun will be darkened, when the stars will be thrown down, when the mountains will be set moving, when the ten-month pregnant camels will be neglected [...] then will a soul know what it has produced (81/1-14).[2]

These are among several cosmic events that, according to the traditional account, will follow the first blast of the trumpet on the Last Day. Upon the first blast of the trumpet, all creatures will die and on the second blast all creatures will rise. All of them, including humans, jinn and animals will gather (*ḥašr*). This is the time when each man's deeds will be counted (*ḥesāb*). Each man receives the book that records his deeds and decisions in the physical world. People who acted morally will be given their book in their right hand, while those who acted immorally will be given their book in their left hand.[3] In other words, man is responsible for his deeds and decisions in this world and will be judged or 'weighed' (*mizān*) by God on the Last Day. The physical world is the place of action and the Hereafter is the place of recompense for actions.[4] Those who performed good deeds will enter paradise (*behešt*). Belief in the Last Day is, with belief in God and his Messengers, one of the most important actions we can perform.

The abode of the evil-doers is hell *(jahannam)*. The *kāfar*, the people who do not believe in God and the Last Day and who do not submit to the religion of God, will fall into hell. On the Last Day, the evil-doers repent and ask God for the chance to return to the world and perform good deeds. According to the Qur'ān, the evil-doers have to pass along a path (*al-ṣirāt*) (Q.37/23-24), which, for people who do not have faith and have not performed good deeds, will be a bridge sharper than a sword and thinner than a hair.[5]

People whose final place is hell are characterized as those who believe neither in God, nor in the Hereafter, who stray from the path of religion. In the Qur'ān, hell has names such as *jahannam* (the purgatorial hell for the Muslims), *laza* (blazing fire for Christians), *al-hutāmah* (the intense fire for the Jews), *sa'ir* (a flaming fire for Sabians), *saqar* (a scorching fire for Zoroastrians), *al-jaḥim* (a huge hot for idolators) and *hāwiya* (bottomless pit for the hypocrites).[6] On the Last Day, sinners fall into the fire; they drink from the tree of Zaqqūm[7] (Q.37/42-3), they suffer tortures such as drinking fiercely boiling water (Q.55/44), and are bound together in chains. When the evil-doers enter hell, a voice says: 'Seize him and drag him into the depths of the chastisement of *jahannam*, then pour out boiling water over his head' (Q.11/109).[8] Such images of apocalyptic upheavals, an exacting judgement and terrible punishment, are far from reassuring, but a martyr (*šahid*) in the cause of Islam is assured of entering paradise. They 'will rejoice in God's bounty and blessing.'[9] The Qur'ān attributes several characteristics to the dwellers of paradise: they have believed in God and observed the religious laws, done good deeds such as feeding the poor and orphans, and have helped others for the sake of God. They receive their rewards in paradise, a garden where there is no bitter cold and where rivers of water, milk, wine and honey flow. The inhabitants of paradise may drink freely from the rivers. They are adorned with gold and clothed with fine silk robes, and black-eyed beautiful virgins (*huris*) serve them.[10]

Another important feature of Qur'ānic eschatology is the concept of intercession (*šefā'at*). In general, God is shown warning that no-one can protect sinners from punishment: they are all responsible for their deeds and acts. But there are several exceptions to this: some beings, such as angels (Q.53/26), true witnesses (Q.43/86), and those who have made a covenant with God (Q.19/87) are allowed to intercede. The Qur'ān contains no direct reference to the intercession of the Prophet Muḥammad, but this role is given to him by tradition.[11]

Eschatology in the *Ta'ziya* Texts

The *ta'ziya* texts use several Persian and Arabic synonyms for the Last Day (*ākherat*), such as *maḥšar* (a place of assembly, the day of judgement), *rūz-e 'araṣāt* (the day of presence in the Court), *rūz-e bāz-pasin* (the day that one brings back what he earns in the physical world, Hereafter), *rastākhiz* (the day of resurrection), *rūz-e ḥesāb* (the day of counting 'judgement'), *rūz-e jazā* (the day of punishment), *qiyāmat* (the day of resurrection), and *rūz-e našūr* (the day of resurrection). The mentioned terms indicate a heightened sensitivity to the Last Day, which overshadows the present action. They remind the audience that evil-doers will be punished in the Hereafter. On the Last Day their apologies will not be accepted and they cannot delay their punishment. Yet, the grace of God might help the evil-doers. For instance, in the *ta'ziya* of Yazid's Penitence (*ta'ziya pašimān šudan-e Yazid*), Yazid's wife Hendeh tells him that God may have mercy on him (168). The mercy of God is conditional: if Yazid repents and apologizes to Imām Zeyn al-'Ābedin, and if the Imām accepts his apology, God will show mercy. She says,

ey Yazid biyā tark-e rūsiyāhi kun
be nazd-e ḥaẓrat-e Sajjād[12] *'uzrkhāhi kun [...]*
ke balka čāre-ye dard-e tu gardad ey bi-din
khudāy raḥm kunad bar tu rūz-e bāzpasin (168).

O! Yazid, cease blackening your own face
Apologize before his holiness, the one who bows in prayer, Imām
Perhaps this will cure your pain, O godless one,
God will show mercy to you on the Last Day (168).

Paradise and hell are important features of the *ta'ziya* texts. They emphasize the concept of hell to highlight the punishments that the Umayyad caliph and his army will suffer. Terms such as *dūzakh* and *saqar* refer to the hell where unbelievers are to be punished. The sin of infidelity (*kufr*) is associated with the main antagonists: Yazid and his commanders' Šemr, Ibn al-Ziyād and Ibn al-Sa'd. Their army is also called the infidel army (*sepāh-e kufr*) (63, 89, 102, 170). Not only the audience, but also the antagonists know they will be punished. Ibn al-Ziyād, for example, tells his servants that his oppression of the household of Imām Ḥuseyn is a deed that will be counted on the threshold of hell (*dūzakh*):

ey khādemān-e dargah-e dūzakh ṭarāz-e mā (75).
O my servants! Our deeds will be counted on the threshold of hell (75).

In the *ta'ziya* texts the Prophet and his daughter Fāṭima will, on the Last Day, question the antagonists about their unjust behaviour towards Imām Ḥuseyn and his household. In one episode, the tyrant Ibn al-Ziyād orders that Mukhtār, who is one of the Shiites imprisoned for his faithfulness to Imām Ḥuseyn, should be brought to the court. When Mukhtār enters the court and sees the condition of the Imām Ḥuseyn's family and followers there, he damns Ibn al-Ziyād and warns him that on the Last Day he will answer to God, the Prophet and Fāṭima. He states,

be ḥeyratam ke javāb-e khudā če migūi
javāb-e ḥaẓrat-e kheyr-o nessā' če migūi[13]
javāb-e jadd-e kebāraš be saḥna-ye maḥšar
čegūn-e midahi ey fāseq-e ze sag kamtar? (78)

I have no idea what you will say in answer to God
What will you answer to Fāṭima, the embodiment of virtue and feminity?
What will you answer to Muḥammad at the last judgement?
O libertine, less than a dog, how will you answer? (78)

In the *ta'ziya* texts the most common torture that the antagonists will suffer in hell is falling into the fire. For example, in the *ta'ziya* 'entering the place of execution' (*majles-e ta'ziya vurūd-e be qatlgāh*), Zeynab damns Šemr and prays to God:

elāhi dar saqar ū rā besūzān
ke gardad bā'eṯ-e marg-e yatimān (25).

O! God, burn him in hell
Because he is the cause of the death of orphans (25).

Zeynab believes that the fire of hell is not enough for the punishment of Šemr. She states,

dānam az nālehā-ye ātašbār
ātaš-e dūzakh 'ektefā nakunad (106).

Because of flaming lamentations, I know
That the fire of hell is not enough [for your punishment] (106).

Another feature of the punishment of unbelievers and oppressors in hell is dragging them to the lowest level (*darakāt*). The evil-doers who fall into hell will be deprived of the mercy of God. He damns (*la'n*) them constantly for eternity. In one episode, Yazid sees the Prophet in a dream, ordering the archangel Gabriel to pull him (Yazid) to the lowest level. Gabriel then orders the angel of hell (*malak-e dūzakh*) to take him down (157-158).

The *Ta'ziya* Texts

The *ta'ziya* texts are composed in verse, in simple language that is close to the language of ordinary people. The composers do not use many literary figures, difficult expressions and allusions. Therefore, the texts are understandable for all walks of life. *Ta'ziya* is written to be performed, not to be read silently.[14] The manuscripts of the texts of *ta'ziya* were recorded in the pamphlet (*daftar*). Humāyūni quotes the historian Muḥammad Muḥit Ṭabāṭabā'i (d.1988) who saw a dated text that had survived from the Ṣafavid period (1501-1722) and the date was mentioned twice in a single page. Such information is valuable, offering us insights into the way texts interacted with oral performative traditions such as Ta'ziya. Humāyūni refers to a manuscript entitled '*jung-e ta'ziya*' (A Collection of *Ta'ziya*), which has a table of contents that contains useful information about the manuscript, such as the names of players and the instruments that are needed for *ta'ziya* performance.[15] Humāyūni informs the reader that the first collection of *ta'ziya* was published in 1332/1953, entitled *Sargodhašt-e mūsiqi-ye Irān* (the Narrative of the Music of Iran) by Rūḥ Allāh Khāleqi.[16] The *ta'ziya* metre changes, and there are sections without metre, according to the needs of the subject matter, the specific message intended for the audience or the emotional effect that is sought. *Ta'ziya* composers are mostly anonymous, because they seek no worldly reward; they just want to gain 'celestial merit.'[17] If a composer wishes to mention his name, he places it at the end of the script in a very modest way. Most *ta'ziya* composers have written several parts of a *ta'ziya* and completed their works using the poems written by classical Persian poets. Several authors have produced *ta'ziya* by bringing together a collection of *ta'ziya* poems. For instance, the *Rawżat al-šuhadā* (*the Garden of Martyrs*) by Ḥuseyn Wā'iẓ Kāšifi has been used.[18]

Tracing the authors of *ta'ziya* is very difficult because, on the whole, they remain anonymous and so searching for the place of their birth or uncovering something about the way they lived is almost impossible.[19]

Each *ta'ziya* has several manuscripts (*nuskha*). The term *nuskha* is commonly used for medieval literary manuscripts, but here the term conveys two meanings. Firstly, it refers to the copies that each player takes to read his role. The *nuskha* is a long narrow paper, usually 10 cm wide and of varying length. Secondly, the term is used for the main copy (*nuskha-ye aṣli* or *sar-nuskha*), a scroll that the *ta'ziya* director or *ta'ziya gardān* assembles, to coordinate the copies of individual players. It shows the prompts of the players and a few words of the text of each speech. The director uses this to guide the players, by pointing to the player who is to speak or act.[20] He uses gestures to direct their performance. This requires a close relationship and understanding between the *ta'ziya* director and each player.

There are about a hundred episodes dealt with in the *ta'ziya* plays, according to Humāyūni.[21] The number attests to the popularity of *ta'ziya* in Iran. The subject matter of most *ta'ziya*s is the martyrdom of Imām Ḥuseyn himself, but other parts of the Karbalā cycle are also portrayed and, more rarely, other Shiite topics. In the Karbalā cycle, there is a *ta'ziya* for Ḥurr al-Riyāḥi, Ibn al-Ziyād's commander who joins Imām Ḥuseyn during the battle. There is another *ta'ziya* for 'the Sons of Muslim ibn al-'Aqil,' Imam Ḥuseyn's cousin and the husband of his sister Ruqeya. Muslim ibn al-'Aqil is killed at Kūfa and, after his death, Hāreth, who serves Yazid, arrests his sons and kills them. The *ta'ziya* on the death of Qāsem is one of the most popular. He is the nephew of Imām Ḥuseyn. Qāsem marries Imām Ḥuseyn's daughter Fāṭima at Karbalā, with the Imām's permission. The marriage is never consummated because Qāsem goes to battle and is killed. Among the other *ta'ziya*s in the Karbalā cycle are 'the Martyrdom of Zeynab's Sons,' 'the Death of her Holiness Zeynab', and 'the Rebellion of Mukhtār.' Among the other Shiite devotional *ta'ziya*s are those on 'the Martyrdom of his Holiness 'Ali' (the first Imām, murdered by Ibn al-Muljam in 661), 'the Death of the Prophet,' and 'the Monastery of Širin,' also known as the *ta'ziya* on 'the Monastery of the Monk' or 'the Monastery of the Foreigners.' Širin was a faithful servant of Zeynab. After the battle, the people of Imām Ḥuseyn's household were imprisoned and taken from town to town. They arrived, hungry and thirsty, at a monastery. Širin entered the monastery and asked for food and water. The Christian priest, whom Jesus had warned about the events of Karbalā in a dream, converts to Islam and marries Širin.[22] The *ta'ziya* known as 'the Throne of Solomon' or 'the Throne of Belqeys' recounts the marriage of the Prophet Solomon and Belqeys, Queen of Sheba.

Time and Setting as the Background of the Events

Time and setting are two important elements in the *ta'ziya* texts. Time as a narrative element does not refer to the actual time that the event occurred. The narrator repeats the events and refers to them constantly in order to construct the time of a narration.[23] The actual date of the event of Karbalā is the year 60/680 and the negotiation between Imām Ḥuseyn and the commanders of Yazid lasted nine days, from the first to the ninth of Muḥarram. Imām Ḥuseyn would not acknowledge the legitimacy of Yazid as Umayyad caliph, so, on the tenth of Muḥarram they started to fight, and the battle lasted one day. The events of the last day (tenth of Muḥarram), and of the night before it, are presented as taking place over a very long period. The *ta'ziya* composers have employed references to time and setting to intensify their portrayal of the events.

Time and setting motivate the emotions of the spectators. They allow the audience to imagine themselves under the same conditions that Imām Ḥuseyn and his family were facing. For instance, Zeynab says to the audience, 'O Muslims! Last night Ḥuseyn did not sleep because he was guarding me, he walked around the tents to protect his family' (9). The image is very close to the audience: it is how they would act if their children were in danger. Another image that elicits an emotional response from the audience is the loneliness of Imām Ḥuseyn on the battlefield. Zeynab's son 'Awn says to his brother that Ḥuseyn's army has now gone, he and Zeynab are facing the enemy alone (10). The image encourages the audience to sympathize with Imām Ḥuseyn, even if the assistance they can offer is restricted to raising their voices.

The actual setting of the event of 'Āšūrā is the plain of Karbalā. The *ta'ziya* composers employ this in order to elaborate the contrast between the protagonists and antagonists. The close relationship between the setting and the players is a matter of great importance. In other words, the setting leads the characters to behave in a certain manner.[24] Constant reference to the plain of Karbalā causes an antithetical sense in the audience. Certain settings are loaded with emotional significance. The battlefield is not only the place of the protagonists' heroism in battle; it is where the heads of the dead are put on lances (55), and their bodies are trampled by the horses of the enemy (25). The focus of light and dark in one setting intensifies the hatred of the audience for the Umayyad caliph and his commanders.

The Theme of Day

In the *ta'ziya*, day is the time to assist Ḥuseyn in the battlefield. For instance, when Zeynab notices that her brother is alone on the battlefield, she sends her two young sons to assist him. She says, 'Today is the time for the one who holds the stirrup' (*kunūn vaqt-e jelowdāri-st emrūz*) (15), meaning, it is time for the lesser characters to act. Then, she adds, 'Today is the day to assist' *(ke hengām-e madad-kārist emrūz*) (15). 'Day' in these expressions does not refer to the day of the battle alone; it conveys a general attitude, reminding both the followers of Ḥuseyn (and the audience) to assist him. The repetition of the word 'today' (*emrūz*) emphasizes the urgency of the fight against injustice. In the *ta'ziya* texts, 'day' is a time when the tyrannies and oppressions of Imām Ḥuseyn's enemy are seen. On the day of the battle, Imām Ḥuseyn asks Ibn-e Sa'd whether he will fight against the Imām or not. He answers, 'Yes: today I will fight with him with malice' (9). Terms such as today (*emrūz*) and yesterday (*dirūz*) refer to the chain of events that show the unjust behaviour of the Umayyad caliph towards Imām Ḥuseyn's family.

When Ruqeya, Imām Ḥuseyn's daughter, dies in the ruins in Damascus, Zeynab tells Imām Zeyn al-'Ābedin, 'Yesterday Ruqeya told me that there is no one in the city of Damascus as hungry as she' (133). The term *dirūz* does not refer to an exact date. It shows that during the imprisonment period Ruqeya was always hungry.

In one episode, Zeynab remembers the time when they entered the city of Damascus, where Ruqeya's hands were tied with her hair and she was wandering around while calling her aunt. The girls of the city came to watch her *day and night* (150). The time reference emphasizes Ruqeya's pitiful state. Another reference to 'day' is the moment Hendeh, Yazid's wife, and previously Zeynab's slave girl, goes to the ruins where Zeynab and other members of Ḥuseyn's family are imprisoned. She recognizes Zeynab and becomes ashamed of herself. Here Zeynab says,

> *khuš ān rūzi ke būd āqat, Hendeh*
> *be nazd-e mā budy ma'vāt Hendeh* (120).

How good was the day when he [Imām Ḥuseyn] was your master, Hendeh
When you were settled next to me, Hendeh (120).

Again, the reference is not to an actual 'day,' but rather to the time when her brother was alive and people honoured them as the Prophet's family. In such references, Zeynab misses her family's past glory. For the Umayyad caliph and his family, 'day' is the time of their unfair victory on the battlefield and the time of their pleasure. For instance, when Hendeh goes to the ruins to see the prisoners, it appears in the *ta'ziya* texts that gloating over foreign prisoners was an amusement in the household of Yazid. Hendeh says to her niece, 'O my dear! Come to see who these prisoners are' (119).

Another aspect of the day is the times of prayer. After the battle, Sakina, the daughter of Imām Ḥuseyn, does not see her father at the time for noon prayers. She remembers that her father used to hold her after the prayers (41). The reference to the time marks how far we have gone through the day of the battle. The afternoon is important because of the heat and thirst the protagonists suffered.

Another episode, in which time is used significantly, relates to the dream of a Shiite believer called 'Abd al-Allāh, who is not at Karbalā. On a certain day, he finds his heart so restless that he retires to bed. In his dream, a series of four messengers tell of the events of Karbalā and the fate of the survivors (96). 'Abd al-Allāh laments Ḥuseyn's death with his family. Their mourning is the prototype of the *ta'ziya*, and the 'true dream' justifies the practice.

The Theme of Night

Night is another narrative element used as background and as actual time in the *ta'ziya* texts. Normally associated with rest and calmness, in *ta'ziya* it is the time of unease, restlessness and sorrow for Imām Ḥuseyn's family. Night is used as a cover to hide the grief of the prisoners. When Zeynab dresses her sons in their shrouds (*kafan*) to send them to the battlefield, she says that she will lament (*afġān*) day and night, that she wails and cries through the night to early morning because of separation from them (*mikunam tā subh šabhā rūd rūd*) (15). Here, night is both the real time and the objective correlative of the emotion involved: pain is more intense at night, whether it is the pain of losing a loved one, the pain of love or the pain of an illness.

In Shiite religious experience, the night after 'Āšūrā is a time for the antagonists to perform immoral or irreligious acts. Night is a cover that hides wicked deeds. After the battle, at night, two men go to the battlefield to steal the possessions of Imām Ḥuseyn (31). They both know that their action is irreligious and illegal, but their desire for the objects leads them to mutilate Imām Ḥuseyn. One of them cuts off his finger to take his ring (33).

Šemr's deceitful behaviour also takes place at night: he suggests that Ibn al-Sa'd should send a messenger to the city of Halab and announce the events of Karbalā to the people (96). He chooses night because no one should be aware of the secret mission of the messenger.

When night covers the world, it provides an opportunity to escape from danger. In the *ta'ziya* texts, after the martyrdom of Imām Ḥuseyn, his Persian wife Šahrbānū decides to escape from their enemies, as the Imām had wished. She tells Zeynab that they can evade the enemy if they escape at night through the desert, or if they go to Najaf to the tomb of Ḥeydar (the title of Imām 'Ali), or if they return to Medina to the tomb of the Prophet (40).

In the *ta'ziya* texts the night is sometimes a time of special awareness. For instance, Muṣayeb, the chief of the tribe of Khazā'el, dreams that Imām Ḥuseyn and his followers are killed at Karbalā and their heads are severed (60). He decides to assist Imām Ḥuseyn but, when Muṣayeb's messenger returns from Karbalā, he learns that he is too late. At the same time, the helpless family of Imām Ḥuseyn decides to send a letter to Muṣayeb asking for help (61). The antagonists also have dreams, making them aware of their unjust behaviour and leading them to regret it. An instance is the dream that makes Yazid ashamed of his deceitful behaviour towards Imām Ḥuseyn's household. He dreams that he is sent to hell by order of the Prophet. He is frightened, invites the prisoners to a feast, apologizes humbly to them, and promises to punish the killer of Imām Ḥuseyn (156-171). His dream is a justification of Imām Ḥuseyn and his family.

Night is the time of mourning and lamentation for the prisoners. They mourn for those killed at Karbalā. In the *ta'ziya* texts, Dorra Ṣadaf is a warrior who fights, with her companions, against the enemies of Imām Ḥuseyn's family to release the prisoners. Zeynab tells her that this is the night of mourning for the exiles killed at Karbalā (*emšab šab-e 'azā-ye ġaribān-e Karbalā-st*) (108). Among Shiites, the third night after 'Āšūrā is called the night of the strangers (*šām-e ġaribān*). On this night, people perform the mourning rites and walk in the streets, holding lighted candles. It is a symbolic re-enactment of the wandering of Imām Ḥuseyn's family in the desert.

The absolute darkness of the night is a symbol of the loneliness and helplessness of Imām Ḥuseyn's family. For instance, when Ruqaya, the daughter of Imām Ḥuseyn, dies in the ruins of Šām, Zeynab says,

na šam'-o na čerāġ-o na yāri-yo hamdami
nūri namānda dar šab-e tāram khudā khudā (133).

O! God there is no candle, no lantern, no assistant or companion
O! God, O God, there is no light in my dark night (133).

For those not suffering pain, night appears with all its beauties. The moon shines and stars glitter. An instance is the daughter of Yazid: she is oblivious to realities, so for her the night is another reason for happiness and cheerfulness. She says, 'this is a very nice night,' and asks minstrels to play to increase the sorrow in the heart of the prisoners (139).

Settings in Ta'ziya

Setting is another narrative element that is skillfully used in the *ta'ziya* texts. Karbalā is the actual site of the historical battle. Afterwards, the prisoners were marched through the desert, and passed through the city of Kūfa on the way to Damascus. They were imprisoned in a ruined mosque – an obvious sign of the corruption of government and society – and presented at the court of Yazid. After some days, they returned to Medina. The composers of the *ta'ziya* texts used these actual places to show the innocence and the legitimacy of Imām Ḥuseyn and his family and the unjust and cruel behaviour of the Umayyad caliph.

The desert (*biyābān*) is the authentic setting of the events of Karbalā, scene of the battle between Yazid and Imām Ḥuseyn. In classical Persian literature, the lover is often portrayed wandering bewildered in the desert to find the beloved. In the *ta'ziya* texts, Imām Ḥuseyn and his fellow men were killed in the desert, their severed heads were placed on lances and the army of the enemy trampled their bodies. The afflictions and hardships that the prisoners suffer are portrayed against the vivid background of the desert. It is in the desert that the families of Imām Ḥuseyn and his sisters are arrested; they are marched through the desert mounted bare backed on camels, and they suffer from thirst and hunger. The women are unveiled and the enemies whip them. Two children of Imām Ḥuseyn, Rāẓiya and Marẓiyya, are lost in the desert and their bodies are later found. Zeynab buries them (21-25). The desert is the background for the bewildered wanderings of Šahrbānū, Imām Ḥuseyn's Iranian wife and daughter of Yazdgerd III (r. 632-651). Imām Ḥuseyn had told her that, if he died, she should not stay. So, after the battle, Šahrbānū mounts Imām Ḥuseyn's horse and escapes to the desert. Along the way she meets her brother 'Abd al-Allāh, who has come to assist Imām Ḥuseyn but is too late. There is someone who follows Šahrbānū as she goes: it is the soul of Imām Ḥuseyn who comes to assist and protect her from the enemy (43-50).

Another setting is the court of Yazid, where the prisoners were taken after the battle. Two major features are mentioned repeatedly. Firstly, at the court, the severed heads of the dead mounted on lances are presented to Yazid. He strikes the severed head of Imām Ḥuseyn and pours wine on his lips, while he is mocking him (77, 127). Secondly, at the court, the prisoners are presented to the king in chains and without their headscarves (119-120). Yazid and his men constantly dishonour and threaten them. For instance, Yazid orders the executioner to kill Imām Zeyn al-'Ābedin because he protested strongly when the lips of the severed head of Imām Ḥuseyn were struck (127-128). The court is the place where Zeynab protests against Yazid and his cruel behaviour towards the family of the Prophet. She threatens him that he will be punished in the Hereafter (82). It can be said that the court of Yazid is a portrayal of two opposites: good and evil, black and white, justice and injustice.

The ruins (*kharāba*) in the city of Damascus where the prisoners were imprisoned form the backdrop for many episodes. The term 'ruins' in the Persian language implies a roofless, uninhabited place. In the *ta'ziya* texts, the ruins are roofless and do not have a door. The setting of the ruins highlights the afflictions and tortures that the family of the Prophet, including the sisters of Imām Ḥuseyn, suffer there. They do not have basic facilities. They sleep in the dust and their pillows are bricks. They are humiliated by Yazid's men. At times, people come to watch them. The pains and sorrows that they have suffered are mingled with the unpleasant place where they are now held. Yazid puts them in a ruin to humiliate them. The prisoners suffer not only from the deaths of their loved ones and their own imprisonment, but also from the cruel behaviour of the Umayyad caliph and his men. For instance, Yazid orders Šemr to take the head of Imām Ḥuseyn to the ruins and show it to his family (132). When Zeynab sees the head of Imām Ḥuseyn, she mourns and laments for him. She says,

dar in kharāba-ye bi-saqf-u bi-dar āmada-i barādar, barādar
magar ke pāy nabūdat ke bā sar āmada-i barādar, barādar (132).

O Brother, O Brother, you have come to this ruin without roof,
without door,

> O Brother, O Brother, did you have no foot, that you come with a head (132).

Ruqeya, Imām Ḥuseyn's daughter, appears in several episodes. She is among the captives who are imprisoned in the ruins. She is a child who constantly complains to her aunt, Zeynab, about their desperate situation. She says,

> our father is dead, we do not have a house to live in, no one is as hungry as we are, we have to dress in old rugs and clothes, our enemies slap us and the people of Kūfa beat us with sticks and stones (138-139).

Ruqeya dies in the ruins and Yazid sends a camel litter for her, but Zeynab does not accept it (151). Their imprisonment in the ruins in Damascus is a time of grief and affliction, with no one to assist them or sympathize with them.

The prisoners constantly complain about the pain of their exile (*ġurbat*) in the city of Damascus. The word *ġurbat* (discussed above in oral tradition in *ta'ziya* texts) refers to the condition of being far removed: it is used for aliens and travellers, but also for social outsiders, for the wretched. It characterizes both the setting of the painful deaths of Imām Ḥuseyn and his men at Karbalā, and the unpleasant situation of the prisoners. When the prisoners address Imām Ḥuseyn they refer to his wretchedness (*ġurbat*) and his loneliness (*biyāvari*) on the battlefield. For instance, Imām Zeyn al-'Ābedin constantly says, 'Father, my martyr! My exiled father!' (*šahidam bābā ġaribam bābā*) (51). The association of not-belonging with the death of Imām Ḥuseyn makes it an especially painful and sorrowful event. His *ġurbat* reminds the audience that he was killed as an innocent, with no one to assist him or his family. The prisoners in the ruins, also in a state of *ġurbat*, can do nothing but mourn. In one episode, Imām Zeyn al-'Ābedin asks his family to gather around him to mourn for the dead of Karbalā, using the less abstract adjective *ġarib* six times. He says,

> *bolbol ġarib-o nāla ġarib-o čaman ġarib*
> *Zeynab ġarib-o šahr ġarib-o vaṭan ġarib* (119).

> The nightingale is a stranger, lamentation is foreign, the meadow is not here
> Zeynab is an exile, the city is alien, our motherland is far away (119).

Notes

1 L. Gardet, in *The Encyclopaedia of Islam* (second edition), under *Qiyāma*.
2 F. Leemhuis, in *Encyclopaedia of the Qur'ān,* under Apocalypse.
3 See Issac Hasson, 'Left hand and right hand', in *Encylcopaedia of the Qur'ān,* vol. 3, ed. J. Dammen Mc Auliffe, Leiden, Boston: Brill, 2003, pp. 176-180; A. Schimmel, *Mystical Dimensions of Islam,* Chapel Hill: University of North Caroline Press, 1975, p. 414.
4 Jane I. Smith, in *The Encyclopaedia of Islam* (second edition), under *Eschatology*.
5 Ibid., see 'the Crossing the Bridge (*sirāt*), the Possibility of Intercession (*shefā'a*) and Preparation for the Final Consignment'.
6 See A.A. Seyed-Gohrab, *The Mirror of Meanings*, Costa Mesa, California: Mazda Publishers, 2002, p. 59.
7 See M.S. El-Awa Salwa, Zaqqūm, in *Encyclopaedia of the Qur'ān*, vol. 5, ed. Jane Dammen McAuliffe, Leiden, Boston: Brill, 2006, pp. 571-2.
8 Jane I. Smith, in *The Encyclopaedia of Islam* (second edition), under *Torment of the Fire* (*al-nār*).
9 Ibid., under *Eschatology*.
10 Ibid., see 'the Bliss of the Gardens'.
11 Ibid.
12 Sajjād is a title of Imām Zeyn al-'Ābedin.
13 *Kheyr-o nessā'* is a titile of Fāṭima.
14 J.G.J. ter Haar, 'Ta'ziyeh: Ritual Theater from Shiite Iran', in *Theatre Intercontinental...*, p. 169.
15 Ṣ. Humāyūni, *Ta'ziya dar Iran,* Tehran: Navid, 1368/1989, p. 264-65.
16 Ṣ. Humāyūni, *Ta'ziya dar Iran,* p. 267. For more information about the coronology of publication of the texts of *ta'ziya* see Ibid., pp. 267-273.
17 J.G.J. ter Haar, 'Ta'ziyeh: Ritual Theater from Shiite Iran', in *Theatre Intercontinental...*, p. 169.
18 Ibid.
19 Ṣ. Humāyūni, *Ta'ziya dar Irān,* p. 233.
20 Ṣ. Humāyūni, *Ta'ziya va ta'ziya khāni*, p. 63.
21 Ibid., pp. 45-46.
22 Ibid., pp. 46-52.
23 M.J. Toolan, *Narrative: A Critical Linguistic Introduction*, London and New York: Routledge, [n.d.], pp. 48-50.
24 For information on time and setting in Persian classic poetry see A.A. Seyed-Gohrab, *Layli and Majnūn, Love Madness and Mystic Longing in Niẓāmi's Epic Romance,* Leiden, Boston: Brill, 2003, pp. 319-336.

Doctrines and Philosophy in *Ta'ziya*

In modern Iran, the doctrines embodied in the *ta'ziya* are usually deduced from the words of Imām Ḥuseyn and his family. Two of the most recurring concepts in *ta'ziya* are predestination (*qadar*) and free will (*ekhtiyār*). The concept of fate is crucial in the *ta'ziya* text because Imām Ḥuseyn submitted himself to God's decree. God's decision for man is best for him, although man does not understand the reasons for it. The idea is developed in several other theological concepts such as one's allotted portion of destiny (*nasib*) and the moment of death (*ajal*). The former refers to the God's decision for each individual based on his aptitude (*este'dād*). The latter denotes both one person's term of life and 'the appointed duration of the world'.[1] An associated motif, drawn from Persian poetry, is represented by terms such as the 'sphere' (*falak, sepehr*), 'sky' (*āsemān*), and 'wheel' (*čarkh*). The connotation of these is that the life of each individual is influenced by the heavenly bodies.[2] In more theological terms, the 'sphere' is explained as a medium through which God's decree is transmitted to the individual. The 'sphere' (*falak*) is said to be responsible for taking the caliphate from the descendants of the Prophet, and for the death of Imām Ḥuseyn and the afflictions that his family suffered. In the *ta'ziya* texts, the protagonists complain about the oppressions and tyranny that the sphere has imposed on them. For instance, Zeynab says,

> *ey falak ẓulm-e tu tā čand ravā bar Zeynab* (137).
> O Sphere! How far you are going in oppressing Zeynab (137).

In one episode, Zeynab expresses her acceptance of the sphere's action. It is before the battle begins, when Imām Ḥuseyn puts his head on her lap for the last time and sleeps. Zeynab says,

> *be zānūyam barādar sar nahāda*
> *be farq-e man falak afsar nahāda* (8).

My brother has put his head on my knee
The sphere puts a crown on my head (8).

The wheel (*čarkh*) is another agent of heaven, responsible for the hardships that Imām Ḥuseyn's family suffer. The new bride, Fāṭima, condemns čar*kh* for its deceitful behaviour in causing the death of her husband Qāsem. She says, 'Who in the world widows a new bride / O deceitful wheel! / I pray that you will be turned upside down' (39).

The concept of free will (*ekhtiyār*) is another doctrinal element in *ta'ziya*. *Ekhtiyār* literally means 'choice,' and 'the power of choice.'[3] As we can see from the discussion of fate and destiny above, its affirmation is somewhat ambivalent. On the one hand, it is said that there is no '*ekhtiyār* except for God'.[4] On the other hand, one has the choice to recognize what is good. For the Shiite, the best choice is 'the matter between two matters'; that is, the middle way.[5] In the *ta'ziya* story, Imām Ḥuseyn was free to choose between giving his oath of allegiance to Yazid, or fighting his army. If he had chosen the first, he could save his life and the life of his family and followers, while the second way led to death. Here, there is no middle way: the option of turning back to avoid the confrontation was also excluded. According to the *History* of al-Ṭabari, the cavalry stopped him in Karbalā:

> Al-Ḥuseyn appealed to them before God and Islam to let him go to the Commander of the Faithful. Then he would put his hand in his hand. They said 'No, there is nothing else for you to do but submit to the authority of Ibn Ziyād.'[6]

However they rejected this possibility. Therefore, Imām Ḥuseyn, having two choices (life and death), chose death. For him, death was the path of salvation. When Imām Ḥuseyn was preparing to go to Kūfa, many people had warned him of the infidelity of the people of Kūfa, but he had accepted God's will.[7]

Another doctrinal element in *ta'ziya* is the Shiite concept of salvation. Imām Ḥuseyn is martyred for the salvation of the Shiite community. He chooses death for the sake of the forgiveness of his followers' sins. From the *ta'ziya*, the audience learns that Imām Ḥuseyn prayed on his deathbed for the salvation of his people (*ummat*). In the *Majāles-e ta'ziya*, Šemr, the murderer of Imām Ḥuseyn says,[8]

mikard bā tazaru'-u bā gerya in du'ā
bakhšā gunāh-e 'ummat-e man rā tu ey khudā (117).

Crying and lamenting, he prayed this prayer:
O God! Forgive the sins of my people (117).

The audience participate in the *ta'ziya* ritual to 'renew their commitment to a religious and ideological order,' according to Humāyūni.[9] The *ta'ziya* reinforces religious commandments, and reminds the audience of religious prohibitions. They learn that the Umayyad caliph and his commanders respected neither Imām Ḥuseyn, the grandson of the Prophet, nor religious law. There is a parallel here; a person today who does not respect the family of the Prophet will also not obey the religious law. For instance, according to the traditions and Qur'ānic verses, drinking wine is forbidden for Muslims. In the *ta'ziya*, the prohibition is presented in the behaviour of Yazid, Ibn al-Ziyād and other antagonists. They are not just wine drinkers but also the archetype of an unfaithful person and enemy of Imām Ḥuseyn's family. In the *ta'ziya* on 'the bazaar of Damascus' (*majlis-e ta'ziya bāzār-e Šām*),[10] when Yazid talks with the severed head of Imām Ḥuseyn, he says,

ey Shah-e tešna-kām buvad rūz-e 'eyš-e mā
labhāy-e khušk-e khiš tu tar bā šarāb kun
Shahā biyā šarāb berizam be ṣūratat
ey seyed-e najib ze mey ejtenāb kun [...] (127).

O thirsting King! Taste this, the day of our pleasure
Wet your dry lips with wine
O King! Come, so that I may pour wine on your face
O noble Seyed, abstain from wine... (127).

As he says this to the severed head of Imām Ḥuseyn, the performer pours wine over the head; a hateful image that motivates Shiites to abstain from wine.

Protecting the 'right of an orphan' is another law of religion that the *ta'ziya* players wish to reinforce in the audience. They learn it from the contrary behaviour of the antagonists. For instance, after the battle of Karbalā, Šemr, Yazid's commander, behaves harshly to the children of Imām Ḥuseyn. He slaps them and dishonours them. The spectators who have these concepts in mind, and hatred for the enemies of Imām Ḥuseyn in their hearts, find these concepts figured externally in the *ta'ziya*.

The Legitimacy of *Ta'ziya*

In its traditional form, there are two types of *ta'ziya* performance. In the first, it is performed by professional players. In this case, the *ta'ziya* is the heritage of a family that has brought up their children to perform it. In the second, the *ta'ziya* is performed by non-professional or semi-professional players. Normally, the *ta'ziya* director chooses a company of players from among the common people. They prepare an arena in which the spectators can show their emotions and their commiseration with the martyrdom of Imām Ḥuseyn.[11]

The *ta'ziya* players are chosen from among the ordinary people, with daily occupations. They grow to symbolize the real martyrs and prisoners of the plain of Karbalā.[12] The players are divided into two groups, protagonists and antagonists. The former are the family and the companions of Imām Ḥuseyn, who fight against the enemy to preserve their religion. The latter are the enemies of Imām Ḥuseyn, and of his men and his household, enemies who fight for power or have submitted to an unjust worldly authority. These two groups are good and bad, black and white. But in some cases, the bad undergo a transformation of character on the battlefield. For instance, Hurr, Ibn al-Ziyād's commander, turns to Ḥuseyn and will not fight against him.[13]

The very practice of *ta'ziya* raises some doctrinal issues. Is it permissible for a player to pretend to be one of the holy figures? Is it permissible to imitate the antagonists? These questions have been discussed at least since the eleventh century. The key term here is *tašābuh*, 'imitation,' used in a negative sense in the context of the very well-known prophetic tradition (*ḥadiṯ*), 'whoever makes himself resemble a group is in the category of that group.'[14] The *ḥadiṯ* was originally used to condemn the imitation of Jewish or Christian devotional practices, but it could also appear to pose a difficulty for *ta'ziya* players, and particularly those playing the antagonists. Abu al-Qāsem Maḥmūd Ibn 'Umar Zamakhšari (1074-1143), a famous theologian, wrote a justification of the rituals of the month of Muḥarram called *Bazaars of Gold Presenting Preaching and Sermon*. Zamakhšari employs another *ḥadiṯ*: 'one who makes people weep for the martyrs is among the virtuous.' The antagonist, who causes the audience to weep for Imām Ḥuseyn, is therefore doing a good deed. This application of the 'imitation' *ḥadiṯ* to the audience also supported the practice of *Maqtal-khāni*, in which an audience is moved to tears by the reading of elegies to the martyrs. The elegies for *Maqtal-khāni* became a genre in themselves. Abul al-Mu'ayed Muwaffaq Khārazmi (d.1172-73), a pupil of Zamakhšari, wrote an epic based on traditions concerning the martyrdom of Imām Ḥuseyn. More than three centuries later, Wā'iẓ Kāšefi (d.1504-5) wrote his *Rawẓat al-šuhadā* (*The Garden of Martyrs*), which was discussed above (in the section on *Late Medieval and Modern Ta'ziya*). *Rawẓat al-šuhadā* had a lasting influence in Iran, expanding its effects to a religious ritual called *rawza-khāni.*

The imitation of Imām Ḥuseyn and the other members of the Prophet's family could be exempted from the generally negative connotation of *tašābuh*: these players are following the Imāms, not making themselves resemble non-Muslims (the sense in which *tašābuh* was forbidden). While the protagonists 'imitate' the Imāms and their families, they always distinguish themselves from them: to pretend to be an Imām would be a blasphemy. The term used for this imitation, which is not condemned, is *tamaṯṯul*, making a metaphor. The *ta'ziya* is conceived to be portraying the event of Karbalā, not reproducing it. Whether a *ta'ziya* player plays the role of a protagonist or an antagonist, he separates himself from the real character. It is very natural for a *ta'ziya* player to read directly from the text (*nuskha*), or to drink tea or water during the performance.[15] Such behaviour is not unexpected for the audience; it shows that the players are distinct from those they portray.

Notes

1 A.A. Seyed-Gohrab, *Layli and Majnūn*, pp. 162-163.

2 F. Graf in *The Encyclopaedia of Islam* (second edition), under *Predestination, the Theory of*; C.E. Bosworth, in *The Encyclopaedia of Islam* (second edition), under *Qisma (a.), Qismet (t.)*.

3 L. Gardet, in *The Encyclopaedia of Islam* (second edition), under Ikhtiyār.

4 Ibid.

5 M. Baktash, 'Ta'ziyeh and its Philosophy', in *Ta'ziyeh: Ritual and Drama,* p. 100.

6 Abu Jafar Muḥammad Ibn Jarir al-Ṭabari, *The History of al-ṭabari*, vol. xix, the Caliphate of Yazid In Mu'āwiyah, trans. I.K.A. Howard, New York: State University of New York Press, 1990, p. 79.

7 One example of people's warning Imām Ḥuseyn not to go to Kūfa is the utterance of Farazdaq. When Imām Ḥuseyn asks him about the people of Kūfa, he stated, 'The hearts of the people with you, but their swords are with the Banū Umayyah. The decision will come from heaven, and God will do what he wishes.' See Abu Jafar Muḥammad Ibn Jarir al-Ṭabari, *The History of al-ṭabari*, p. 71. Also see ibid., p. 22.

8 H. Ṣālehi Rād-e Darbandsari, *Majāles-e ta'ziya*, p. 117.
9 Ṣ. Humāyūni, 'An Analysis of the Ta'ziya of Qāsem', in *Ta'ziyeh: Ritual and Drama in Iran,* ed. P.J. Chelkowski, New York: New York University Press and Soroush Press, 1979, p. 30.
10 H. Ṣālehi Rād Darbandsari, *Majāles-e ta'ziya*, pp. 111-135.
11 P.J. Chelkowski, 'Ta'ziyeh: Indigenous Avant-Garde Theater of Iran', *Ta'ziyeh: Ritual and Drama,* p. 10.
12 P. Mamnoun, 'Ta'zieh from the View Point of the Western Theatre', in *Ta'ziyeh: Ritual and Drama in Iran*, ed. P.J. Chelkowski, New York: New York University Press and Soroush Press, 1979, p. 160.
13 Ibid., p. 160.
14 M. Bektash, 'Ta'ziyeh and its Philosophy', *Ta'ziyeh: Ritual and Drama,* p. 101.
15 P. Mamnoun, 'Ta'zieh from the View Point of the Western Theatre', *Ta'ziyeh: Ritual and Drama,* pp. 157-159.

Zeynab in the Passion Play

Zeynab is the third child of 'Ali Ibn Abi Ṭālib and Fāṭima, the Prophet's daughter. Zeynab was born in Medina. Sources on her childhood are meagre. She married her cousin, 'Abd al-Allāh Ibn al-Ja'far Ṭayyār. Although he was a wealthy man, it is said that he led a modest life, devoting most of his wealth to charity. They had four sons –'Ali, 'Awn, Muḥammad, 'Abbās and one daughter, 'Umm al-Kulṯūm.[1]

Zeynab played an important role in the battle of Karbalā. After the day of *'Āšūrā*, the household of Imām Ḥuseyn, along with his two sisters Zeynab and 'Umm al-Kulṯūm, were taken to Damascus to the court of Yazid. A few days later, he released them and they returned to Medina. It is said that Zeynab did not survive for long after returning from Damascus. She died in 682/1283. There are several different suggestions about the day of her death: on the 11th or 21st of Jamādi 'uṯ-ṯani, the 24th of Safar, or the 16th of Dhu'l-Hijjah.[2]

Veiling and its Supporters in the *Ta'ziya* Texts

The term *ḥejāb* derives from the Arabic root h-j-b. The Persian equivalent is *parda:* a general term for an object that conceals or covers something or someone. The term *parda* has different meanings in the Persian language such as, 'curtain,' 'musical mode,' 'respect' and 'secret(ly)'.[3] The veil has various functions: sometimes it indicates the marital status of a woman. In Mesopotamian society, the veil was a sign of a woman's chastity, in contrast to the prostitutes who appeared in public uncovered.[4] After the revelation of Islam in 610, the significance of the veil in Arab society changed. It became an indicator of a woman's belief in the sacred law (*šari'a*) of Islam, as distinct from the dress of pagan Arabs. In that period, wearing a veil showed one's belief in the Islam, but it was not a device for limiting women and secluding them in the court, in a harem or in the house.

The veil plays an important role in the Persian passion play. When, after the massacre in Karbalā, the family of Ḥuseyn were arrested and taken to the court of Yazid, Zeynab protests twice: first, in Kūfa against the people of Kūfa, and a second time, at the court of Yazid. At the court, she protests and saves the life of her nephew Imām Zeyn al-ʿĀbedin.[5] Zeynab appears both with and without a veil. When her veil is forcefully removed, her character does not change. Zeynab, wearing a veil, supports Imām Ḥuseyn and follows him to Karbalā. She shows the ultimate sacrifice when she sends her sons to the battlefield. Her veil does not prevent her from taking part in the battle. The veil was not a means to seclude her as a woman. Later, Zeynab appears without a veil, protesting against injustice, embodied in the Umayyad caliph. Without any covering, she criticizes the people of Kūfa and Yazid. She reminds Yazid of the punishment that he will suffer in the Hereafter. Appearing without a veil or headscarf (*sar berahna*) in the bazaar of Damascus and at Yazid's court was very hard for Zeynab because, as one of the descendants of the Prophet, she would normally have been veiled in the company of men who were not among her intimates. After the battle, when the prisoners are being taken to the court of Yazid in Damascus, Zeynab says,

be sūy-e kūfa bā meḥnat ravam bi čādur-u maʿjar
če sāzam čāra natvānam khudāhāfez khudāhāfeẓ (26).

I am going to Kūfa, with no veil or headscarf,
There's no remedy for me; may God be with you, God be with you (26).

She says that as soon as she arrives there, she will tell the truth to the people and dishonour Yazid. In the court of Yazid, Zeynab tells him,

biparda miyān-e khalqam ammā
rūh al-qudus ast parda dār-am (125).[6]

I am unveiled among the people, and yet
The Holy Spirit, like a lady's maid, is proffering a veil (125).

From the above examples we see that Zeynab feels that it is her social and religious duty to protest against the tyrant Yazid. When a woman unveils herself, she is protesting against a situation.

The female audience in the *taʿziya* performance wears the veil and supports veiling. When a woman spectator sees Zeynab's veil being forcefully removed by the enemy, she is expected to curse the Umayyad caliph and his commanders such as Šemr and Ibn al-Sa'd for their malicious behaviour. For the audience, the veil increases the aura of chastity around Zeynab and, by association, around other women. So the veil is accepted as a sign of moral behaviour in public and unveiling is an evident sign of protest against injustice. When Zeynab says that the Holy Spirit is my *parda-dār*, she is expressing that her chastity is protected by it.

Zeynab as a Role Model for Iranian Women

Zeynab, presented as a chaste and brave woman who fights against injustice at the side of her brother, has become a role model for Iranian women. Before the Islamic Revolution (1978-79), she was presented as an afflicted, oppressed woman who, in spite of restrictions, protested against the ruling Umayyad caliph. During the Islamic revolution, Zeynab found a role, for the revolutionary women of Iran, as a symbol of the resistance against Muḥammad Reẓā Shah (1941-1979), who was 'compared to the tyrant Yazid responsible for Ḥuseyn's death'.[7] During the Islamic Revolution, women took Zeynab as their role model when they protested against the Pahlavi king. The difference here is the role of the veil: Reẓā Shah had politicized the veil (*čādur, rūsari*) in 1936 by officially banning it in public.[8] The veil became part of women's protest. They would conceal themselves in the veil as a sign of freedom of beliefs and ideas.

After the Islamic Revolution and during the war between Iran and Iraq (1980-88), Iranian women strictly followed Zeynab as a model. They supported the soldiers both behind the battlefield and at the front line. For Iranians, the war against Iraq was a 'holy defence' (*defā'-e muqaddas*). The state tried to shape perceptions of the war using the tragic paradigm of Karbalā. Women going to the front went as if they were Zeynab, going to assist Imām Ḥuseyn at Karbalā. State propaganda claimed that it was the ancestors of the Iraqi soldiers who had killed the Shiite Imām; now Iranians had to sacrifice themselves and their families to avenge the act.

After the Iran-Iraq war, Zeynab's status as a model Shiite woman was used to reinforce the wearing of *ḥejāb* as a sign of chastity. An Islamic state organization called 'the sisters of Zeynab' (*khāharān-e Zeynab*) act in public to remind women to cover their body and head in public or in the company of those who are not their close relatives. Women who do not cover themselves completely are seen as protesting against the Islamic Revolution.

Zeynab's Sermons

After the battle of Karbalā, during the imprisonment period Zeynab preached two sermons, one in Kūfa and one in Damascus. After the battle, the army of Ibn al-Ziyād set fire to the tents, arrested the women and children and took them to Kūfa.[9] Here, Zeynab preached a sermon, which is seen by the Shiites as a new chapter in the history of Shiite belief. After praising God and introducing herself and her family, she blames the people of Kūfa and calls them 'deceitful and renegade.' She warns them of God's punishment in the Hereafter.

She preached her second sermon in Damascus before the Umayyad caliph Yazid. He is noted as an unbeliever and an enemy of Islam, the Prophet and his family. Yazid says to Zeynab that the battle of Karbalā is revenge taken on the Prophet's descendants, because the Prophet and his companions killed Yazid's polytheist ancestors. Zeynab criticizes Yazid, listing the sins that he has committed. Citing a Shiite tradition, she says, 'Denying the signs of Allah and ridiculing him and his Prophet is a sin.' Then she says: 'You [Yazid] have reached the point that you want to take revenge for your ancestors on the children of the Prophet. So you are still at the same stage that they [the ancestors] were,' meaning that Yazid is still a pagan. She emphasizes that whatever Yazid does to the family of the Prophet, whether it is killing them, or arresting them and marching them through the blistering desert from one town to another, cannot disgrace them. She says to Yazid that his wrong ideas have made him proud of himself, but God says, 'We only give them [unbelievers] time to let them increase their sins. For them there will be a humiliating torment' (Q.3/178). She reminds Yazid that his ancestors were pagan, that he is an unbeliever, that his ancestors were among the last group to embrace Islam. Then she talks about herself and her well-known family. Her connection with the Prophet gives her a position superior to Yazid's. The cruel behaviour of Yazid and his men cannot diminish the honour of Zeynab and other members of Imām Ḥuseyn's family. She is particularly critical of Yazid's mistreatment of the severed head of Imām Ḥuseyn.[10]

Zeynab's sermon shows her character. She is a very strong and brave woman. She speaks in Yazid's court and criticizes him, while the severed head of her brother is before her. Her deep grief at the martyrdom of Imām Ḥuseyn and her children does not prevent her from protesting against Yazid and demanding justice.

Zeynab, Justice and Destiny

In the *ta'ziya* texts, Zeynab is the archetype of devotional beliefs and moral attitudes. She turns her face to God to ask for justice. She does not ask people for help. When she talks with people, she reveals how her enemies' have oppressed her. Even when Zeynab talks with God, her tone is that of a person who complains about injustice. For instance, in the period of imprisonment a diplomat comes from Europe (*farang*) to the court of Yazid. Yazid respects him, but he does not respect Imām Ḥuseyn's family. Zeynab complains to God,

> *bār-elāhā sina-ye Zeynab az in ġam riš šud*
> *ey khudā bengar farangi qurbaš az mā biš šud* (122).

> O God! My heart is wounded by this grief
> O God, a man from Europe is more honourable than we are (122).

Zeynab's tone changes when she seeks justice from God. She is forced to go to a public place such as a bazaar without her veil. She says, 'O! May the hand of God make haste and destroy Damascus, like Khaybar because Zeynab has lost her veil' (127). Here she draws a comparison between Khaybar, a fortification belonging to Jewish opponents of Muḥammad, and the city of Damascus where the court of Yazid is. The Jews of Khaybar were defeated by her father, Imām 'Ali. Through this comparison, Zeynab highlights the distinction between the family of the Prophet and the Umayyad caliph, between faith and infidelity. Several times, Zeynab prays to God asking him to take revenge. In such cases, she explains the situation like a person who wants to motivate someone else and asks him to help her. For instance, after the day of *'Āšūrā*, Imām Ḥuseyn's family gathers around Zeynab. She prays and they say 'amen' twice. She swears to God, invoking his mercy, kindness and blessings to the previous Prophets (Noah, Abraham, Moses and Jesus). Then she invokes God in the name of the Prophet Muhammad and, finally, in the name of the family of the Prophet who have been killed, asking God to take revenge on their enemies (155). The *ta'ziya* text reports that Zeynab's supplication causes Yazid to have a dream in which the Prophet orders that Yazid should be thrown into hell (157). Because of the dream, Yazid is frightened and regrets his behaviour towards Imām Ḥuseyn and his household. He humbly apologizes to the Imām Ḥuseyn's family, and specifically to Zeynab and Imām Zeyn al-'Ābedin, for his cruel behaviour. The event shows the spiritual power and the honour of Zeynab in the eyes of God.

When Zeynab faces the tyranny of her enemies, she also asks for justice from the spheres. Zeynab refers to the sphere as an oppressor, and she protests against her destiny. She talks to the sphere in a loud voice as if it hears her. She seeks revenge for the martyrs. The sphere is responsible for the death of her brother and her two sons. She refers to herself several times as afflicted and oppressed (*setamkeš-e zār*), and as sorrowful and wounded (*ḥazin-e fegār*). She says that the sphere oppressed her by separating her from Ḥuseyn. Zeynab says,

> *falak ze jowr-u jafāhā-ye tu hezārān dād*
> *ze sina barkešam az kina-at du ṣad faryād*
> *če kina-hā ke nadāri be in setamkeš-e zār*
> *če ẓulmhā ke nakardi be in hazin-e fegār*
> *ze hejr-e rūy-e Ḥuseyn šahid-e bi yāvar*
> *ravān nemūda-i az dida-am tu lakht-e jegar*
> *ze dāġ-e Akbar-u ʿAbbās-u Qāsem-u Aṣġar*
> *be rūz-u šab zanam az ġuṣṣa dast-e ġam bar sar [...]* (199).

> O Sphere! A thousand times I protest your tyrannies and oppressions,
> Two hundred times I shout from my heart because of your rancour.
> What tyrannies have you not imposed on this oppressed, afflicted one!
> What oppressions have you not inflicted on this wounded sorrowing one!
> Because of separation Ḥuseyn, the martyred, the friendless
> You have caused bloody tears to flow from my eyes.
> From the fateful marking of Akbar, ʿAbbās, Qāsem and Asġar
> Day and night, for grief, I lay the hand of sorrow on my head [...] (199).

The oppression of the sphere is not limited to the martyrdom of Imām Ḥuseyn and his companions. The sphere is blamed for having stolen the leadership of the Muslim community from Imām Ḥuseyn's family.

The first four hemistiches rhyme on *dād* and *faryād* (to shout or to appeal for justice, to cry out), and on *zār* and *fegār* (afflicted and wounded). These words imply dissatisfaction and rebelliousness. In the second four hemistiches, the rhyme words strengthen the empathy of the audience: Ḥuseyn dies without a supporter (*biyāvar*), her tears contain part of her liver (*lakht-e jegar*), and she beats the hand of sorrow on her head (*dast-e ġam bar sar*, a mourning practice). The emotive rhyme words arouse the audience to seek revenge on the enemies of Imām Ḥuseyn's family, and to show their feelings in the *ta'ziya*.

Although Zeynab addresses the sphere in a harsh tone, as if she is talking to her enemy, she submits to the power of destiny, because she believes in predestination (*qadar*). *Qadar* is a Qur'ānic term meaning 'eternal decision or decree.'[11] Zeynab employs this word to show her submission to God and his decision. She accepts her fate and tries to remain patient, while her restless heart is filled with sorrow and grief. The following hemistiche shows Zeynab's submission to predestination. After *'Āšūrā*, the Imām Ḥuseyn's daughter Sakina mourns for her father and complains about their situation. Zeynab says,

> *če kunam 'amma kār-e taqdir ast* (200).
> What can I do, this is predestined (200).

Zeynab Inspired

Inspiration (*elhām*) is one of the essential traits of the Prophet and his family. Being the friends of God, they were fully aware of their fate. A friend of God receives inspiration from divine grace.[12] For instance, when Imām Ḥuseyn was on the way from Mecca to Kūfa, many people asked him not to go further, but he responded that,

> The decision is God's, and God will do what he wishes.'Every day our lord exercises power in [every] matter'. If fate sends down what we like, we praise God for his blessings [...] However, although fate may frustrate their hopes, those whose intention is the truth and whose hearts are pious are not aggressors.[13]

This answer shows that he had utter trust (*tawakkul*) in God. Zeynab does the same. There is a parallel between them: both are aware of their fates and the fates of the other members of the family. Zeynab speaks in a way that shows she is divinely inspired. For instance, when she talks to Sakina, she mentions the place of her death. Zeynab says,

> *be khudā ke khūn šud az ġam del-e biqarār-e Zeynab*
> *ke be Karbalā mabādā bešavad mazār-e Zeynab* (200).

I swear to God that Zeynab's restless heart is bloody for grief,
That Zeynab's resting place may not be at Karbalā (200).

The narrator employs the term 'may not be' (*mabādā*) to emphasize that the event will happen in near future.

Zeynab's Spiritual Power

One example of Zeynab's spiritual power, in the *Majāles-e ta'ziya*, comes after the events at Karbalā, when Šemr goes to Medina to once more arrest Imām Ḥuseyn's family. Zeynab says to her fellow women,

čādur-e 'eṣmat kunid 'āl-e payāmbar be sar
dušman-e jān-e šumā dast be khanjar resid
jumla ravid in zamān bar sar-e qabr-e rasūl
āh-o faġān barkešid Šemr-e setamgar resid (204).

Put on the veil of protection, O family of the Prophet,
Your mortal enemy is arriving, dagger in hand.
All of you, go to the tomb of the Prophet,
Wail and mourn, the oppressor Šemr is coming (204).

In these couplets, Zeynab offers two means of escaping from Šemr, their enemy. Firstly, they are told to wear the veil of chastity. The veil acts like a protective boundary between a woman and those not immediately related to her. The word translated here as protection, *'eṣmat,* also means chastity. It also has a connotation of the spiritual power exercised by Muḥammad, Fāṭima and the twelve Imāms. Secondly, the women are told to take refuge in mourning and lamenting at the tomb of the Prophet. The supposition is that they will be assisted by the Prophet's spirit. The idea that the deceased saints such as the Prophet, Imām 'Ali and Fāṭima can assist the faithful is very common in the *ta'ziya* texts.[14]

Zeynab's curse is also effective. It is linked to the idea that the sigh uttered by an innocent person has an effect. After the battle of Karbalā, Šemr tears Fāṭima's earring from her ear. With her ear bleeding, Fāṭima cries and complains of Šemr's cruelty to her aunt Zeynab. Zeynab says to Šemr: 'Curse on you unfaithful Šemr that you make the daughter of the king of the Faith cry' (53). Zeynab warns him that God will help her and that she is not alone. She swears to God that her sigh (*āh*) will have a profound effect (*be khudu āh-e man khatā nakunad*) (54). Then, speaking to the earth, Zeynab says,

ey zamin kun madad be Zeynab-e zār
tā kamar gir in sag-e ġaddār
tā bedānad ke mā saġir-u kabir
bahr-e 'ummat šudim zār-u 'asir (53-54).

O earth! Assist Zeynab,
Take this deceitful dog up to his waist
That he may know that all of us, young and old,
Are afflicted and bound for the sake of the nation (53-54).

Zeynab's prayer causes a miracle: at that moment Šemr is rooted to the spot. He asks Sakina for help, and Sakina intercedes on behalf of Šemr. Zeynab asks God to accept Šemr's repentance, and then the earth releases him. The miracle is a warning to the audience, to respect Imām Ḥuseyn and his family, for disrespect has consequences.

Other miracles also show Zeynab's spiritual power. After the battle, Ibn al-Sa'd orders his army to trample on the bodies of the martyrs. Feẓẓa (Zeynab's servant) hears this order and asks Zeynab to find a solution. She adds that last night she heard a lion moaning the whole night. Zeynab tells her, 'go to the lion and say, the family of 'Ali have been arrested, come and guard the bodies of the martyrs' (55). The lion obeys Zeynab and comes, and Ibn al-Sa'd's army run away. According to Shiite tradition, when the Imām Ḥuseyn was killed, the whole universe lamented. Here the lion, the royal animal, represents the animal kingdom. In another episode, a lion moans for the martyrdom of Imām Ḥuseyn, and the audience is expected to accompany the lion. If the lion (the animal kingdom) respects Zeynab and obeys her, then the Shiites must do the same.

Zeynab the Leader

The role of Zeynab as a leader is signified both in history and in the *ta'ziya* texts. As a leader, she teaches her family and, indirectly, the audience that they have to sacrifice themselves for the sake of justice. She is a model for her fellow women and subsequent generations of Shiite women. She is an archetype of sacrificial behaviour. For instance, she offers her children to

Imām Ḥuseyn and asks him to permit them to fight against Yazid's army (10-12). In all situations, she is the first person who takes decisions for her small community, motivates her fellow women and teaches them to protest against their enemy. For instance, after *'Āšūrā*, she makes the people of Medina aware of the events at Karbalā and the harsh behaviour of Yazid and his commanders against them. She also implies that what happened to Ḥuseyn and his household might happen to the rest of society in the future. She uses mourning and lamentation as a womanly weapon to motivate the people of Medina. They gather around the family of Imām Ḥuseyn, asking about the events on the day of *'Āšūrā*. Zeynab behaves like a man fighting against his enemy. She mourns and laments, and in doing so protests against the Umayyad caliph. For instance, after the battle of Karbalā she asks the mother of Qāsem to arrange a mourning assembly for the martyrs. First, Zeynab asks her fellow women to make a circle of mourning (*mātam*) around her. She says,

> *zanid ḥalqa-ye mātam be dowram ey yārān*
> *kunid nawḥa-u zāri ayā havā-dārān* (202).

> O! My friends make a circle of mourning around me,
> O! Partisans lament and wail (202).

Next, Zeynab gives them pieces from the clothes of the martyrs. She gives the bloody flag of 'Abbās to 'Umm al-Kulṯūm her sister, the clothes of 'Ali Asġar to Sakina, the dress of Qāsem that is drenched in his blood to his mother, and the dress of 'Ali Akbar to her sister, Fāṭima. Then she says, 'My part is putting the robe of Imām Ḥuseyn on my head while I am wailing and mourning' (202).[15]

Mātam is an Arabic term, referring to mourning and lamenting for a dead person. In Shiite terminology, the term *mātam* refers mainly to mourning and wailing for the martyrs of Karbalā. The mourners perform *mātam* in the form of repetitive chest beating (*sina-zani*). The sound of chest beating harmonizes with the chanting of elegies (*nawha*).[16] In *nawha*, 'vocal recitation and public performance'[17] is an important factor. The expression, 'circle of mourning' (*halqa-ye mātam*) means that she asks them to mourn for the martyrs with her. In the *ta'ziya* performance the audience stands in a circular form around the *ta'ziya* players. Therefore the mourning circle is ready. The spectators are friends who gather around the *ahl al-bayt*, the holy family, and ease their sorrows by mourning with them. Zeynab addresses the audience as 'My friends and Partisans' (*yārān* and *havā-dārān*). The reference to the spectators motivates them. They lament bitterly, as Zeynab asks them to. They wish that they could take part in the battle of Karbalā and assist Imām Ḥuseyn and his family. Their chest-beating, and the lamentation of Imām Ḥuseyn's family, harmonizes with the sound of the *nawha* chant. This motivates the spectators to participate in the *ta'ziya* performance. For the spectators, distinctions of time and place vanish and the past and present mingle.

Another example of a direct address to the audience is in the passage just mentioned, in which Zeynab says,

> *naṣib-e man bowad ey khāharān be šivan-o šin*
> *be farq-e khud fekanam jāma-ye Imām Ḥuseyn* (202).

> O my sisters! My part in lamentation is,
> To put Imām Ḥuseyn's robe over my head (202).

The expression 'O my sisters!' (*ey khāharān*) is a reference to the audience. In Persian literature, the term *khāhar* has a profound meaning because the *khāhar* is the closest relative who sympathizes with her sister under all conditions. Here, Zeynab calls the audience 'sister.' On the one hand, she is going to share her grief with the females who are present, as if they were her sisters. She reminds them that Zeynab is their oppressed sister who was alone and helpless before her enemies. Her helplessness invokes the image of the Shiite community as helpless, but surviving despite the limitations opposed on Shiites throughout history.[18] On the other hand, Zeynab asks them to lament and to mourn for their brother (Ḥuseyn) and the other martyrs. Here the spectators beat their chests and lament bitterly.

The *ta'ziya* texts show that the seed that Zeynab has cultivated grows. The mourning of Imām Ḥuseyn's family attracts the people of Medina. They ask Imām Zeyn al-'Ābedin to explain 'how the Imām of salvation (Imām Ḥuseyn) was martyred.'[19] The *ta'ziya* spectators symbolically become the people of Medina, gathering to hear about the martyrdom. Zeyn al-'Ābedin recounts how Imām Ḥuseyn's loved ones were killed before his eyes. For instance, he says how cruelly his half brother 'Abbas, his son 'Ali Akbar, and his nephew Qāsem were killed. The audience is taught, or reminded of, the hardships that Imām Ḥuseyn suffered before his death. They compare these with their own hardships and find them tolerable.

The awareness of the people of Medina of Yazid's cruel behaviour then causes uproar in Medina. People sympathize with the family of Imām

Ḥuseyn and regret not being present at Karbalā. Zeynab's mourning is a protest against the authority of the Umayyad caliph, a cry against oppression and for justice.

Zeynab as Saviour of the Shiite Tradition and the Line of Imāms

In the *ta'ziya* texts, Zeynab has a symbolic role as the holder of the Shiite Trusts (*amānāt*, the things entrusted for safekeeping). On the Day of Judgement, these Trusts will exempt Shiites from punishment. According to an episode in the *ta'ziya* on 'the death of her holiness Zeynab' (*majles-e ta'ziya rehlat-e haẓrat-e Zeynab*), on her deathbed she passes on several Trusts (*amānāt*) to her sister 'Umm al-Kulṯūm. Zeynab tells her sister to preserve the Trusts, saying that on the Day of Judgement, her mother (Fāṭima, the daughter of the Prophet) will intercede on behalf of the Shiites because they have preserved the remembrance of the Trusts (210).

Amāna (Persian *amānat*) is a Qur'ānic term derived from the Arabic root a-m-n. The most famous Qur'ānic verse that refers to the *amāna* is, 'we offered the Trust to the heaven and the earth and the mountains, but they refused to bear it and were afraid of it: but man undertook to bear it [...]' (Q. 33/72). The Trust here is 'free will and moral responsibility,'[20] which man alone was willing to bear. The Shiite Trust that Zeynab transmits is responsibility for the preservation of the Faith and community, embodied in certain relics. The fragment refers to the importance of preserving the relics because the salvation of the Shiites depends on them. The *amānā* are two teeth of the Prophet that were broken in the battle against pagans for the sake of the expansion of Islam; the turban of Imām 'Ali who was murdered by Ibn al-Muljam in 661/1262 because he wished to preserve Shiite Islam; the torn liver of Imām Ḥasan, poisoned by the order of Mu'āwiya, the Umayyad caliph; and lastly, the shirt of Imām Ḥuseyn, martyred on the plain of Karbalā by the Umayyad army. For a Shiite, the objects depict the sequence of conflicts between the family of the Prophet and false claimants to the caliphate. The question is, how can a Shiite today preserve these relics that no longer exist? The answer is that commemorating and mourning for the owners of the objects will prevent them being forgotten. The remembrance of a thing is preserving its essence. In the *ta'ziya* 'on the death of Zeynab,' there is a reference to the intercession of Fāṭima, the Prophet's daughter, on the Day of Judgement,[21] for those who have preserved the relics. It is suggested that one who mourns and wails for the owners of the objects preserves their memory, so his salvation is assured.

Zeynab is the preserver of the line of Shiite Imāms in another way, because she prevented Imām Zeyn al-'Ābedin from being killed. After the battle of Karbalā, the severed heads of the dead were taken to Yazid's court, where Yazid desecrated them. According to the *ta'ziya* texts, Imām Zeyn al-'Ābedin criticized Yazid's behaviour. He says to Yazid: 'O! Oppressor! You struck the one whom the Prophet had kissed' (127). Yazid orders his executioner to kill him. Zeynab protects Imām Zeyn al-'Ābedin and threatens Yazid,

> If you kill him I will untie my hair [indicating the innocent victim], wail in God's court of law and ask him for justice [...] I will go to Najaf without veil or footwear and lament so bitterly that the earth and heavens roar (129).

Then she calls on her father Imām 'Ali for help. Miraculously, Imām 'Ali appears to Šemr and orders him,

> *makuš makuš ke del-e 'ahl-e bayt khūn gardad*
> *makuš makuš ke samāvāt sarnegūn gardad* (129).

> Do not kill him, do not kill him, lest the hearts of the Prophet's family turn to blood [...]
> Do not kill him, do not kill him, lest the heavens be turned upside down (129).

When this vision appears to Šemr, he is frightened and does not dare to murder Imām Zeyn al-'Ābedin. The lesson for the audience is that the family of the Prophet is 'spiritually present and actively involved in human affairs long after her [their] deaths'.[22] Zeynab's words not only preserved Imām Zeyn al-'Ābedin, they preserved 'the line of the Imāms in human [Shiite] History'.[23]

Zeynab the Generous

The *ta'ziya* teaches the virtues and norms of society. As the archetype of Shiite virtues, Zeynab is described as a generous person. For instance, when

Yazid releases Zeynab and the household of Imām Ḥuseyn, they return to Medina, assisted in their journey by a man named Bašir. When they are near Medina, Bašir wants to separate from them. Zeynab thanks him and gives him her ankle-ring as a gift. She apologizes to Bašir and says that nothing else is left to give, because their properties were plundered by Šemr's army. Sakina imitates Zeynab's action and gives her necklace to Bašir, and Imām Zeyn al-ʿĀbedin gives him his turban (184). The expectation is that the spectators will likewise be generous.

Zeynab and the Protagonists

Zeynab and Imām Ḥuseyn

The close relationship between Zeynab and her brother Imām Ḥuseyn is emphasized in the *taʿziya* texts. She is his supporter and assistant. At Karbalā, as Imām Ḥuseyn is going to the battlefield, he asks Zeynab to bring his horse (9). She also hands him a weapon, saying 'take the weapon of war from your sister' (*selāh-e razm rā bestān ze khāhar*) (10). When all the men have been killed, she holds the flag of war as a man would (172). Imām Ḥuseyn is the last person to go the battlefield; no man is left alive to help him, so Zeynab tells him that the women sheltered in his own tent will assist him (172).

There is another episode, in which Zeynab finds her brother alone and helpless on the battlefield. She sends her two sons, Muḥammad and ʿAwn, to help him. According to the *taʿziya* texts, they were then aged seven and eight. Zeynab offers her sons as a sacrifice (*qurbān*) to her brother. She ties them with a rope, like sheep being offered for sacrifice (12), and both are killed in battle. Zeynab sacrifices her children to save her brother's life; the question is, why does she do so? There is no doubt that her love for her brother is not the main reason. In fact, she sacrifices them to ensure the survival of Shiite Islam. The implication is that Shiites should sacrifice themselves and their children so that Islam can survive.

In the *taʿziya* on Amir Muṣayeb (*majles-e taʿziya Amir Muṣayeb*)[24] there is an episode in which Zeynab and Imām Ḥuseyn talk about the coming events of Karbalā, and through their conversation reveal their spiritual relationship and their foreknowledge. The events of Karbalā are vividly depicted. Imām Ḥuseyn says,

resida vaqt ey khāhar ke mā az ham judā gardim
biyā tā dar zamān-e ḥāl az qesmat rezā gardim (61).

My sister, the time of our separation has come
You know that in this world we must acquiesce to our fate (61).

The term *qesmat* is derived from the Arabic root q-s-m, meaning 'to share.' In Persian literature, it appears with the meaning of 'accepting the effect of predestination' (*qadar*). Acquiescence (*reẓā*) is a crucial concept in Islamic culture. It refers to man's submission to God's will (*az qesmat reẓā gaštan*) (8). The fate of each man is written on the Well-Preserved Tablet (*lawḥ-e mahfūẓ*).[25] Thus, man cannot change his fate, but he can accept it happily. When Imām Ḥuseyn says to Zeynab that they must acquiesce to their fate, he prepares the audience to hear unpleasant news. In this episode, Imām Ḥuseyn and Zeynab divide the coming events of Karbalā between them, each taking a number of parts. Zeynab tells Imām Ḥuseyn that she will take grief. He answers that he will take the parts of the plain of Karbalā and the shameless siege, as well as offering his head and his chest to the daggers of the enemy. He says that he also takes the martyrs of the plain of Karbalā as his part. 'Abbās, whose hands are cut off, the body of Qāsem that is torn into one hundred pieces, 'Ali Akbar, whose face is as beautiful as the moon, and 'Ali Asġar, the infant whose life is sacrificed. He takes two further parts: those of the pilgrim (*ẓā'er*) and of the preacher (*Dhāker* and *rawẓa-khān*) (61-62), who will retell the events of Karbalā and recite the suffering of Imām Ḥuseyn and elegies to him

The roles that Zeynab takes are affliction, mourning (*mātam*), and the events that happen after the day of *'Āšūrā*. Therefore, her share is to preserve the indigent orphans from the attack of Šāmiyān's army, to support Robāb, Šahrbānū and Umm al-Laylā,[26] and the bride who does not have *jahāz* or dowry (61-62). The last refers to Imām Ḥuseyn's daughter Fāṭima, who has married Qāsem in Karbalā but does not consummate the marriage because he is killed in the battle.

In the role of Imām Ḥuseyn, the wounds of daggers refer to his badly injured body, before his final death. The reference to his head and chest summons up an image of his martyrdom. His head is mentioned because he is beheaded, his chest because his body is trampled by his enemies. The body of 'Abbās that is 'without hands' refers to the death of 'Abbās, Imām Ḥuseyn's half-brother. According to Shiite sources, the blockade prevented water from being obtained for ten days. Then, 'Abbās galloped to the Euphrates for some water, but the enemy cut off his hands and he was killed. The tearing of the body of Qāsem reminds the audience that he was newly married, and his body was torn to pieces. The sacrificed life of 'Ali Asġar reminds the audience of Imām Ḥuseyn holding him, and demanding a sip of water for him. Harmala shoots an arrow and murders the infant. The last parts taken by Imām Ḥuseyn are the pilgrims (*zā'er*) and the preachers (*dhāker* and *rawẓa-khān*). The former refers to Shiite Muslims who visit the shrine of Imām Ḥuseyn. The reference in the *ta'ziya* increases the desire to visit Imām Ḥuseyn's shrine. The latter (*Dhāker* and *rawẓa-khān*, see above) refers to those whose profession is to recite the elegies of Imām Ḥuseyn and narrate the events of Karbalā. The reference to them tells the audience that the family of the Prophet respected this occupation, and that its practitioners will be rewarded in the Hereafter (61-62).

The parts that Zeynab takes are the events after the day of *'Āšūrā*, beginning with mourning and lamentation. Zeynab is described as a mournful woman who takes responsibility for keeping the tragedy of Karbalā alive. In imitation of her, Shiite women have to mourn and lament for the martyrs of Karbalā. Second, Šāmiyān's attack on the destitute children, the occasion when Ibn al-Ziyād's army attacked the tents of Imām Ḥuseyn's family, set them on fire, seized the women and children and marched them through the desert to the palace of Yazid in Damascus. Third, Robāb, Šahrbānū and 'Umm al-Laylā are the wives of Imām Ḥuseyn whom Zeynab agreed to support after his death. The name of Šahrbānū, between the names of Imām Ḥuseyn's other two wives, gives an Iranian flavour to the *ta'ziya*. Šahrbānū reminds the audience of the Iranian presence at Karbalā, which underlines the duty of Iranian women to take part in the *ta'ziya* and mourn the martyrs. Fourth, the image of the bride who does not have *jahāz*, referring to the marriage of Fāṭima and Qāsem (the son of Imām Ḥasan) at Karbalā. Qāsem was martyred while Fāṭima was captured and taken to Damascus. According to the *ta'ziya* texts, their marriage will be consummated in the heaven.

Through the conversation of Imām Ḥuseyn and Zeynab, the audience remembers the entire tragedy of Karbalā and is moved to sympathy and to active participation in the *ta'ziya*.

Zeynab and Sakina

Zeynab as Mother

In the *ta'ziya* texts, Zeynab acts as a mother for Imām Ḥuseyn's children. The most vivid picture is of the relationship between Zeynab and Sakina. The word Sakina derives from the Arabic root s-k-n. There are many derivations from this root in the Qur'ān. It means, 'To go down, rest, be quiescent, inhabit'.[27]

Sakina is the daughter of Imām Ḥuseyn. She was present at the battle of Karbalā, with the rest of Imām Ḥuseyn's family. Many *ta'ziya* texts refer to the relationship between Sakina and her aunt Zeynab.[28] Zeynab always supports Sakina, like a mother who supports her daughter. When Sakina cries for the death of her father, Zeynab tries to calm her, like a mother who cannot bear to hear her daughter crying. When Zeynab talks with Sakina, she uses the expressions that a mother uses to comfort a sorrowful daughter. For instance, Zeynab says 'I sacrifice myself for you' (*be qurbān-e tu*) or 'I sacrifice myself for your well-being' (*fadāy-e ḥālat*). After the events at Karbalā, Sakina wails and laments for her father's death. Zeynab says,

mazan bar sina-u sar ey Sakina
be qurbān-e tu ey meḥnat qarina
čegūna bengaram geryān-u zārat
bemiram tā nabinam aškbārat (199).

O Sakina! Do not beat your chest and head
I sacrifice myself for you, for whom grief is a companion
How can I see you, afflicted and shedding tears?
I wish I could die and not see your tears (199).

Several times, Zeynab says, 'I sacrifice myself for the sake of your head' (*fadā-ye sarat gardam*).

makun tu gerya be qurbāni-ye sarat gardam
fadāy-e ān del-e andūh parvarat gardam (200).

Do not cry, I sacrifice myself for your head,
I sacrifice myself for your sorrowful heart (200).

The expression (*fadā-ye sar gaštan*) to make oneself a sacrifice for someone's 'head,' has a profound meaning in Persian literature. The head (*sar*) is much more than the seat of reason it represents the person's life.

Zeynab speaks as a mother talks to her very young daughter.

agar mādar nadāri mādarat man
agar yāvar nadāri yāvarat man (122).

As you have no mother, I will be your mother
As you have no helper, I will be your helper (122).

The term child (*ṭefl*) has positive connotations. It is used to show kindness and compassion towards someone who is not necessarily a child. Zeynab calls Sakina, 'my child of Ḥuseyn, who has no friend' (*ṭefl-e biyār-e Ḥuseynam*) (199). This expression increases the empathy of the audience for Sakina, and reinforces their hatred for Šemr, who killed Imām Ḥuseyn.

Zeynab takes risks to rescue Sakina. In the *ta'ziya* on 'the death of her holiness Zeynab' (*ta'ziya vafāt-e ḥaẓrat-e Zeynab*), Šemr goes to Medina to once again arrest Imām Ḥuseyn's family. He severely beats Sakina. When Zeynab sees his cruel behaviour, she curses him and says, 'O unfaithful ugly oppressor,' terms that show that Šemr's behaviour results from his lack of faith. In this episode, Zeynab says,

čūb bar peykaraš mazan ze jafā
zan be farq-e man ey la'in-e daġā (206).

Do no beat her with a stick, for cruelty's sake,
Instead, strike my head, you deceitful, cursed one (206).

Zeynab again behaves sacrificially when Šemr is about to seize Sakina. Seeing Sakina in danger, she asks Šemr to arrest her instead. She says,

az yatimi čunin če mikhāhi
tu marā jāy-e ū bebar mal'ūn (205).

What do you want with such an orphan?
Seize me, instead of her, you accursed man! (205).

Both these examples present ideals for the audience to follow. The audience is deliberately involved. When Šemr goes to arrest Sakina, Sakina turns to the audience and seeks refuge. Her behaviour moves the audience to sympathy. Several key terms such as, O Muslims! (*ey musalmānān*), O Friends! (*ey yārān*), O my dears! (*ey ʿazizān*)[29] connect the player to the audience, and motivate the audience to participate. This comes at the climax of the *taʿziya*. The direct link with the player reinforces the emotions of the audience, and they wail and lament bitterly because they cannot help Sakina.

Sakina then rushes to her aunt asking for help. She says,

ʿamma jān ʿamma jān be dādam res
juz tu ey ʿamma jān nadāram kas (206).

Dear aunt, dear aunt, respond to my appeal
I have no one but you, dear aunt (206).

In Persian literature, *dād* means justice, but also a lament or appeal for justice. The compound verb, *be-dād residan* means to respond, to release someone from oppression or hardships. Sakina asks Zeynab for justice, giving Zeynab the role of a judge, Šemr that of the oppressor, and Sakina is the oppressed one. The audience wants to know whether Zeynab rescues herself or assists the oppressed Sakina.

Zeynab several times refers to Sakina and Fāṭima, Imām Ḥuseyn's daughters, as orphans.[30] The term orphan (*yatim*) is derived from the Arabic root y-t-m. According to Shaham, it denotes 'a child, below the age of puberty who has lost his father.'[31] The importance of observing an orphan's rights is emphasized in the Qur'ān. For instance, the property of an orphan has to be preserved for him until he reaches to the age of puberty, when he is free to manage his property. Despoiling the property of an orphan is prohibited.[32] It is said, 'Do not approach the property of the orphan, save in the fairest manner, until he is of age, and fulfill the covenant; surely the covenant shall be questioned of.'[33]

In the *taʿziya* texts the theme of orphans is used to emphasize the cruel and irreligious behaviour of Yazid and his commanders who neither obey God's commands, nor follow social customs. The *taʿziya* composer emphasizes the innocence and loneliness of the victims to highlight the unjust behaviour of the Umayyad caliph.

Zeynab as Defender

In the *ta'ziya* texts, Zeynab is present at almost all the events. When the family of Imām Ḥuseyn is humiliated by the enemy, she does not remain silent. She always refers to her rank and dignity. Her honourable lineage is a weapon. At Yazid's court, when Sakina is asked about the reason for her sadness and why she beats her chest and her face. Sakina answers in tears that she is lamenting for her father. Hearing this, Yazid tells her, 'You are correct, being an orphan is very hard, but now that you have come near me, you can be my daughter's slave girl' (124). Zeynab then defends Sakina, cursing Yazid in a loud voice and wishing him to be dumb and blind. She continues: 'Who are you that you want to have a slave-girl from the family of the Prophet? Should Sakina who is the love of Zahrā [title of Fāṭima the Prophet's daughter] 'serve you as a slave-girl?' (124). Yazid talks about Zeynab's father and grandfather, Imām 'Ali and the Prophet. He says, 'Is this she whose father conquered the world with his sword? Is this she whose mighty grandfather was lifted to the throne by God?' Then he thanks God that Zeynab is now humiliated and dishonoured (124). Although Yazid intends to mock her, his words show the dignity of Zeynab and her family.

Zeynab and the Mother of Qāsem[34]

In the *ta'ziya* texts, Qāsem's mother is a close companion for Zeynab. She follows Zeynab's suggestions. Zeynab trusts her and turns to her in extreme circumstances.

After the battle of Karbalā, Sakina, Fāṭima and 'Umm-e Kulṯūm lament for Imām Ḥuseyn and other members of the family who were killed. Zeynab tries to calm them but she cannot. She then asks the mother of Qāsem to arrange a mourning assembly. She answers, I will do it, O woman of power (or rank) (*be čašm ey bānūy-e bā-eqtedāram*) (201). Her answer shows Zeynab's influence among her family. Zeynab asks her to mourn for the oppressed (those killed at Karbalā). Qāsem's mother prepares a space for mourning for the martyrs (202). The episode shows that in the *ta'ziya* texts, mourning and lamentation are expected to calm a person.

Zeynab and the Antagonists

Zeynab and Yazid

According to the *ta'ziya* texts, Yazid orders to his commanders to kill Imām Ḥuseyn and his companions and to arrest his household. During the imprisonment period, Yazid's men behave savagely to them. Zeynab is such a strong woman that Yazid is frightened of her influence. For Yazid, Zeynab is a real opponent and a major threat to his authority. So he puts her under a lot of pressure to make her remain silent in the face of his cruel and immoral behaviour.

Yazid's cruellest act towards the prisoners is that he orders them to be led around in public places, such as the bazaar, without any veil or headscarf. In the *ta'ziya* texts we see several references to this event. For instance, Yazid thanks God when he sees Zeynab humble and dishonoured. Zeynab answers: 'Seventy maids of Medina eat from my table, such am I / I am unveiled among the people, and yet the Holy Spirit, like a lady's maid, is proffering a veil' (125). Here, Zeynab shows her rank both in this world, among the people of Medina, and before God. Not being allowed a veil does not prevent her from defending herself and her family.

Another act by Yazid that Shiites particularly loathe, and the protagonists criticize, is that he strikes the severed head of Imām Ḥuseyn, in the presence of the Imām's household and sisters. For instance, in one episode, Zeynab and Imām Ḥuseyn's daughter, Sakina, say several times that Yazid strikes the head of Imām Ḥuseyn (81). This behaviour is highlighted in the *ta'ziya* of 'the Bazaar of Damascus,' in which Imām Zeyn al-'Ābedin, the son of Imām Ḥuseyn, criticizes Yazid when he strikes Imām Ḥuseyn's head. Yazid then orders the executioner to kill Zeyn al-'Ābedin (127). In the same *ta'ziya*, when the head of Imām Ḥuseyn is taken to the ruins to be shown to Imām Ḥuseyn's family, Zeynab says that the blackness of his lips shows that Yazid has beaten him (133).

In the *ta'ziya* texts, Yazid's rancour toward Imām Ḥuseyn's family is shown in several episodes. For instance, when the family of Imām Ḥuseyn is released and they return to Medina, the people of Medina commiserate with them, wailing and mourning for Imām Ḥuseyn. Yazid is informed of this, and regrets allowing Zeynab and Sakina to live. He says,

> *čerā be kuštan-e Zeynab nemūdehim quṣūr*
> *Sakina ra nanemūdim az če zenda be gūr* (204).

Why did we neglect to kill Zeynab?
Why we did not bury Sakina alive? (204).

In addition to showing his deep hatred for Zeynab and Sakina, there is an allusion to the worst custom attributed to pre-Islamic Arabs, that of burying newborn girls alive. By his words, Yazid shows that he is not a Muslim, but rather a pagan at heart.

Zeynab is not frightened by Yazid's authority. She threatens to reveal his unjust behaviour to people. For instance, when the captives are being taken to Damascus, Zeynab tells the audience that, when she reaches Damascus, she will say what has happened and will disgrace Yazid (26). When the survivors of Imām Ḥuseyn's household arrive as prisoners at the court of Yazid, Zeynab several times speaks harshly to Yazid and reminds him of his dishonourable lineage and his savage behaviour. She warns him of the divine punishment that awaits him on the Day of Judgement.

Zeynab and Šemr

Šemr is Yazid's commander, whose cruel behaviour to Imām Ḥuseyn's family, and specifically to Zeynab, is emphasized in the *ta'ziya* texts. He is the archetype of oppression, a person who killed Imām Ḥuseyn while he was thirsty. In the *ta'ziya* texts he is described as a heartless person who is happy with his own unjust behaviour. He slaps the children of Imām Ḥuseyn and humiliates them. For instance, after the day of *'Āšūrā*, Šemr goes to arrest Imām Ḥuseyn's family and to take them to the court of Yazid. Zeynab is the first woman whom he seeks, and he wants to taunt her. Zeynab is not present when he enters, and Šemr tells the people,

khabar dahid be Zeynab du češm-e tu rowšan
kunūn ze rāh resid Šemr-e ẓel-jowšan (204).

Tell Zeynab, 'Now your eyes are delighted
Now Šemr has come in his armour' (204).

The expression 'your eye is delighted,' (*češm-e tu rowšan*) is used when a loved one returns from a journey. But Zeynab hates Šemr, as her father's murderer; he is being sarcastic and taunting her. Šemr's utterance increases the audience's hatred for him.

Šemr annoys Zeynab by reminding her of her frustrating situation on the plain of Karbalā and in the court of Yazid. For instance, in the *ta'ziya* on 'the Death of her holiness Zeynab' (*majles ta'ziya vafāt-e ḥaẓrat-e Zeynab*),[35] Šemr says to her that she must go to the bazaar without headscarf or veil, and be dishonoured (205). This harks back to what happened after the day of *'Āšūrā*, in Damascus. The forced unveiling of Zeynab and other women of Imām Ḥuseyn's family is so important that the audience is reminded of it repeatedly, in almost all the *ta'ziya* episodes.[36]

When Zeynab sees the cruel behaviour of her enemy, she raises her voice and protests. She is presented as the voice of righteousness and justice; she does not remain silent. She curses Šemr and reminds the audience that he is responsible for her death. Zeynab says,

> *vāy ke ān Šemr-e dūn ān sag-e kāfer resid*
> *'umr-e man-e khasta jān az setamaš sar resid* (204).

> Alas! Despicable Šemr, that infidel dog, has come
> The life of this broken soul has reached its end because of his injustice (204).

Zeynab provokes two responses in the audience. On the one hand, she talks harshly to Šemr, damns him and reminds him his ancestors were pagans, creating admiration for her in the audience. On the other hand, she addresses the audience as an oppressed, helpless, sorrowful woman who has been left without any support because the men have all been killed in battle, except for Imām Zeyn al-'Ābedin, who was too ill and very young. Zeynab says,

> *musalmānān hamin Šemr-e la'in ast*
> *ke az dastaš del-e zāram ġamin ast*
> *hamin ast ān ke āmad Karbalā vāy*
> *Ḥuseyn rā sar burid ū az qafā vāy*
> *hanūz az khanjaraš az rāh-e bidād*
> *čekad khūn-e Ḥuseyn ān Shah-e owtād* (205).

> O! Muslims this is that damned Šemr
> Because of him, my bitter heart is so sorrowful.
> Alas, he is the one, who came to Karbalā,

Alas, he beheaded Ḥuseyn.
The blood of Ḥuseyn, the King of the pillars,[37]
is still dripping from his dagger, because of his injustice (205).

Here, Zeynab addresses the audience as O! Muslims (*ey musalmānān*). Her helplessness and her critique of Šemr's deeds encourage them to take part in the *ta'ziya*.

Zeynab and Ibn al-Ziyād

Ibn al-Ziyād is another of Yazid's commanders. After the battle he orders his army: 'set fire to the tents of the household of Imām Ḥuseyn and trample the bodies of the dead.' In one episode, when the prisoners have been taken to his palace, he strikes the lips of the severed head of Imām Ḥuseyn with a stick, as Yazid does, and says, 'I was afraid of you.' At that moment, Sakina laments, referring to the head of her father as 'you' (*tu*), as if her father was still living, rather than as 'it' (ū). She says,

čūb zad Ibn-e Ziyād vāy, vāy, vāy
bar lab-e tu az 'enād vāy, vāy, vāy (81).

Ibn al-Ziyād is striking, alas, alas, alas,
On your lips, out of enmity; alas, alas, alas (81).

Zeynab repeats Sakina's words, in an address to her own dead mother, Fāṭima. Zeynab says,

fāṭimā ey mādaram vāy, vāy, vāy
khāk šuda bar saram vāy, vāy, vāy
čūb zad Ibn-e Ziyād vāy, vāy, vāy
ra's-e barādar baram vāy, vāy, vāy (81).

O! My mother Fāṭima, alas, alas, alas
Dust is on my head, alas, alas, alas
Ibn al-Ziyād is striking, alas, alas, alas
On my brother's head, in front of me; alas, alas, alas (81).

Then Zeynab says to Ibn Ziyād,

čūb mazan ey daġā vāy, vāy, vāy
bar sar-e Shāh-e hodā vāy, vāy, vāy
tešna-ye khuškida lab vāy, vāy, vāy
bas ke bedida jafā vāy, vāy, vāy
ey daġā pur jafā kun ḥayā vāy, vāy, vāy (81).

You imposter! Do not strike, alas, alas, alas
The head of the King of Guidance, alas, alas, alas
His lip is dry with thirst, alas, alas, alas
He has suffered much tyranny, alas, alas, alas
You imposter, oppressor, be ashamed of yourself; alas, alas, alas (81).

Sakina then repeats almost the same words, and at last Ibn al-Ziyād himself, referring to the severed head of Imām Ḥuseyn, says,

mizanam az khayzarān bar lab-o dandān-e tu
mišekanam az 'enād bas del-e yārān-e tu (81).

I beat on your lips and teeth with a bamboo rod,
I break your friends' hearts because of my enmity (81).

In these lines, Ibn al-Ziyād's striking the severed head of Imām Ḥuseyn is referred to four times. The composer uses a rhetorical figure 'repetition' (*takrir*), by repeating the compound verb 'to strike with a stick' (*čūb zadan*), in the words of Ibn al-Ziyād, Sakina and Zeynab. The repetition is used to motivate the audience. For them, Ibn al-Ziyād's behaviour is a sign of his enmity for the family of Imām Ḥuseyn. Thus, they hate him and curse him.

In these lines, Zeynab criticizes Ibn al-Ziyād and calls him an imposter or deceiver (*daġā*), and an oppressor (*pur jafā*). Ibn al-Ziyād asks Zeynab what her name is. She says, 'I am one whose young sons you have killed, I am Zeynab who has seen the mark [of fate] on her brother (*dāġ-e barādar*), and I am Zeynab who is arrested by your hand […].' We see that she is constantly referring to Ibn al-Ziyād's cruel behaviour to Imām Ḥuseyn, her sons and herself, reminding the audience how oppressed they are. Ibn al-Ziyād then praises God, because he has taken the caliphate from the family of the Prophet, and dishonoured Zeynab. Zeynab asks for help from her mother (Fāṭima) and her father (Imām 'Ali). She says to Ibn al-Ziyād: 'God bestowed salvation on us, we are loved because of his Prophet and you will be publicly disgraced […]' Ibn al-Ziyād threatens Zeynab, saying, I will order your head to be cut off. Zeynab will not be silenced: she curses him,

> O cursed one, O cursed one, you are the son of Marjāna; now hear of the dignity of the son of the Prophet […]. God bestowed his grace on Imām Ḥuseyn from the cup of martyrdom. While you, you impure one, will be disgraced because of your behaviour. O infidel! Keep silent do not babble. God will pour fire from hell into your heart (82-4).

Ibn al-Ziyād orders his executioner to kill Zeynab, but Sakina intervenes. She laments and demands that Ibn al-Ziyād should leave Zeynab alive, because the children of Imām Ḥuseyn have no other supporter but her (81-84).

In the above episode, we see that Zeynab identifies herself by her relationship to the martyrs, while she identifies Ibn al-Ziyād as the son of Marjāna,[38] in order to disgrace him. Zeynab curses him, reminds him that he killed her children and brother, while she praises her father and brother. For Zeynab, martyrdom was God's bounty for Imām Ḥuseyn. She addresses her enemy loudly and fearlessly. In imitation of her, a Shiite should protest against oppressors, and there is nothing to fear: Imām's martyrdom is the grace of God for the best of His servants.

The first couplet of the passage cited above shows the belief in the presence of saintly spirits. Zeynab talks to her father and her mother as if they were alive and could see her and help her. For instance, she says, 'Come my mother, cover my hair, see how red-faced I am because of shame' (81). Her utterance teaches the audience that they too can benefit from the assistance of these saintly spirits, in opposing an oppressive ruler.

Notes

1 M.H. Bilgrami, *The Victory of Truth: The Life of Zaynab bint 'Ali*, Karachi: Zahra Publications, 1986.

2 J.E. Tucker, 'Women in the Middle East and North Africa: The Nineteenth and Twentieth Centuries', in *Women in the Middle East and North Africa*, ed. G. Neshat & E. Judith Tucker, Indiana: Indiana University Press, 1999, p. 126.

3 For more information on the term *parda* (veil) and its symbolic meaning in Persian poetry (classic poetry and Qājār dynasty) see A.A. Seyed Gohrab, 'The Symbolism of Veiling and the Poetics of Unveiling in Early Modern Persian Poetry'

in *Khil'a: Journal of Dress and Textiles in the Islamic World*, No. 1, Leuven: Peeters, 2005, pp. 107-21.

4 J.E. Tucker, 'Women in the Middle East and North Africa: the Nineteenth and Twentieth Centuries', in *Women in the Middle East and North Africa*, p. 33.

5 Abu Jafar Muḥammad Ibn. Jarir al-Ṭabari, *The History of al-Ṭabari*, p. 76.

6 The compound word '*parda dāri*' (lit. to proffer a veil) means to show a person respect. In contrast, '*parda dari*' (lit. to draw aside a veil, to reveal a secret) means to dishonour a person.

7 N. Yegana & N.R. Keddie, 'Sexuality and Shiite Protest in Iran', in *Schism and Social Protest*, eds. J.R.I. Cole and N.R. Keddie, New Haven and London: Yale University Press, 1986, p. 122.

8 J.E. Tucker, 'Women in the Middle East and North Africa: The Nineteenth and Twentieth Centuries', in *Women in the Middle East*, p. 126.

9 Kūfa is the city whose people invited Imām Ḥuseyn to lead them and release them from the tyranny of Yazid, the successor of Mu'āwiya; but when Imām Ḥuseyn was surrounded by the army of Yazid at Karbalā they did not assist him.

10 After the battle of Karbalā, the martyrs are beheaded and their heads are taken to the court of Yazid. Yazid beats on the severed head of Imām Ḥuseyn with a stick. See Abū Ja'far Muḥammad Ibn Jarīr Ṭabarī, *The History of al-Ṭabari*, p. 176.

11 Gy, Káldy Nagy, in *The Encyclopaedia of Islam* (second edition), under *Ḳadā*.

12 R. Radtke et al., in *The Encyclopaedia of Islam* (second edition), under *Walī (A., Pl. Awlīyā)*.

13 Abū Ja'far Muḥammad Ibn Jarīr Ṭabarī, *The History of al-Ṭabari*, p. 71.

14 For more instances of the presence of the soul of the holy figures see: H. Ṣāleḥi Rād Darbandsari, *Majāles-e ta'ziya*, pp. 50, 129, 156.

15 See J. Calmard, *Encyclopaedia Iranica*, under *'Ali Akbar*.

16 D. Pinault, 'Zaynab bint 'Ali and the Place of the Women of the Household of the First Imāms in Shiite Devotional Literature', in *Women in the Medieval Islamic World, Power, Patronage, and Piety*, ed. G.R.G. Hambly, New York: St. Martin's Press, 1998. p. 87; for more information on the term elegy (*nawha*) see J.T.P. de Bruijn, in *Encyclopaedia Iranica*, under *Elegy*.

17 Ibid.

18 Ibid., p. 87.

19 *begū šahid česān gašt ān Imām-e hudā* (203).

20 D. Pinault, *The Shiites: Ritual and Popular Piety in a Muslim Community*, London: I.B. Tauris & Co Ltd, 1992, p. 39.

21 On the Day of Judgement my mother / has to intercede the sin of the nation by these deposits (211).
bāyad ānke mādaram kunad be rūz-e jazā / šafā'at-e gunah-e khalq rā zin amānathā (211).

22 D. Pinault, 'Zaynab bint Ali and the place of the Women of the Households of the First Imāms', in *Women in the Medieval Islamic World*, p. 81.

23 Ibid., p. 83.

24 According to *Majālis-e ta'ziya*, Amir Muṣayeb was a follower of Imām Ḥuseyn. Before the battle, the Imām sent him a letter asking for help. When Amir Muṣayeb arrived at Karbalā, Imām Ḥuseyn had already been killed. See H. Ṣālehi Rād Darbandsari, *Majālis-e ta'ziya*, pp. 59-72.

25 A.A. Seyed-Gohrab, *Layli and Majnūn*, p. 166; Daniel Madigan, in *Encyclopaedia of the Qur'ān*, under *Preserved Tablet*.

26 Šahrbānū and ' Umm-e Laylā are both the wives of Imām Ḥuseyn. Šahrbānū was the daughter of the last Iranian King Yazdgerd III. She was arrested by Arabs when they invaded Iran. She was taken to Medina where she married Imām Ḥuseyn. See D. Pinault, 'Zaynab bint 'Ali and the place of the Women of the Households of the First Imāms', in *Women in the Medieval Islamic World*, p. 80.

27 T. Fahd, in *The Encyclopaedia of Islam* (second edition), under *Sakina*.

28 See '*majles-e ta'ziya ġārat-e khaymagāh-e ahl-e karbalā*' and '*ta'ziya Amir Muṣayeb*' in H. Ṣāleḥi Rād Darbandsari, *Majālese ta'ziya*.

29 *qātel-e bābam ān šah-e dowrān / āmada čūn kunam musalmānān [...].*
ey azizān yatīm-o afgāram / rah dahīdam ke khowf az ū dāram (205).
O Muslims! My father's killer, the king of the age / is coming, what can I do [...]? O my friends, I am an orphan and wounded / Help me, because I am frightened of him (205).

30 For instance, what do you want with such an orphan? (*az yatimi čunin če mikhāhi?)* (205) Zaynab and 'Umme Kulṭūm several times refer to Fāṭima and Sakina saying: They are both orphans; their hearts are broken in two by grief (*in har du yatīmand az ġam del du nimand*) (205).

31 R. Shaham, in *The Encyclopaedia of Islam* (second edition), under *Yatīm*.

32 Ibid.

33 *The Koran Interpreted*, A.J. Arberry, trans., London: Allen & Unwin, 1955, p. 306, 17/36.

34 The wife of Imām Hasan (the elder brother of Imām Ḥuseyn) is called 'the mother of Qāsem' in the *Majāles-e ta'ziya*.

35 H. Ṣāleḥi Rād Darbandsari, *Majāles-e ta'ziya*, pp. 197-214.

36 See ibid., *Majles-e ta'ziya Durra-ye ṣadaf, Mjlise ta'ziya bazaar Šām, Majlese ta'ziya vurūd-e be Medina*.

37 King of the pillars refers to five unseen supports who sustain the world's existence.

38 Ibn al-Ziyād is called the son of 'Marjāna (ibn al-Marjāna) the [grand] son of Sumayyah, a man who claims a false [grand] father'. See Abū Ja'far Muḥammad Ibn Jarīr Ṭabarī, *The History of al-Ṭabari*, p. 89.

The Transformation of History

In what follows, I will examine several examples of the transformation of historical facts into oral tradition. In Shiite tradition, the events of Karbalā and the martyrdom of Imām Ḥuseyn and his companions were crucial, and their commemoration has become the most important devotional event in the Shiite calendar. The popularity of the commemoration has meant that several aspects of the historical events are now narrated in slightly different forms. The *ta'ziya* composers have added details to what is known about the events of Karbalā: details chosen to stimulate the audience's empathy.

One example of this is the murder of Imām Ḥuseyn. According to Abū Ja'far Muḥammad Ibn Jarir Ṭabari (d.839-923), on the day of 'Āšūrā, Imām Ḥuseyn went to the battlefield, where the men of his family and his companions were killed. The battle between him and Ibn al-Ziyād's soldiers lasted a long time. They were frightened to kill him. Several of them wounded him, but did not dare to kill him, until Šemr shouted at them, 'Shame on you! Why are you waiting for the man? Kill him, may your mothers be deprived of you!'[1] They then attacked Imām Ḥuseyn: he fell from his horse and Sinān Ibn Anas Ibn 'Amr al-Nakha'i stabbed him and killed him. Then he cut off his head.[2] In the *ta'ziya* texts, it is Šemr who does this, and so incurs the guilt. This is simply a collapsing of Ṭabari's account, in which Šemr does not do the deed, but does prompt Imām Ḥuseyn's killers, who might otherwise not have dared commit such an act.

Another historical fact that is transformed into oral tradition is Zeynab's behaviour in rescuing her nephew, 'Ali Ibn Ḥuseyn, from death. According to Ṭabari, after the day of 'Āšūrā, the prisoners were taken to Ibn-e Ziyād's palace. When he noticed Imām Zeyn al-'Ābedin he asked his companions whether he was mature or not. Receiving a positive answer, he ordered them to kill him. Zeynab then said, 'I plead to you by God, if you are a believer: that if you kill him, you kill me with him.'[3] Zeynab's intervention led Ibn-e Ziyād to free Imām Zeyn al-'Ābedin. In the *ta'ziya* texts this event happens in Yazid's palace. Because Imām Zeyn al-'Ābedin objects to Yazid striking the lips of the severed head of Imām Ḥuseyn, Yazid orders his men to kill Zeyn al-ʿĀbedin. Zeynab then threatens Yazid, saying: 'If you kill him, I will untie my hair and complain to God. Then I will go, barefooted and unveiled, to the tomb of the King of Najaf [her father Imām ʿAli].' Then she calls on her father and his image appears to Šemr. He is frightened and does not kill Imām Zeyn al-ʿĀbedin (129).

The place of Zeynab's death is another detail that is transformed in the *taʿziya* texts. Tabari says that Zeynab did not survive for long after returning from Damascus to Medina.[4] According to the *taʿziya* texts, Zeynab dies in the ruins in Damascus where the household of Imām Ḥuseyn were imprisoned (210-213).

A final example of the effect of the oral tradition is the person of Sakina, the four-year-old daughter of Imām Ḥuseyn who died during the imprisonment in Damascus.[5] In the *taʿziya* texts, Sakina is a mature girl, Zeynab's closest companion and, next to Zeynab, the primary target of the tyrannies of the Umayyad caliph and his commanders. In the *taʿziya* texts, it is Ruqeya, another daughter of Imām Ḥuseyn, who dies during the imprisonment in Damascus (133).

Notes

1 Ṭabarī, *The History of al-Ṭabari*, p. 160.
2 Ibid.
3 Ibid., p. 167.
4 Ibid.
5 D. Pinault, *The Shiites: Ritual and Popular Piety in a Muslim Community*, p. 6.

Pre-Islamic Iranian Elements in the *Ta'ziya* Texts

Another important feature of the *ta'ziya* texts is the way Shiite Arab traditions are linked to Iran. The *ta'ziya* composers give the events of Karbalā an Iranian flavour by employing words and expressions that are integral to Iranian life today. They also make plot links to Iran, so that the events of Karbalā seem more familiar to the audience. The most important of these is the presence of Šahrbānū, an Iranian princess, at Karbalā. She is the daughter of Yazdgerd III (r. 632-651), the last Sassanid (224-651) king of Iran before the Arab invasion. According to popular Shiite tradition, before the Arabs invaded Persia, Šahrbānū dreamt that Fāṭima, the daughter of the Prophet, told her that she would go to Medina and marry Fāṭima's son, Ḥuseyn, and a line of Imāms would stem from this marriage (44). The day after her dream, she was arrested and taken to Medina, where she married Imām Ḥuseyn, and so is present at the battle of Karbalā. According to the *ta'ziya* texts, Imām Ḥuseyn told her that if he should be killed on the battlefield, she had to take his horse and escape because the enemy must not arrest her. After the death of Imām Ḥuseyn, Šahrbānū first asks permission from Zeynab and then says farewell to other members of the family and leaves them. From the texts of the *ta'ziya*, one learns that Sakina, Fāṭima and Imām Zeyn al-'Ābedin are the children of Šahrbānū (43-45). Therefore, the line of Imāms is almost Iranian. So naturally, Iranians are responsible for continuing the commemoration of the martyrdom of Imām Ḥuseyn and other members of the Prophet's family.

In the above episode, Šahrbānū's brother 'Abd al-Allāh has been expecting Imām Ḥuseyn, who does not arrive. 'Abd al-Allāh sends a messenger to him, but the messenger does not return for two weeks. When he does return, he explains to 'Abd al-Allāh the miserable situation of Imām Ḥuseyn and his companions on the plain of Karbalā (37-38). 'Abd al-Allāh's camp is in the desert, and his sister Šahrbānū comes to him there (48-49). In these texts, Yazdgerd's son is named 'Abd al-Allāh, whereas his real name was Pirūz.[1] The transformation of the name encourages Iranians to adopt Arabic names and choose them for their children. Yazdgerd's supposed acceptance of this name is a sign of his respect for Arab customs.

Another important feature that makes the *ta'ziya* seem more familiar for Iranians is its suffusion with motifs drawn from the Persian ethic of kingship. Hereditary kingship has very ancient roots in Iran. Terms such as king (*Shah*), crown prince (*vali'ahd*), and prince (*Shahzāda*) are associated with social rank in Persian. Iranians respect the idea of social rank: those who bear one of these titles are entitled to at least a presumption of dignity. In the *ta'ziya* texts, Imām Ḥuseyn is several times called the King of the Day of Judgement (*pādešah-e rūz-e ma'ād*) (16), the King of Religion (*Shah-e din*) (33), the headless king (*Shah-e bi sar*) and the thirsting king (*Shah-e tešna lab*) (182). In the *ta'ziya* texts, the members of Imām Ḥuseyn's family identify themselves with a lineage that can be traced back to royalty. For example, Ruqeya, Imām Ḥuseyn's daughter, says to the daughter of Yazid, 'our lineage traces back to kings, we are among the nobility of the world' (*mā az šahānim ze khūbān-e jahānim*) (149).

The *ta'ziya* texts sometimes name Persian kings. In the *ta'ziya* on 'the mourning of Dorra Ṣadaf' (*ta'ziya Dorra Ṣadaf*), Dorra and her companions are setting out to fight Ibn al-Sa'd and so free Imām Ḥuseyn's household (she is able to see Zeynab and offer her a headscarf (95-108)). On the way, she meets a man named Šabān, who is also going to take revenge on the enemies of Imām Ḥuseyn. He says to Dorra Ṣadaf that the legendary kings Jamšid and Dārā are mere slaves compared to her (101). This image and several other Iranian names mentioned in this *ta'ziya* assembly, such as Muštary, Šabān and Sanān, make the events of Karbalā seem more familiar to Iranians.

Note

1 See N. Garsoian, 'Bizantium and the Sasanian', in *The Cambridge History of Iran, the Seleucid, Parthian and Sasanian Periods*, vol. 3 (1), ed. E. Yarshater, Cambridge: Cambridge University Press, 1983, p. 177.

Conclusion

Ta'ziya is the most important Shiite religious ritual. It is performed to commemorate Imām Ḥuseyn's tragic death at Karbalā on the tenth of Muharram in 60/680. *Ta'ziya* performances preserve the tragedy of Karbalā to the present day, by re-enacting it. These performances show us the core of Shiite religious identity. They picture the afflictions that Imām Ḥuseyn and his family endured at Karbalā, and motivate the audience to mourn and lament for him.

The present study sheds light on several aspects of *ta'ziya* in Iran. It appears to have some continuity with the pre-Islamic dramatic tragedies of Mitrā (an Iranian god), of Zarir and of Siyāvuš. Where ancient Iranians mourned and lamented for the afflictions that Mitrā had suffered, medieval and modern Iranians mourn and wail for the afflictions that Imām Ḥuseyn endured on the plain of Karbalā. Where once they applauded Zarir, who fought a neighbouring king to defend the religion of Zoroastrianism, now they applaud Imām Ḥuseyn, who dies in the defence of his faith. Siyāvuš was killed innocently, his head cut off, and after his death his wife was captured by Afrāsiyāb, the king of Tūrān. This is similar to the events of Karbalā: after the death of Imām Ḥuseyn his head was cut off and his household was taken captive on the orders of Yazid, the Umayyad caliph. The common features (fighting for religion, innocence, death, captivity, suffering, affliction, and mourning) have prepared the ground for Iranians to commemorate the tragic death of Imām Ḥuseyn in a dramatic tragedy. For Shiites, the tragedy of Karbalā is a religious myth, and Imām Ḥuseyn and Zeynab are the main figures in it.

In *ta'ziya* the religious beliefs and virtues of Zeynab are highlighted and mingled with Iranian terms and motifs. Although Zeynab is an Arab, she is so close to the spirit and beliefs of Iranian women that they live with her memories and emulate her behaviour. She is the heroine of the battle of Karbalā.

The *ta'ziya* ritual unites Shiites and reminds them about their common history. The women of Imām Ḥuseyn's household are role models for Iranian women in various ways. Fāṭima and Imām Ḥuseyn's daughter Sakina are the archetypes of suffering and endurance. Imām Ḥuseyn's sister 'Umme Kulṯūm is a support to his children and a helper for her sister Zeynab. After the battle, Zeynab protests against the Umayyad caliph Yazid (r.60-3/680-3). Her behaviour enabled the tragedy of Karbalā to become a living tradition. Zeynab played a major role both before the battle and after the battle, during the imprisonment period. Zeynab's character and her exceptional behaviour in standing up to Yazid have connected Shiite history with the events of Karbalā. Her behaviour made her an archetype for Iranian women before the Islamic Revolution, during the Revolution, during the Iran-Iraq war (in the 1980s), and after it.

Imām Ḥuseyn, too, is an archetype for Shiite behaviour. He teaches Shiites not to accept the authority of a ruler who does not obey the religious law. Imām Ḥuseyn is the symbol of submission to God's will. He sacrifices himself and his family to preserve the faith. This image, repeated in the *ta'ziya*, has motivated Shiites to preserve their religion and show their loyalty to their Imām.

Zeynab is the archetype of protest against the ruling class. She transcends all prohibitions and restrictions to preserve Shiite Islam and the memory of her brother. Her loyalty to her mission makes her speak against Yazid. Zeynab's story draws attention to the afflictions and hardships that the family of Imām Ḥuseyn suffered during the siege period at Karbalā and in the imprisonment period.

Before the Islamic Revolution, Zeynab was generally presented in Iran as a passive protestor and an afflicted woman who stood up to Yazid. She appeared only in the *ta'ziya* plays held during the month of Muḥarram. During the Islamic Revolution (1979), Zeynab played a more prominent role, as the archetype of protest for Iranian women as a whole. They protested against the tyrant Muḥammad Reẓā Shah (1925-1979), whose father had forced women to go to public places without a veil or headscarf. The Shah had continued his father's policies, and was treated as if he was the return of the tyrant Yazid.

In the *ta'ziya* texts, Zeynab is also the archetype of self-sacrificing behaviour and of support for Imām Ḥuseyn and his lineage. Zeynab is pictured as a mother for the orphans of Imām Ḥuseyn, especially Sakina, her closest companion. During the Iran-Iraq war (1980-88), Zeynab was 'present' in every house: mothers would send their sons and husbands to battle in her name, to take revenge on the descendants of Yazid for Imām Ḥuseyn's blood.

Those who died in the war were likened to the martyrs of the battle of Karbalā, because they died to preserve the religion of God, like Imām Ḥuseyn. For them, there was no doubt that the dead would live in paradise beside their master, Imām Ḥuseyn. Women who supported the soldiers from behind the lines were likened to Zeynab.

After the Iran-Iraq war (1980-88), Zeynab's image was adopted by a corps of moral police. Women who have taken on this role call themselves 'the sisters of Zeynab' (*khāharān-e Zeynab*). Thus, Zeynab is still among the Iranians. She has taken on responsibility for directing women to follow the religious law, she 'commands the good and forbids the evil' (*amr-e be ma'rūf va nahy-e az munkar*). She emphasizes wearing the headscarf that Zeynab was deprived of, after the battle of Karbalā, and she restrains women from doing what the religious law (*šari'at*) has prohibited.

Another important feature of Zeynab is her relationship with the saintly spirits of the Prophet's family, who assist her. This image is rooted among Shiites. They believe in the presence of the holy spirits in the physical world and their involvement in people's affairs. In general, all the members of the Prophet's family (*ahl al-bayt*) have a significant role among Shiites. They are their religious leaders, their moral teachers and their spiritual guides. They intercede on behalf of the Shiites in the Hereafter. Thus, the Shiites are responsible for preserving their memory.

Glossary: The *Ta'ziya* of the Damascus Bazaar

I follow the Persian pronounciation and spelling of Arabic names.

'Abbās [Abu al-Faẓl al-'Abbās] (d.680): a half brother of Imām Ḥuseyn, killed at Karbalā

'Ābedin (Zeyn al-'Ābedin): the fourth Shiite Imām, the son of Imām Ḥuseyn

'Ābes: a representative follower of Imām Ḥuseyn, killed at the battle of Karbalā

'Abū 'Amr-e Naš'ali: a representative follower of Imām Ḥuseyn

Adam: the first man created by God

'Ali (d.661): the first Imām of Shiite Muslims and the fourth caliph of the Muslim community (656-661)

'Ali Akbar (d.680): the son of Imām Ḥuseyn. He was killed at the battle of Karbalā

'Ali Aṣġar (d.680): the infant son of Imām Ḥuseyn. He was killed at the battle of Karbalā

'Ali Ibn al-Ḥuseyn: see 'Ābedin

Amir-e ġāyeb: a title of Imām 'Ali

'Amr-o 'Ās: one of Yazid's commanders; he fought against Imām Ḥuseyn

'Awn (d.680): Zeynab's son

Bū Turāb: a title of Imām 'Ali

Doctor: a narrative figure

European: a narrative figure

Executioner: a narrative figure

Fāṭima: the daughter of the Prophet Muhammad and Khadija

Ġassāla: refers to a woman whose job is washing the dead

Ḥabib Ibn Mazāher (d.680): a follower of Imām Ḥuseyn, killed at the battle of Karbalā

Ḥasan (d.670): the son of Imām 'Ali and Fāṭima and the second Shiite Imām

Hendeh: Yazid's wife
Hendeh's maid: a narrative figure
Ḥeydar-e Ṣafdar: a title of Imām 'Ali
Hunter: a narrative figure
Ḥurr ibn-Riyāhi (d.680): Ibn-e Ziyād's commander at the battle of Karbalā. Later, he joined Imām Ḥuseyn and fought for him
Ḥuseyn (d.680): the son of Imām 'Ali and Fāṭima and the third Shiite Imām. He was killed at Karbalā
Ibn-e Sa'd: the governor of Kūfa and one of Yazid's commanders
Imam 'Ebād: see 'Ābedin
Ishmael: son of Abraham. Refers to a Qur'ānic story that Abraham was told in a dream to sacrifice his son
Ja'far (d.680): Zeynab's son
Jacob: a Qur'ānic figure
Joseph: a Qur'ānic figure
Kaniz: a narrative figure
Messenger: a narrative figure
Minstrel: a narrative figure
Mu'āviya [Mu'āwiya Ibn Abi Sufyān] (d.680): the founder of the Umayyad dynasty (661-680)
Muḥammad (d.632): the Prophet, son of Abdullah and 'Āmena
Muslim Ibn 'Awseja: a narrative figure
New bride: a title for Fāṭima, Imām Ḥuseyn's daughter
Preacher: a narrative figure
Prophet: see Muhammad
Qāsem (d.680): Imām Ḥasan's son, killed at the battle of Karbalā
Ruqiya (d.680): Imām Ḥuseyn's daughter. She died during the imprisonment period in Damascus
Sakina: Imām Ḥuseyn's daughter
Salmā: a narrative figure
Salmi: a narrative figure
Šemr: Ibn Ziyād's commander
Seyed-e Sajjād: see 'Ābedin
Šowdhab: a narrative figure, a representative follower of Imām Ḥuseyn
The Family of the Prophet: refers to the survivors after the battle of Karbalā
'Umar-e Sa'd (d.680): the son of Vaqqās and the governor of Ray. He took part in the battle of Karbalā on Yazid's side
Vizier: see 'Amr-o 'Ās

Yazid (d.683): the son of Mu'āwiya and Marjāna. He is the second Umayyad caliph
Zahra: a title of Fāṭima, the Prophet's daughter
Zeyn al-'Ebād: see 'Ābedin
Zeynab (d.682): the daughter of Imam 'Ali and Fāṭima. The Prophet's daughter

The *Ta'ziya* of the Damascus Bazaar

Introduction

(Spoken by Sakina)
O European! Help us
O European! Our lives depend on you.
O European! Turn back from this ruin,
We are all unveiled, afflicted, naked!

O European! Help us
O European! Our lives depend on you
O Father! King of Medina! Where are you!
A European has come, his eyes are on Sakina!
O European! Help us
O European! Our lives depend on you.
If my father was alive to support me
Surely, I would not be living in this ruin.
O! European! Help us
O! European! Our lives depend on you

مجلس تعزیه بازار شام

پیش خوانی

فرنگی دست ما بر دامن تو
فرنگی خون ما در گردن تو
فرنگی زین خرابه رو بگردان
همه بی چادریم و زار و عریان

فرنگی دست ما بر دامن تو
فرنگی خون ما در گردن تو
کجایی ای پدر شاه مدینه
فرنگی آمده سیر سکینه

فرنگی دست ما بر دامن تو
فرنگی خون ما در گردن تو
اگر دست پدر بودی به دستم
چرا من در خرابه می نشستم
فرنگی دست ما بر دامن تو
فرنگی خون ما در گردن تو

Yazid: Come ʻAmr-o ʻĀs, my companion in grief
Sit with me a while, here in private
Be the salve for my old wound
For the fire [of grief] has burned my wings.
Bring the word of God (the Qur'ān)
So I may read the omens, my heart marked with grief.

ʻAmr-o ʻĀs: You are a sea of subterfuge, compared to me;
Next to you, I am less than an ant.
Take the word of God
Read the omens, your heart marked with grief.

Yazid [in Arabic, reciting a formula]:
O God! Thou the Generous, Thou the Merciful, Thou the Judge;
Thou the Proof, Thou the Beneficent, Thou the Praised,
Thou the Patient, the Wise, the Lord of glory and honour.
I appeal to You for a sign.
O God! Heart of my heart, whose remembrance is the light of my heart, I consult you regarding all my affairs.

ʻAmr-o ʻĀs [Opens the Qur'ān and reads]: Truly, the hypocrites will be in the lowest depths of the fire,[1] then inform them of the supreme torment.

Yazid: O! ʻAmr-o ʻĀs, this is not a good omen, I will take another omen and see what comes.

ʻAmr-o ʻĀs gives the interpretation: 'Soon will the oppressors know how the changeable will be changed.'[2]

Yazid: This is again bad,
The Pure One [God] has informed us
Through his own Word, of a painful torment.
I will put aside this 'Word of God.'
I sigh from the depths of my heart.
The spark of fever has set my soul on fire,
All my bones are burning
The spark of fever fired my soul
Surely Huseyn's anger has made me burn so hot

یزید ـ بیا عمروعاص ای به غم یاورم
به خلوت نشین ساعتی در برم
بشو مرحم زخم ناسور من
که آذربرافروخت بال و پرم
بیاور کلام خداوندگار
تفأل زنم با دل داغدار

عمروعاص ـ تو دریای تزویری اندر برم
به نزد تو از مور من کمترم
بگیر این کلام خداوندگار
تفأل بزن با دل داغدار

یزید ـ استخیر بك یا الله یا کریم و یا رحیم و یا دیان و یا برهان و یا منان و یا سبحان
و یا حلیم و یا حکیم و یا ذوالجلال و الاکرام
استخیرالله فی کل الامور ذات فی قلبی و ذکر الله نور

عمروعاص ـ ان المنافقین فی الدرك أسفل من النار فبشرهم بعذاب الیم

یزید ـ عمروعاص این که بد آمد زنم یك بار دیگر فال و بینم چیست

عمروعاص در تعبیرش ـ وسیعلم الذین ظلموا ای منقلب ینقلبون

یزید ـ این هم که بد آمد
چون بشارت داد ما را فرد پاك
از کلام خود عذاب دردناك
افکنم دور این کلام الله را
از نهاد خود برآرم آه را
شرار تب زده آتش به جانم
همی سوزد تمام استخوانم
یقین خشم حسینم این چنین سوخت

O Vizier! I am dying of this pain!

'Amr-o 'Ās: how can I cure an incurable pain?

Yazid: O Vizier! I am dying because of this double-dealing.

'Amr-o 'Ās: I will invite one of the European doctors.

Yazid: Go and bring one of them as soon as possible.

'Amr-o 'Ās: (Now I invite the doctor for the patient)
O Doctor! The fate that was asleep, is wakened now
Yazid the shameless, is now ill
If you are able to kill, do it![3]
Have mercy on his wife.

Doctor: Why am I in this wretched condition?
My heart and my eye are filled with blood,
I will go, but I do not want to.
It's as if there is a pitfall on this path.
O Caliph! Greetings to you,
the sorrowful heart is cheered on meeting you.
Now, I have come to practise medicine
I am going to find the cause of your illness.

Yazid: Greetings to you, Aristotlean genius
Come and sit at the banquet of my favour.
Ho! My comely, charming, servants,
Bring some sherbet for the sage.

Doctor: O King! What is your condition?
[Yazid:] My condition? My heart is overflowing with blood?
[Doctor:] Give me your hand so that I can take your pulse.
[Yazid:] Doctor, I fear that I may die!
[Doctor:] Fear not, it is not the time for your death.
[Yazid:] Help me, Doctor.

وزیرا آه مردم من از این درد

عمروعاص ـ چه چاره درد بی درمان توان کرد

یزید ـ بمیرم ای وزیر از این دورنگی

عمروعاص ـ بیارم از اطبای فرنگی

یزید ـ بیاور زودتر پایی تو بگذار

عمروعاص ـ طبیب آرم کنون از بهر بیمار
طبیبا بخت خفته گشته بیدار
یزید بی حیا گردیده بیمار
گر توانی بکش حلالش کن
رحم بر حالت عیالش کن

طبیب ـ ندانم حال زارم را که چون است
دل من همچو چشمم پر ز خون است
روم من لیك پایم مانده در راه
تو پنداری سر راهم بود چاه
سلامم بر تو بادا ای خلیفه
دل غمگین ز تو شاد ای خلیفه
کنون من امدم بهر طبابت
ببینم تو مریضی از چه بابت

یزید ـ علیك السلام ای ارسطو ضمیر
به بزم تقرب بیا جای گیر
ایا خادمان قشنگ و وسیم
بیارید شربت برای حکیم

طبیب ـ تو را ای پادشه احوال چون است؟
چه احوالی؟ دلم لبریز خون است
بده دستت که تا نبضت بگیرم
طبیبا ترس از آن دارم بمیرم
مخور غم نیست وقت مردن تو
طبیبا دست من بر دامن تو

Doctor: Is any bone in your neck painful?

Yazid: Yes, I am fainting from pain.

Doctor: Can you sleep on your side?

Yazid: O Sage! Not for a long time, but for a short time.

Doctor: Tell me, is your breathing difficult?

Yazid: As if there is a stone on my chest.

Doctor: O afflicted man! And what taste is in your mouth?

Yazid: Sometimes it is bitter, sometimes sour, and sometimes it is salty.

Doctor: Now tell me, do you thirst for water?

Yazid: My heart is on fire for water.

Doctor: What is your condition when you cough?

Yazid: When I cough my headache increases.

Doctor: Open your mouth, I want to see inside.

Yazid: Look then! May all my pain and afflictions be on you.

Doctor: God be praised! There is an incurable disease in your throat.

Yazid: You villain, do not say useless words to me.

Doctor: Tell me does your wounded heart thirst for water?

Yazid: O Sage! I am dying because of the burning fever.

Doctor: Does your heart flutter like a slaughtered bird?

Yazid: It feels as if there are needles in my heart.

طبیب ـ کند هیچ استخوان گردنت درد؟

یزید- بلی این درد بی حالم چنین کرد

طبیب ـ به پهلو گر بخوابی می توانی؟

یزید ـ نه بسیار، ای حکیم، اندك زمانی

طبیب ـ نفس بر سینه ات برگو که تنگ است

یزید ـ تو پنداری به روی سینه سنگ است

طبیب ـ دهان دارد چه طعم ای مرد رنجور؟

یزید ـ گهی تلخ و گهی ترش و گهی شور

طبیب ـ بگو بر آب داری هیچ خواهش؟

یزید ـ دلم بگرفت بهر آب آتش

طبیب ـ به وقت سرفه کردن حال چون است

یزید ـ چو آید سرفه درد سر فزون است

طبیب ـ دهانت باز کن بینم دهانت

یزید ـ ببین درد و بلاهایم به جانت

طبیب ـ بحمدالله به حلقت کوفت افتاد

یزید ـ مگو بیهوده بر من، زشت بنیاد!

طبیب ـ بگو دارد عطش قلب فگارت؟

یزید ـ حکیما مردم از سوز حرارت

طبیب ـ طپش دارد دلت مانند بسمل

یزید ـ تو پنداری که سوزن هاست بر دل

Doctor: O good Vizier! It's certain that
The reason of the illness has been found, I will tell you the remedy.

'Amr-o 'Ās: Tell me, what is the nature of this essence of rancour?
How did you find what the illness is?

Doctor: His essence is worthless,
But the illness is pneumonia of the chest.
You have to prepare a poultice for him.
Do not delay, prepare it quickly.

'Amr-o 'Ās: O skilful doctor! Blessed with the [healing] breath of Jesus!
Write a prescription for whatever ingredients you wish.

Doctor: Certainly. First, you have to prepare
A poultice from beeswax, camphor and sandalwood
Then add to it chalk, rose and sugar
Sweet basil, the seed of purslane and the seed of coriander,
Mallows, jujube and Sebestens,
the leaves of leek and the seeds of sweet basil.
Then add some chicken fat,
and peanut oil.
If his stomach is flatulent, I tell you next.
He must take some sodium bicarbonate
and three to six kilos of large plums,
and one hundred and seventy tortoise eggs.
Boil the medicines for him
Pour them in his poisoned throat.

'Amr-o 'Ās: Slave girls! Come to the threshold
Bring us the mortar and pestle.
O King! Arise, turn your face to your servants,
Drink the medicine that preserves your health.

Yazid: I'll have nothing to do with these ingredients.
The cure for my pain is a cup of wine.
These ingredients will make me more ill.
The cure for my pain is the blood of Huseyn.
When has jujube ever removed grief?
When has the violet ever caused cheerfulness?

طبیب ـ یقین دان ای وزیر نیك بنیاد
مرض معلوم شد باید دوا داد

عمروعاص ـ بگو این جوهر کین را غرض چیست؟
چه سان معلوم بنمودی مرض چیست؟

طبیب ـ اگر چه ذات او بی ارج و قدر است
مرض ذات الریه با ذات صدر است
ضمادی بایدش ترتیب فرمود
نه چندان دیر، باید ساختن زود

عمروعاص ـ ایا نیکو طبیب دم مسیحا
هر آن ادویه خواهی نسخه فرما

طبیب ـ بلی، باید مهیا کرد اول
ضماد از موم و از کافور و صندل
نباشیر و گل سرخ و شکر نیز
سپرغم، تخم خرفه، تخم گشنیز
ز خبازی و عناب و سپستان
ز برگ گندنا و تخم ریحان
ز پیه مرغ بعد اندك بیفزا
اضافه روغن بادام فرما
دلش گر نفخ دارد گویمت این
بده بر وی تو قدری جوش شیرین
یك دو من آلو بخارای درشت
یکصد و هفتاد تخم لاك پشت
دواها را بجوشانید بهرش
بریزید آنچنان در کام زهرش

عمروعاص ـ کنیزان روی بر درگاه آرید
همه هاون برای ما بیارید
شها برخیز و رو بر چاکران کن
دوای حفظ صحت نوش جان کن

یزید ـ مرا از این دواها اجتناب است
دوای درد من جام شراب است
مرا از این دواها شور و شین است
دوای درد من خون حسین است
یزید ـ کجا عناب رفع غم نماید
بنفشه کی در شادی گشاید

I am afflicted, I will be cheerful when
I lead Zeynab around the bazaar.
My heart will be free of sorrow on the day
When a messenger comes from Karbalā.

Messenger: I am a messenger and now
I am carrying a secret letter, with a hundred admonitions to Yazid.
Greetings, O commander of Damascus:
The bird of fortune has fallen in a trap.
I have brought a letter from the commanders of the army:
Take it the black-faced commander.

Yazid: Greetings, eloquent messenger,
You are welcome; weary one.
O Preacher, O nightingale in speech,
Mount the pulpit and recite the letter for me.

Preacher: I take refuge in God from Satan the damned,
In the name of God the compassionate the merciful.
Hear now, this letter is written by ʻUmar-e Saʻd-e Vaqqās, a slave who is ready to sacrifice his soul, and ʻthe whisperer [of evil] who whispers in the heart of man,'[4] to Yazid ibn Muʻāwiya, who deserves to go to the hell.
Now that the world has turned in your favour,
Your are appointed and ʻAli is deposed.
The bright palace of the king of the two worlds is ruined,
The body of the king of the world was covered with the blood and dust.
They burnt the tents with the fire of rancour,
The veil of shame has been completely drawn from our face.
Šemr has slapped the face of the children until they were as red as red juniper.
Their ruby lips were dry with thirst, wanting one sip of water.
They cut off the hand of ʻAbbās, who carried the flag [of Huseyn]
The body of Akbar fell in the dust, and was seen drowned in blood.

Yazid: Thanks be to God, the sphere is turning to fulfil our desire
The wild bird of fortune has fallen in our trap
Grief is ended and sorrow is removed from our heart.
Pour the wine of good cheer in our cup,

شوم خشنود آن وقتی من زار
که زینب را بگردانم به بازار
رها دل را ز غم روزی نمایم
که آید قاصدی از کربلایم

قاصد ـ قاصدم این زمان به صد تأکید
می برم نامه از برای یزید
السلام ای امیر کشور شام
مرغ دولت فتاده اندر دام
نامه آوردم از سران سپاه
بستان ای امیر روی سیاه

یزید ـ السلام ای قاصد نیکو بیان
این زمان خوش آمدی ای خسته جان
ای خطیب ای بلبل شیرین زبان
رو به منبر نامه از بهرم بخوان

خطیب ـ اعوذ بالله من الشیطان رجیم، بسم الله الرحمن الرحیم
اما بعد، این نامه، نامه ای است از غلام جان فشان عمر سعد وقاص الخناس الذی یوسوس
فی صدور الناس
بسوی پادشاه عام و خاص یزید بن معاویه علیه الهاویه نوشته است:
تا که اوضاع جهان با نام او گردیده شد
مسند تو چیده از آل علی برچیده شد
کاخ نورانگیز سلطان دو عالم شد خراب
پیکر شاه جهان در خاك و خون غلطیده شد
خیمه ها را از شرار آتش کین سوختند
پرده شرم از رخ ما سر به سر بدریده شد
شمر از سیلی رخ اطفال کرده سندروس
از برای جرعه آبی لعلشان خشکیده شد
دست عباس علمدارش ز تن انداختند
پیکر اکبر به خاك افتاد و در خون دیده شد

یزید ـ شکر خدا که دور فلك شد به کام ما
افتاد مرغ وحشی دولت به دام ما
اندوه شد تمام و غم از سینه دور شد
ریزید باده طرب اینك به جام ما

Decorate my court like the garden of heaven
Decorate the streets and bazaar of our city, Damascus.
Bring the minstrels who sing lyrics and play the harp,
and our pretty dancers who walk gracefully.
O Cupbearer! Bring wine and make us cheerful,
Light our candle with the light of wine.

Yazid: Servants! Bring sherbet!
Make sweet the mouths of our friends and loved ones,
Slaves! Bring my water pipe,
that I may dispel from my heart the pain of disturbing speech.
Pour aloeswood, musk, rose, tulip and jasmine.
Sing, minstrel, so that grief may leave my heart.

Minstrel: The events of *Karb* and *balā* have made our heart bloody
Because there is no cure for an incurable pain,
Alas, that the sphere has lit such a fire in Damascus
That its smoke has darkened the lamp of Medina
This day is Yazid's day: minstrels play the tambourine
The King of Religion has been martyred, all of you clap your hands
O Minstrels! play the tambourine and clap your hands
The King of Religion has been martyred, this day is Yazid's day.

Yazid: Since Šemr has given his allegiance to us,
It is fitting that we honour him.
Lead out seventy of my best horses,
with amphora, braziers and incense
Šemr, come before us with such splendour
It is fitting that he should enter the city with honour and glory.

Šemr: O Shiites! I have brought the musk of Tartar from Karbalā,
I have brought the family of the Prophet, despised and afflicted,
I have chained the hand of Zeynab, the afflicted sister of Huseyn.
By God, I have brought the daughter of the lion of God [Imām 'Ali] and dishonoured her.

Šemr: Greetings, O king of Damascus.

Yazid: Greetings!

زينت كنيد بارگه من چو باغ خلد
آذين كنيد كوچه و بازار شام ما
آريد مطربان غزل خوان و چنگ زن
رقاصگان خوب رخ و خوشخرام ما
ساقى بيار باده و تر كن دماغ ما
از نور باده ساز منور چراغ ما

يزيد ـ شربت بياوريد شما پيشخدمتان
شيرين كنيد كام عزيزان و دوستان
قليان بياوريد غلامان براى من
تا درد دل برون كنم از غلغل سخن
ريزيد عود و مشك و گل و لاله و سمن
خوشخوان بخوان كه رفته برون از دلم محن

خوشخوان ـ حديث كرب و بلا كرده خون دل ما را
كه چاره اى نتوان درد بى مداوا را
فغان كه چرخ برافروخت آتشى در شام
كه تيره كرد ز دودش چراغ بطحا را
دور دور يزيد است، اى مطربان دف زنيد
سلطان دين شهيد است كف جمله بر كف زنيد
اى مطربان دف زنيد كف جمله بر كف زنيد
سلطان دين شهيد است دور دور يزيد است

يزيد ـ چون شمر كرد خدمت خود را به ما دراز
مى زيبد اين كه ماش نماييم سرفراز
هفتاد اسب خاصه من را يدك كنيد
با آبدارى و قبل و منقل و گداز
با اين جلال شمر بيايد حضور ما
زيبد اگر به شهر در آيد به عز و ناز

شمر ـ شيعيان از كربلا مشك تتار آورده ام
اهل بيت مصطفى را خوار و زار آورده ام
بسته ام بازوى زينب خواهر زار حسين
الله الله دختر شير خدارا كرده خوار آورده ام

شمر ـ سلطان شهر شام، سلام

يزيد ـ السلام، ها!

Šemr: I have brought news for you.

Yazid: From where?

Šemr: From the plain of Karbalā.

Yazid: Is it victory, or defeat?

Šemr: Fortune favours the king, it is victory.

Yazid: Praised be God who has fulfilled our desire.
Has the King of Religion been martyred?

Šemr: Yes, he was drowned in blood.

Yazid: Did no one assist him on the plain of calamity?

Šemr: Yes.

Yazid: Who assisted him there?

Šemr: His brother.

Yazid: What was his name?

Šemr: His holiness ʻAbbās, the Faithful.

Yazid: Was ʻAbbās killed?

Šemr: Yes, he was martyred.
For spite, both his hands were cut from his body.

Yazid: How did he fight?

Šemr: Bravely.

Yazid: Give me a description.

Šemr: He attacked our army like a brave dragon.

شمر ـ آورده ام خبر

یزید ـ زکجا؟

شمر ـ دشت کربلا

یزید ـ فتح است یا شکست؟

شمر ـ به اقبال شاه، فتح!

یزید ـ حمد خدای را که خدا داد کام ما!
سلطان دین شهید شد؟

شمر ـ آری به خون تپید

یزید ـ کس یاری اش نکرد به دشت بلا؟

شمر ـ چرا!

یزید ـ که کرد یاری اش مگر آنجا؟

شمر ـ برادرش

یزید ـ نامش چه بود؟

شمر ـ حضرت عباس باوفا

یزید ـ عباس کشته گشت؟

شمر ـ بلی او شهید شد
از کینه هر دو دست شد از پیکرش جدا

یزید ـ چون جنگ می نمود؟

شمر ـ دلیرانه

یزید ـ وصف کن

شمر ـ زد بر سپاه ما چو یکی نره اژدها

Yazid: Did the army resist?

Šemr: No.

Yazid: Then what?

Šemr: They fled.

Yazid: From one person?

Šemr: Yes, they fled like the sparrow that flees the eagle.

Yazid: How many fighters were killed there?

Šemr: One thousand.

Yazid: Over how many days?

Šemr: In a single attack.

Yazid: Well done.
What did Hurr do with Huseyn?

Šemr: He supported him.

Yazid: Was he not our friend?

Šemr: No, he turned away from us.

Yazid: How many soldiers did we have?

Šemr: One hundred thousand.
But the enemy's army was larger than ours.

Yazid: Why did their army [Huseyn and his companions] leave Karbalā?

Šemr: Because most of them were turncoats.

Yazid: Who sacrificed himself for Huseyn there?

یزید ـ لشگر ستاده بود؟

شمر ـ نه

یزید ـ چون شد؟

شمر ـ گریختند

یزید ـ از یك نفر؟

شمر ـ بلی چو مگس از بر هما

یزید ـ از ما چقدر کشته شد آنجا؟

شمر ـ هزار تن

یزید ـ در چند روز؟

شمر ـ به یك حمله

یزید ـ مرحبا!
حر با حسین چه می کرد؟

شمر ـ یاری اش

یزید ـ با ما مگر نبود؟

شمر ـ نه، گرداند رو ز ما

یزید ـ آیا چقدر لشگر ما بود؟

شمر ـ صد هزار
اما سپاه خصم بد افزون ز فوج ما

یزید ـ پس آن سپاهشان ز چه از کربلا برفت؟

شمر ـ بودند چون که اکثر آن قوم بی وفا

یزید ـ آنجا که شد فدای حسین؟

Šemr: The youth, Vahab.

Yazid: Who else?

Šemr: Barir.

Yazid: Who else?

Šemr: The moon-faced ʻAwn.

Yazid: Who else?

Šemr: Habib, Jaʻfar, the Turkish slave,
and Muslim Ibn ʻAwseje, the servant of God.

Yazid: Who else was there?

Šemr: ʼAbū ʻAmr-e Našʻali.

Yazid: Who else?

Šemr: Šowzab fought in many encounters beside ʻĀbes.

Yazid: How did ʻĀbes fight?

Šemr: He was naked.

Yazid: Did ʻĀbes fight naked?[5]

Šemr: Yes from head to foot.

Yazid: Was he not frightened of our army?

Šemr: No, he was ready to sacrifice his life, He fought and killed [our soldiers] until he was killed and his head was cut off.

Yazid: Who else was killed among the companions of the King of Religion?

شمر ـ نوجوان وهب

یزید ـ دیگر؟

شمر ـ بریر بود،

یزید ـ دگر؟

شمر ـ عون مه لقا

یزید ـ دیگر؟

شمر ـ حبیب و جعفر، با آن غلام ترك
با مسلم بن عوسجه، آن بنده خدا

یزید ـ دیگر که بود؟

شمر ـ ابو عمر نشعلی

یزید ـ دگر؟

شمر ـ شوذب کنار عابس کردند جنگ ها

یزید ـ عابس چگونه جنگ نمود؟

شمر ـ او برهنه بود

یزید ـ عابس برهنه شد؟!

شمر ـ بلی، از فرق تا به پا

یزید ـ خوف از سپه نداشت؟

شمر ـ نه از جان گذشته بود
جنگید و کشت تا که شد از تن سرش جدا

یزید ـ دیگر که کشته گشت ز انصار شاه دین؟

Šemr: Seyf Ibn abū Tamāme and the faithful Tarmā.

Yazid: Was his son ʻAli-ye Akbar martyred?

Šemr: Yes he was drowned in blood on the plain of Karbalā.

Yazid: Didn't he have a mother? Alas, for the youth, alas.

Šemr: His mother wept many tears beside his corpse.

Yazid: Was no-one thinking of his wedding?

Šemr: Yes, they were.

Yazid: Then what happened?

Šemr: It turned into a wake!

Yazid: Did Huseyn plead with you on the plain of Karbalā?

Šemr: Yes.

Yazid: How did he beg? Tell me, you deceitful dog!

Šemr: I am ashamed to say it, while people sit silently,
And are not waking heaven with the cry 'Ya! Huseyn!'
The first time, he held up his infant Asġar,
and said, O Soldiers! O Shameless people!
For three days now my child has had no water,
Give me some water for my infant ʻAli Asġar.

Yazid: Who gave water to Huseyn's suckling babe?

Šemr: Heartless Harmala, shot an arrow at his throat.

Yazid: When else did Huseyn plead with you?

Šemr: In the battlefield, when he had been knocked down.

شمر ـ سیف ابو طمامه و ترمای با وفا

یزید ـ آیا علی اکبر او هم شهید شد؟

شمر ـ آری به خون تپید به صحرای کربلا

یزید ـ مادر مگر نداشت؟ جوان حیف بود، حیف

شمر ـ مادر کنار پیکر او کرد گریه ها

یزید ـ آیا کسی نبود به فکر عروسی اش؟

شمر ـ بودند

یزید ـ پس چه گشت؟

شمر ـ بدل گشت بر عزا!

یزید ـ در کربلا حسین به شما التماس کرد؟

شمر ـ آری

یزید ـ چگونه کرد؟ بگو ای سگ دغا

شمر ـ شرم آیدم بگویم و ساکت نشسته خلق
فریاد یا حسین نرسانند بر سما
یك بار آنکه اصغر خود را به روی دست
بگرفت و گفت ای سپه، ای قوم بی حیا
طفلم سه روز قطره آبی نخورده است
آبی دهید بهر علی اصغرم شما

یزید ـ بر طفل شیرخوار حسین پس که داد آب؟

شمر ـ زد حرمله به حنجر او تیر از جفا

یزید ـ دیگر چه وقت کرد حسین التماستان؟

شمر ـ در قتلگاه چون که بیفتاد او ز پا

Yazid: So he pleaded with you, covered in dust and blood?

Šemr: No!

Yazid: Then how was it, and where was it?

Šemr: When the King of Religion fell on that ground
Ibn-e Sa'd said, 'Who is ready to cut off his head?'
We ten, all swore to kill him,
We went to the place where that shining sun [Imām Huseyn], was to die
O Yazid! When we came to the place of execution,
nine of us fled and I alone remained.
I took the dagger from my belt and I tied in my cloak,
Then I lifted my sleeve above my hand,
I had no shame before God: in a foul rage, I placed my boot
On the chest of the King of Karbalā.
Suddenly, he opened those eyes that see the truth, he looked at me,
He sighed, and said, 'O Shameless Šemr!'

Yazid: What did he say?

Šemr: He said a word that burned my heart.

Yazid: Damn you! Tell me what Huseyn said!

Šemr: With his dry lips, he said, 'I am thirsty'.

Yazid: Did you give him water?

Šemr: No, I didn't.

Yazid: Tell me, why?

Šemr: I wanted him to be martyred, suffering from thirst.

Yazid: So! Because of what you did, our faces are blackened.
Now tell me, did Huseyn cry?

Šemr: Yes, he cried twice.

یزید ـ بر روی خاك و خون به شما التماس کرد؟

شمر ـ نه!

یزید ـ پس چگونه، چه سان بود، در کجا؟

شمر ـ چون اوفتاد خسرو دین اندر آن زمین
گفت ابن سعد کیست نماید سرش جدا
ده تن شدیم هم قسم از بهر قتل او
رفتیم سوی مقتل آن شمس والضحی
وارد به قتلگاه چو گشتیم ای یزید
بگریختند نه تن و من ماندمی به جا
خنجر کشیدم از کمر و بر کمر زدم
دامن پس آستین بنمودم ز کف رها
شرم از خدا نکردم و بنشستم از غضب
با چکمه روی سینه آن شاه کربلا
ناگه گشود دیده حق بین به روی من
آهی کشید و گفت که ای شمر بی حیا

یزید ـ گفتا چه؟

شمر ـ گفت کلامی که سوختم

یزید ـ اظهار کن کلام حسین ای لعین به ما

شمر ـ با آن لبان خشك به من گفت: تشنه ام

یزید ـ دادیش آب؟

شمر ـ من که ندادم

یزید ـ بگو چرا؟

شمر ـ می خواستم که با لب عطشان شود شهید

یزید ـ آری؟ سیاه گشت از آن فعل روی ما
اکنون به من بگو که حسین گریه کرد هیچ؟

شمر ـ آری، دو بار گریه نموده است او

Yazid: Where?

Šemr: Once, when his son Akbar fell to the ground,
He cried out, 'O kind father! Help me!'
The King of Religion mounted [his horse] like the Valiant Lion [Imām 'Ali].
He attacked the army like the leviathan that attacks from the sea of calamity.
Sometimes he attacked on the right, sometimes he attacked on the left
Sometimes he was busy with the army and sometimes with the tents.

Yazid: Did he cry when he saw the army of the infidels?

Šemr: No, he did not cry because of fear.

Yazid: Then why?

Šemr: The King of Religion leapt from *zu al-Faqār* [his horse]
Tenderly, he lifted the head of his son from the ground,
Tearfully, he said one thing, and the heavens wept tears,
He said 'I will carry your body to the bridal chamber'.
He sighed, and raised a lament that rose to the sky.
'Alas! That a youth like you should be felled,'
He held up the body of that green youth,
He carried his body from the battlefield to the tents.

Yazid: O Shameless one! Didn't your heart burn,
When you inflicted so many tyrannies and oppressions?

Šemr: I'm the mother of villainy and master of tyranny
My heart has never burned for tyranny! Never!

Yazid: Where else did Huseyn cry?

Šemr: When I was about to sever his head from his body.

Yazid: Was he frightened of death, then?

Šemr: No, he had no fear.

یزید ـ کجا؟

شمر ـ یك دفعه چون که اکبرش افتاد بر زمین
فریاد زد که ای پدر مهربان بیا
سلطان دین چو حیدر صفدر سوار شد
زد بر سپاه همچو نهنگ از یم بلا
گه در یمین روانه شد و گاه بر یسار
گاهی نظر به لشگر گاهی به خیمه ها

یزید ـ وقتی که دید لشگر کفار گریه کرد؟

شمر ـ نه، او ز خوف گریه نمی کرد

یزید ـ پس چرا؟

شمر ـ تا که ز ذوالجناح شه دین پیاده شد
برداشت از زمین سر فرزند از وفا
با گریه گفت یك سخنی که آسمان گریست
گفتا به حجله گاه برم پیکر ترا
آهی کشید و شد به فلك ناله اش بلند
حیف از تو نوجوان که فتادی کنون ز پا
بگرفت نعش تازه جوانش به روی دست
برد از میان معرکه جسمش به خیمه ها

یزید ـ با این همه تعدی و ظلمی که کرده ای
آیا نسوخت قلب تو بی شرم و بی حیا؟

شمر ـ ام الفساد هستم و استاد ظلم و جور
هرگز دلم نسوخته از ظلم مطلقا

یزید ـ بار دگر حسین کجا گریه کرده است؟

شمر ـ وقتی که خواستم سرش از تن کنم جدا

یزید ـ از مرگ بیم داشت مگر؟

شمر ـ نه، نداشت بیم

Yazid: Why did he cry, tell me what happened.

Šemr: When the King of Religion fell from the back of his saddle,
He said, 'Allow me to pray'.
He was allowed, and he performed his ablutions with sand,
He prostrated himself, and he prayed to God.
Some time passed, but he did not lift his head from prostration.
Ibn-s Sa'd said, 'He is praying that we be dammed.'
Slowly and silently, I crept to his side.
I heard him, he was crooning, like this...
Weeping and lamenting, he was praying this prayer,
'O God! Forgive the sins of my people.'

Yazid: What did you do after you had martyred him?

Šemr: I inflicted a thousand tyrannies on the people of his house, to make you pleased with me.

Yazid: Did you burn the tents to take revenge?

Šemr: Yes, they burned, and went up in smoke.

Yazid: And what of Huseyn's children? Do any remain?

Šemr: One son survives him, and he is ill.

Yazid: Is there any thing else that you want to say?

Šemr: I want to ask you to bestow a robe of honour on me.

Yazid: Well done! This is the path of fidelity,
This was service to the family of Sufyan.
You deserve a robe, and gold, a garland, and jewels,
Because you have destroyed the family of the Lion, 'Ali.
You who attend me in my throne-room,
bring two robes of honour from the treasury, fitting for Šemr.

Šemr: What do you order to do with these captives?
Should we bring them with respect or humiliation?

Yazid: Go, bring them like 'Uzbak or Tatar prisoners,
lead them, bareheaded, through the streets and bazaar.

یزید ـ بهر چه گریه کرد؟ بیان کن تو ماجرا

شمر ـ از پشت زین چو آن شه دین خورد بر زمین
گفتا بده اجازه نمازی کنم ادا
رخصت گرفت و کرد تیمم به روی خاك
در سجده رفت و داشت مناجات با خدا
طولی کشید چون که سر از سجده برنداشت
فرمود ابن سعد که نفرین کند به ما
آهسته و یواش چو رفتم کنار او
کردم چو گوش زمزمه می کرد این نوا
می کرد با تضرع و با گریه این دعا
بخشا گناه امت من را تو ای خدا

یزید ـ بعد از شهادتش تو چه کردی؟

شمر ـ هزار جور بر اهل بیت او که تو گردی ز من رضا

یزید ـ آتش ز راه کین به سراپرده ها زدی

شمر ـ آری چنان که دود شد و رفت بر هوا

یزید ـ فرزندی از حسین ندانم به جای ماند؟

شمر ـ بیمار مانده است از او یك پسر به جا

یزید ـ دیگر چه مانده است تو را گفتنی، بگو؟

شمر ـ خواهم که خلعتی بنمایی به من عطا

یزید ـ صد مرحبا که رسم وفاداری این بود
خدمت به خانواده سفیان چنین بود
چون خانمان خراب کن آل حیدری
شایسته قبا و زر و تاج و گوهری
ای حاضرین مجلس من از برای شمر
آرید از خزانه دو خلعت سزای شمر

شمر ـ چه در ورود اسیران به شهر فرمایی
به احترام بیاریم یا به رسوایی

یزید ـ برو به مثل اسیران ازبك و تاتار
سر برهنه بگردان به کوچه و بازار

Šemr: After enduring tyranny and oppression,
when they have passed through the bazaar,
Where are the strangers to be housed?
Where is the dwelling of those whose portion is sorrow?

Yazid: On the far side of the square, there is a ruined building,
It is a mosque, without a door or prayer niche,
I think there is no place better,
for the family of the Prophet, than that ruin.

Šemr (to the audience): Know, all you people of Damascus,
That the household of Huseyn the thirsty are arriving.
Come Zeynab, Sakina and 'Ābedin,
Now, for cruelty's sake, I am going to take you to Damascus.

Zeynab: Helpless, unfortunate Zeynab,
In one place she is imprisoned, in another she is a stranger,
In one place she is mounted on a bare camel
In another, people are playing instruments and beating the drum.
Where is my son Akbar, that he may see how I am injured,
Where is the King of my Faith? I bear no more.
O My brother! O My brother! You have been martyred with the sword of tyranny,
And I am a prisoner in the land of strangers,
Here are the heads of the virtuous, here are the lances of villains,[6]
Here is Zeynab the afflicted, here in the streets and bazaar!

Imam 'Ebād: O father! O father! My martyred father
O Head! On your account, black bile has filled my heart.
Your love has drawn us to the bazaars.[7]
We are prisoners, ashamed of our appearance,
You, who aspire to nothing, let these words teach you shame.

Sakina: O Father! Grief for you left me despised and afflicted
The sphere[8] has left me an orphan in childhood.

شمر ـ بعد از این جور و کینه و آزار
چون گذشتند از سر بازار
به کجا منزل غریبان است
به کجا جای غم نصیبان است؟

یزید ـ پشت میدان عمارتی است خراب
مسجدی هست بی در و محراب
بهر این اهل بیت پیغمبر
ز آن خرابه نیافتم بهتر

شمر ـ خبر شوید شما اهل شام سرتاسر
که می رسند عیال حسین تشنه جگر
زینب بیا سکینه بیا عابدین بیا
اکنون به شام آرمتان از ره جفا

زینب ـ بیچاره زینب در بی نصیبی
يك جا اسیری، يك جا غریبی
يك جا بر اشتر عریان سواره
يك سو نوازند، ساز و نقاره
کو اکبر من بیند فگارم؟
کو شاه دینم، طاقت ندارم
یا اخا یا اخا انت شهید بسیف العدوان
و انا اسیر، به دیار الغربه
سر اخیار کجا نیزه اشرار کجا
زینب زار کجا کوچه و بازار کجا؟

امام عباد ـ یا ابا یا ابا بابای شهیدم بابا
داشت سودای تو ای سر با دل ما کارها
می کشد عشق تو ما را بر سر بازار ها
ما اسیران از نگاه خود خجالت می کشیم
آخر ای بی همتان شرمی از این گفتارها

سکینه ـ آه ای پدر غم تو مرا خوار و زار کرد
در کودکی یتیم مرا روزگار کرد

Šemr: Soldiers! Play the drum and tabor,
For the world has turned to Yazid's desire.

Zeynab: O apostate, deceitful Šemr! Come before me,
Both God and the soul of Mohammad hate your face.
Tell me the reason for the lamentation in the city.
Is today the Feast of Sacrifice,[9] according to the doctrines held here?

Šemr: O daughter of the seal of the prophets,
You are the pure essence of lineage of the Prophet,
Did you hear the sound of the drums?
Did you see the people of Damascus?
The feast that you see
Is newly prepared for you, by Yazid.

Zeynab: O Šemr! What has happened to dignity and honour?
After all, you are an Arab! What has happened to manly behaviour?
I have no companion or helper,
and now, I have no brother.
O Šemr! Show mercy!
Do not take us among the people.

Šemr: I have cut your Huseyn's head from his neck,
I have drowned the body of 'Ali Akbar in blood,
You have no other companion or helper.
Why don't you give up your haughtiness?

Zeynab: (Why does the infidel Šemr have no shame?
No one would inflict such tyranny on unbelievers.)
O Infidel dog!
You imagine that no-one could cure my pain.
I will complain to God about you.
By God! My sigh will not miss its mark.
But I fear that God
Does not separate wet from dry.

شمر ـ بنوازید دهل، طبل زنید ای لشگر
که جهان گشت به دلخواه یزید ای لشگر

زینب ـ بیا به نزد من ای شمر مرتد غدار
خدا و روح محمد ز روی تو بیزار
به من بگو که در این شهر این چه افغان است
مگر به مذهب این قوم عید قربان است

شمر ـ ای دختر خاتم النبیین
ذریه پاك آل یاسین
آواز نقاره ها شنیدی
جمعیت اهل شام دیدی
این عیش که آیدت به دیده
بهر تو یزید تازه چیده

زینب ـ ای شمر وقار و عزتت کو
آخر عربی حمیتت کو
من مونس و یاوری ندارم
امروز برادری ندارم
ای شمر بیا بکن ترحم
ما را تو مبر میان مردم

شمر ـ حسینت را ز حنجر سر بریدم
به خون نعش علی اکبر کشیدم
دگر تو مونس و یاور نداری
چرا دست از بزرگی برنداری

زینب ـ شمر بی دین چرا حیا نکند؟
کس به کافر چنین جفا نکند!
به خیال تو ای سگ کافر
که کسی درد من دوا نکند؟
شکوه ات می برم به پیش خدا
به خدا آه من خطا نکند
لیك ترسم که حضرت باری
خشك و تر را ز هم جدا نکند

Šemr: O family of Muhammad, dismount, all of you.
Go into this roofless ruin with no door.

Imam ʻEbād: O People! Go to one side,
So that we may sit in a private place,
wailing and lamenting,
and conduct the mourning rite.
May the nightingales gather, that we in concert
may lament the memory of the garden, our homeland.
The nightingale is a stranger, lamentation is foreign, the meadow is not here
Zeynab is an exile, the city is alien, our motherland is far away.

Yazid: Bring all the prisoners to our throne-room
Give them a place in some corner at our gathering.

Šemr: Have all of you given up all hope for your lives?
You are all going to the court of Yazid.

The family of the Prophet (together): We are being taken to Yazid, bound in the chains of tyranny.
These shameless people are taking us before Yazid.

Yazid: O Slave! Your task is to go to the chamberlain's office[10]
Pass through the curtain to the private apartments
On this radiant day, to the court of that shining moon.
To the private sanctuary of my palace,
say to Hindeh, my silvery, moon-faced idol:
'Come here because I am going to take the veil of grief from your face.'

Šemr: I obey your command, with pleasure,
obeying your order is a grace to my soul.
Greetings, O intimate [of the king]! O houri-faced!
The king has summoned you.

Hendeh: I obey the king's command, with pleasure.
Come, girl,[11] we are going to watch them.

شمر ـ گروه آل محمد همه پیاده شوید
در این خرابه بی بام و در فرود آیید

امام عباد ـ ای قوم روید یك كناری
تا ما به فغان و آه و زاری
یك گوشه خلوتی نشینیم
یك مجلس ماتمی بچینیم
آیید بلبلان که همه همعنان شویم
با یاد گلستان وطن در فغان شویم
بلبل غریب و ناله غریب و چمن غریب
زینب غریب و شهر غریب و وطن غریب

یزید ـ بیاورید به مجلس همه اسیران را
به کنج محفل ما جا دهید ایشان را

شمر ـ ایا جماعت از جان گذشته نومید
روان شوید تمامی به بارگاه یزید

اهل بیت ـ بسته به زنجیر جفا نزد یزیدم می برند
این قوم بی شرم و حیا نزد یزیدم می برند

یزید ـ ایا غلام به دار النظام مأموری
بکش به غرفه مجلس حجاب زنبوری
به روز مهر به درگاه ماه تابنده
حریم خاصه دولتسرای من هنده
بگو به آن بت سیمین ماه رخسارم
بیا که پرده غم از رخ تو بردارم

شمر ـ به چشم آنچه تو گویی مطیع فرمانم
قبول امر شما منتی است بر جانم
السلام ای حرم حورلقا
شاه احظار نموده است تو را

هنده ـ فرمان پادشاه دهم بر دو دیده جا
عمه بیا رویم تماشا کنیم ما

We are going to see who these prisoners are
O Slave! You go ahead, we will follow.

Yazid: Welcome, my faithful wife.
Sit beside me, my moon-like cypress.

Zeynab: O Sphere! May you turn upside down for grief.
May grief fill your liver as it fills mine, in my misery.
You have brought the family of the martyred king,
to Damascus because of your enmity.
I hope that you will be turned upside down!
O Sphere, you have ruined my house.

Hendeh: Look, my aunt, at these prisoners,
Light shines from their faces, up to the heavens.
Look at the moon-faced girls
They all put their heads on their knees.
These moon-like women, who are despised and afflicted,
From which city and land do they come?
O aunt! It is clear,
that they are nobles.

Hendeh's maid: O Hendeh! Know that all these prisoners
Are natives of Medina.
It seems that they are all Arabian,
They are people of stature.

Handeh: Do not mention Medina to me,
It makes my heart burn.
My master and lord lives in Medina,
Don't you know that my master lives there?

Hendeh's maid: Your stature puts the cypress tree to shame,
Say, who was your master in Medina?
Truly, your face is like paradise, your stature like the tree of Tūbā,
whoever hear of a king talking with a poor man.
Do you not scorn to look on the prisoners?
Please, sit on the golden chair.

این مردم اسیر ببینیم کیستند
رو ای غلام پیش که آییم از قفا

یزید ـ خوش آمدی تو ایا زوجه وفادارم
به پهلویم بنشین سرو ماه رخسارم

زینب ـ آه ای چرخ ز غم برگردی
خون جگر چون من مضطر گردی
اهل بیت حرم شاه شهید
سوی شام از ره کین آوردی
دارم امید شوی زیر و زبر
ای فلك خانه خرابم کردی

هنده ـ عمه بنگر به این اسیران
نور از رخشان رود به کیوان
بنگر تو به دختران مه رو
بنهاده تمام سر به زانو
این ماه رخان که خوار و زارند
از اهل چه شهر و چه دیارند؟
پیداست از این قرار عمه
هستند بزرگوار عمه

کنیز هنده ـ ای هنده بدان که این اسیران
از اهل مدینه اند ایشان
گویا عربند این جماعت
هستند تمام با مناعت

هنده ـ مبر در پیش من نام مدینه
که می افتد مرا آتش به سینه
مدینه سرور و مولایم آنجاست
نمی دانی مگر؟ آقایم آنجاست

کنیز هنده ـ تویی که سرو خجل گشته پیش بالایت
بگو به شهر مدینه که بوده آقایت؟
ای رخت خلد قامتت طوبی
صحبت شاه با فقیر کجا
عارت آید ز دیدن اسرا
بنشین روی صندلی طلا

Hendeh: Know that my master is the light of my eyes
He is the honourable Huseyn, the Imām and the King of Religion.

Zeynab: Hendeh! Blessed was the day when your master lived,
and you lived with us, Hendeh.
Blessed was the day in Medina when,
My slave girl was a unique person, like you.
O sphere, be just, for the sake of chivalry,
Where is chivalry, where is manliness?

Hendeh: Who was this woman? My soul burns,
I swear to God, the marrow in my bones is burnt.
The lamentation of this prisoner has turned me to water.
O My aunt, my aunt, she has burnt me with grief.
Dear aunt, let me go beside her,
I see her sorrowful state.

Kaniz: Truly, your face is like paradise, your stature like the tree of Tūbā,
Whoever heard of a king talking with a poor man.
Do you not scorn to look on the prisoners?
Please, sit on the golden chair.

Zeynab: It is fitting that you scorn me,
There you are, and here am I, in my misery.
You are adorned in a gown, gold and jewellery.
I beat on my chest and head because I have no one,
You are sitting on the golden chair,
I am sitting in the dust of calamities.

Hendeh: Dust be on my head, this is the voice of my lady
This is the complaining song of a nightingale far from the meadow,
Dust be on your head, Hendeh, because of this tyranny and oppression.
Zeynab goes bareheaded while you are sheltered behind the curtain.
My day has been turned to night by watching this scene,
I will go out from behind the curtain, to Zeynab's side.

Yazid: O My shameless, ill-behaved wife!
I am shamed in my throne-room by your behaviour.
You come out from our private apartment, your head bare.

هنده ـ بدان آقای من نور دو عین است
امام و شاه دین آقا حسین است

زینب ـ خوش آن روزی که بود آقات هنده
به نزدما بدی مأوات هنده
خوش آن روزی که در شهر مدینه
کنیزم بود چون تو بی قرینه
فلك انصاف ده از روی غیرت
کجا رفته است غیرت کو مروت

هنده ـ این زن آیا که بود؟ جانم سوخت
به خدا مغز استخوانم سوخت
ناله این اسیر آبم کرد
عمه عمه ز غم کبابم کرد
عمه جان اذن ده روم بر او
بنگرم حالت مکدر او

کنیز ـ ای رخت خلد و قامتت طوبی
صحبت شاه با فقیر کجا
عارت آید ز دیدن اسرا
بنشین روی صندلِی طلا

زینب ـ جای دارد که عارت از من باد
تو کجا و کجا من ناشاد
تو مکلل به رخت و زیور و زر
من ز بی کسی زنم به سینه و سر
تو نشسته به صندلی طلا
من نشسته به روی خاك بلا

هنده ـ خاکم به سر این صدای خاتون من است
این ناله نوای مرغ دور از چمن است
خاکت به سر ای دهنده به این جور و جفا
زینب سر عریان و تو در پرده سرا
روزم همه گشت زین تماشا چون شب
از پرده روم برون به نزد زینب

یزید ـ بی حیا زوجه تبهکارم
کرده ای شرمسار حضارم
سر عریان روی برون ز حرم

The court is filled with strangers.
Does the matchless private sanctuary mean nothing?
What is the meaning of this disorder and uproar?
You make yourself the topic of banter and jest,
and in the end the reproach is on me.

Hendeh: O cursed one! Am I shameless, or is it you?
Am I the black-faced deceiver, or are you?
Do you find it too grievous to look on your wife,
in the presence of strangers?
Are they not the family of the Prophet?
You ill-fated, cursed fellow.
Rejected one, you sped to cover my head with a cloak,
so hurriedly, hastily.
I am adorned in a gown, gold and jewellery,
While the daughter of Fātima has no head covering.

Yazid (to his slaves): take Hendeh whose heart is filled with blood,
to the private apartments, and bring me red wine.

Šemr: O wise commander, I have a message for you,
An envoy has arrived from European lands.

Yazid: Tell the people of Kufa and Damascus
to come quickly and welcome the messenger of the European king.

Šemr: O people of Kufa and Damascus,
Quickly, welcome the European.

European: what is this burning coal in my chest?
Once more: what is the coal, I feel in my heart?
Saturn is bent double because of the dagger of grief.
The sword of mourning is on Gemini's skull.
The leader of prayers is busy with dancing and play,
The ear of the sphere is deafened by the sound of drums and trumpets
I had heard that in Damascus,
An event has occurred that is causing grief.
One party is playing the flute and tambour in flowering gardens,
Another group in an uproar are wailing and beating their heads.

بارگه پر بود ز نامحرم
حرم بی مثال یعنی چه؟
فتنه و قیل و قال یعنی چه؟
خلق شطرنج خوش دلی بازند
بعد از این ها ملامتم سازند

هنده ـ ای لعین، بی حیا منم یا تو!
رو سیاه دغا منم یا تو؟
نتوانی عیال خود از غم
بنگری در حضور نامحرم
مگر اینها عیال پیغمبر
نیستند ای لعین بداختر؟
با هزاران شتاب ای مردود
بر سر من عبا فکندی زود
من مکلل به رخت و زیور و زر
دختر فاطمه است بی معجر

یزید ـ برید سوی حرم هنده جگر خون را
بیاورید برم باده های گلگون را

شمر ـ خطاب من به تو باد ای امیر با فرهنگ
رسیده است یکی ایلچی از دیار فرنگ

یزید ـ بگو به کوفی و شامی همه به استعجال
رسول شاه فرنگ را کنند استقبال

شمر ـ کوفیان، شامیان به استعجال
بر فرنگی کنید استقبال

فرنگی ـ باز این چه اخگر، در سینه پیداست
باز این چه آذر، در دل هویداست
از دشنه غم، پشت زحل خم
شمشیر ماتم، بر فرق جوزاست
شیخ نمازی در رقص و بازی
گوش فلك کر از کوس و کرناست
بشنیده بودم شرحی که در شام
وضعی غم افزا گفتند برپاست
قومی به گلشن، مزمار و دف زن
جمعی به سر زن با شور و غوغاست

Sakina: O King of Medina, where are you?
The European has come to look at Sakina.

European: O God! Who are this group of beauties?
They are bound in chains from head to foot,
O God! Who has chained a woman?
It seems that the necklace of the Pleiades has been scattered.
I cry out against the hand of the executioner
who has brought down these noble people.
This head on a lance, its lips red as ruby,
has drunk without pause to the health of these two beauties.[12]
There's no doubt that he must be the brother
Of these two sisters who are younger.
From the mystery of this [other] head, I am certain
That he desires this moon-like countenance.
This is a new bride and he is a new groom,
This one is like Salmi, the other like Salmā.
This infant has no milk, no blame, no guilt,
has never seen the breast of his mother.
And this bright head: from every side we see that he
is one who is straight-necked, his head held high.
It seems that he was the water carrier for the children,
He has never found any water in the world.
O Acclaimed and Living Lord, O Only God,
reveal this hidden mystery,
kām kūs jaras paras fluriyāni Bonjour Monsieur Yazid.[13]

Yazid: Do not speak in that foreign tongue, speak in another language,
Submit to the religious law of the Prophet.

European: O Wise king, my greetings to you,
I am one of the viziers of the European king,
I have brought two cameras,[14] two watches and two sword sheathes,
to present them to you, O great commander.

سکینه ـ کجایی ای شهنشاه مدینه
فرنگی آمده سیر سکینه

فرنگی ـ یا رب کیانند این خیل خوبان
بسته به زنجیر از فرق تا پا
یا رب که بسته زن را به زنجیر
گویا گسسته عقد ثریا
ای داد بیداد از دست جلاد
کاین سروران را افکنده از پا
این سر که بر نی لعل لبش می
نوشد پیاپی بر این دو عذرا
بی وهم خاطر باشد برادر
بر این دو دختر، بر این دو صغری
از سر این سر، گشته یقینم
کاین مه جبین را دارد تمنا
این نوعروس و آن تازه داماد
این همچو سلمی و آن همچو سلما
این طفل بی شیر بی جرم و تقصیر
پستان مادر نادیده اصلاً
این رأس انور کز این سر آن سر
یك گردن و سر بگرفته بالا
گویا که باشد سقای طفلان
آبی به دوران ناکرده پیدا
ای حیّ سبحان وی فرد یزدان
این راز پنهان کن آشکارا
کلم کلّوس جرس پرس فلوریانی بانژور موسیو یزید

یزید ـ مگو زبان فرنگی بگو زبان دگر
سلام کن تو به قانون شرع پیغمبر

فرنگی ـ سلام من به تو ای پادشاه با فرهنگ
منم یکی ز وزیران پادشاه فرنگ
دو دوربین و دو ساعت، دو قبضه شمشیر
به رسم پیشکش آورده‌ام امیرکبیر

And further, out of loyalty, the king has sent a message:
If there is anything else that you seek, tell me.

Yazid: Greeting to you, O envoy from foreign lands,
These multicoloured presents are accepted from you.

Zeynab: O God! My heart is wounded by this grief
O God, a foreigner is more honourable than we are.
The European is honoured while the family of the Prophet suffers tyranny,
The European is respected while the family of Ahmad[15] suffers oppression.

Yazid: One of you trustworthy courtiers
who is allowed to enter the private apartments:
Go and bring my daughter.
My moon-faced flower-faced daughter.

Šemr: I obey your commands and whatever you wish,
Because you are king.
Greetings, O fairy-faced ward of the palace apartments,
Your father has summoned you.

Yazid's daughter: This is a fortunate, auspicious omen;
You go ahead, I will follow.
Greetings, Father, to your beautiful and bright face,
May the shade of fortune remain over your head forever.
Sit me on your lap like the bloom of a rose,
I am like a particle of dust in search of the sun, shelter me.

Yazid: My greetings to you, with your rose-like face and moon-like countenance,
Come here and sit like the rose bloom on my lap,
Come here, take your place like the rose bloom on my lap.
Look at this group of captives for a moment.

Now 'arūs: O God! Why do I have no father!
Since I am an orphan, people do not honour me.
If my kind father was alive

دگر پیام چنین داده پادشه ز وفا
اگر که هست تو را مطلبی بیان فرما

یزید ـ علیك من به تو ای قاصد دیار فرنگ
قبول شد ز تو این تحفه‌های رنگارنگ

زینب ـ بار الها سینه زینب از این غم ریش شد
ای خدا بنگر فرنگی قربش از ما بیش شد
بر فرنگی عزت و بر آل پیغمبر جفا
بر فرنگی حرمت و بر آل احمد ظلمها

یزید ـ یکی از معتمدان درگاه
که به دربار حرم دارد راه
رود و آورد آن دختر من
دختر مه رخ و گل پیکر من

شمر ـ هر چه فرمان دهی و می‌خواهی
سر نمی‌پیچم از آن چون شاهی
السلام ای حرم حور لقا
بابت احضار نموده است تو را

دختر یزید ـ برو به پیش آیا مقبل همایون فال
برو به پیش که اینك بیایم از دنبال
سلام بر رخ زیبای انورت بابا
همیشه سایه اقبال بر سرت بابا
مرا چو غنچه گل روی دامنت جا ده
چو ذره در طلب آفتاب مأوا ده

یزید ـ علیك من به تو ای گلعذار ماه جبین
بیا چو غنچه گل روی دامنم بنشین
بیا چو غنچه گل روی دامنم جا کن
به این گروه اسیران دمی تماشا کن

نوعروس ـ خدایا من چرا بابا ندارم
یتیمم پیش مردم جا ندارم
اگر می‌بود بابای نکویم

Šemr the vile would not slap my face.
Where are you, my mother Šahrbānū,
That you may put my head on your lap?

Zeynab: O Sakina! Your afflicted aunt dies for you,
she cannot bear this sorrow for your pain.
Since you have no mother, I will be your mother,
Since you have no support, I will be your support.
Come here, so I, in place of your mother
may put your head on my lap.

Yazid: Who is this small homeless child?
A child who is bareheaded, barefoot, her heart full of blood.

Šemr: She is the new bride of Qāsem, the new groom
who was martyred at Karbalā.

Yazid: O unhappy child of Huseyn!
The new bride of the Huseyn's new son-in-law,
why are you crying, so young and marked by fate,
You lament like the nightingale.

Now 'arūs:[16] How can I not weep and wail like a bell?
May no one see what I have seen!
I have suffered much grief and heartfelt sorrows,
I am one whose father has been killed, whose brother is dead.

Yazid: Don't cry so much, O daughter of the martyred king.

Now 'arūs: How can I not cry, I am in mourning, Yazid.

Yazid: Why have you covered your face with your hands?

Now 'arūs: I have no face veil, and all these people are strangers.

Yazid: Who is looking at you here?

Now 'arūs: My new groom is watching me.

نمی‌زد شمر دون سیلی به رویم
کجایی مادر من شهربانو
که بگذاری سرم را روی زانو

زینب ـ سکینه عمه زارت بمیرد
غم درد تو را بر دل نگیرد
اگر مادر نداری مادرت من
اگر یاور نداری یاورت من
بیا تا من به جای مادر تو
بگیرم بر سر زانو سر تو

یزید ـ کیست این طفل صغیر در به در
سر برهنه پا برهنه خون جگر

شمر ـ این عروس قاسم نوکدخداست
تازه داماد شهید کربلاست

یزید ـ ای صغیره طفل ناشاد حسین
نوعروس تازه داماد حسین
از چه گریی ای صغیره داغدار
هست افغان تو مانند هزار

نوعروس ـ چون نگریم چون ننالم چون جرس
آنچه من دیدم نبیند هیچ کس
غصه‌ها و خون دل‌ها خورده‌ام
من پدر کشته، برادر مرده‌ام

یزید ـ گریه کم کن دختر شاه شهید

نوعروس ـ چون نگریم من عزادارم، یزید

یزید ـ دست بر صورت گرفت از چه باب؟

نوعروس ـ این همه نامحرمان، من بی نقاب

یزید ـ که تماشایت در اینجا می‌کند؟

نوعروس ـ تازه دامادم تماشا می‌کند

Yazid: Why has your tulip-like face gone pale?

Now 'arūs: Because I am so very thirsty, Yazid.

Yazid: No one has seen one marked like you,
Both your father and brother are martyrs.
Tell me, do you have another brother in this world?

Now 'arūs: Know, O Oppressor, I have one brother.

Yazid: Tell me, do you have any sister in your wailing and lamenting?

Now 'arūs: One or two sisters survive, from my father Huseyn.

Yazid: There is no hope for you! Tell me their names.

Now 'arūs: O Yazid, one is Sakina and the other is Ruqaya.

Yazid: Are you Sakina the daughter of the peerless king?
Are you the one who cheered the heart of Huseyn the thirsty?

Sakina: O Yazid, O Yazid: I am Sakina the daughter of the king of east and west
O Yazid, O Yazid: My God kill me, I am the daughter of Huseyn.

Yazid: O child! Why do you beat your head and your chest?

Sakina: Because of the recent fate of my 'Ali Akbar, who died young.

Yazid: Why do you hold the chain so firmly in your hand?

Sakina: Because my neck is wounded by cruelty.

Yazid: Why do you cover your face with your hands in your bewilderment?

Sakina: I protect my face with my hands because I am distressed.

Yazid: Sakina, why has your face turned livid with resentment?

یزید ـ از چه رنگ از لاله رویت پرید؟

نوعروس ـ بسکه بی آبی کشیدم ای یزید

یزید ـ داغ دیده کس به مثل تو ندید:
هم پدر شد هم برادر شد شهید
گو به من داری برادر در جهان

نوعروس ـ يك برادر دارم ای ظالم بدان

یزید ـ خواهر ار داری بگو با شور و شین

نوعروس ـ یک دو خواهر مانده از بابم حسین

یزید ـ نامشان را بازگو ای ناامید

نوعروس ـ این سکینه این رقیه ای یزید

یزید ـ سکینه دختر سلطان بی قرینه تویی؟
حسین تشنه جگر را سرور سینه تویی؟

سکینه ـ سکینه دختر سلطان مشرقینم من ای یزید ای یزید
خدا مرا بکشد دختر حسینم من ای یزید ای یزید

یزید ـ تو ای صغیره چرا میزنِی به سینه و سر

سکینه ـ ز داغ تازه جوانمرگ خود علی اکبر

یزید ـ چرا به دست گرفتی چنین سلاسل را؟

سکینه ـ برای آن که شده زخم گردنم ز جفا

یزید ـ چرا دو دست به صورت گرفته حیرانی؟

سکینه ـ حفاظ صورت خود سازم از پریشانی

یزید ـ چرا سکینه شده صورتت ز کین نیلی؟

Sakina: Because Šemr the shameless slapped me several times.

Yazid: Orphan of Huseyn, why are you crying constantly?

Sakina: How could I not cry, How could I not lament?
I am an orphan; I have no father,
Your daughter is seated beside you,
I am standing before you.
In that sitting, and my standing,
There is nothing for me but a heart full of blood.
A cry has blocked my throat.
May God give what they deserve!

Yazid: You are right; it is not easy to be an orphan,
There is no one in distress like you.
O child, come to my side,
From now on, be a slave girl to my daughter.

Zeynab: May God strike you dumb and blind your eyes!
May you be far removed from the grace of God.
Who are you that you call yourself great,
and want a slave girl from the family of the Prophet?
How far has this high rank of yours gone?
That you want Zahra's[17] darling to be your slave girl.[18]

Yazid: who is this fortunate, blessed woman?
Whose voice rose from among [the captives]?
May God requite you! What can I say?

Šemr: She is one, whom you have despised,
whom you have dishonoured.
She is Zeynab, Huseyn's sister.
You should know her by her tearful eyes.

Yazid: She is one, whose father seized the world,
with the blows of his sword, *zulfaqar*.
She is one, whose most laudable grandfather
was taken up to the throne by his God.

سکینه ـ ز بس که خورده‌ام از شمر بی حیا سیلی

یزید ـ چرا تو گریه کنی هر دم ای یتیم حسین؟

سکینه ـ چرا نگریم چرا ننالم
که من یتیمم پدر ندارم
نشسته پیش تو دختر تو
ستاده‌ام من برابر تو
از این ستادن از آن نشستن
به غیر خون جگر ندارم
گرفته گریه ره گلویم
خدا جوابت دهد چه گویم

یزید ـ راست گفتی یتیمی آسان نیست
هیچ کس مثل تو پریشان نیست
پس بیا ای صغیره در بر من
شو در این دم کنیز دختر من

زینب ـ الهی آن که شوی لال و هر دو چشمت کور
ز فیض حضرت پروردگار گردی دور
تو کیستی که خودت را عزیز می‌خواهی
ز اهل بیت نبوت کنیز می‌خواهی
رسیده است کجا رتبه عزیزی تو
عزیز کرده زهرا کند کنیزی تو!

یزید ـ کیست گو این زن سعادتمند
که صدایش شد از میانه بلند

شمر ـ این است که کرده‌ای تو خوارش
انداخته‌ای ز اعتبارش
این زینب خواهر حسین است
بشناس ز چشم اشکبارش

یزید ـ این است که باب وی جهان را
بگرفته به ضرب ذوالفقارش؟
این است که جد امجدش را
برده است به عرش کردگارش

A thousand thanks to God that I can see her
dishonoured, despised and afflicted.

Zeynab: I am the daughter of the father of seven and four.[19]
I am alone, without assistance or support.
Seventy maids of Medina ate from my table,
such am I.
I am unveiled among the people, yet the Holy Spirit,
like a lady's maid, is proffering a veil.
I am Zeynab, Huseyn's sister,
you should know me by my tearful eyes.

Yazid: When women's souls are on fire,
There's no answer, it's best to hold one's tongue.
Bring in the heads of the martyrs,
Put them in a corner at our gathering.

Šemr: These thirsty ones have drunk water from the sword's blade,
They gave the world its soul, in giving their souls.

Yazid: Tell me, whose is this shining head?

Šemr: That is the head of the hero, Hurr.

Yazid: And whose is this pure, unsullied head?

Šemr: This is the head of Habib Ibn Mazāher.

Yazid: I see two heads; tell me each of their names.

Šemr: One is 'Ābes, the other is his slave Šowzab.

Yazid: The head of a black man lies before me.

Šemr: That is the head of the Turkish slave of Huseyn, the King of Religion.

صد شکر به چشم خویش دیدم
رسوا و ذلیل و خوار و زارش

زینب ـ من دختر باب هفت و چهارم
من بی کس و بی معین و یارم
آنم که زنان مکه بودند
هفتاد کنیز ریزه‌خوارم
بی پرده میان خلقم اما
روح‌القدس است پرده‌دارم
من زینب خواهر حسینم
بشناس ز چشم اشکبارم

یزید ـ در جواب زنان سوخته جان
باید اندر دهان کشید زبان
بیاورید به مجلس سر شهیدان را
به کنج محفل ما جا دهید ایشان را

شمر ـ این تشنگان که آب ز شمشیر خورده‌اند
جانبخش عالمند که جان‌ها سپرده‌اند

یزید ـ بگو از کیست این رأس منور؟

شمر ـ بود آن سر سر حر دلاور

یزید ـ همین سر از که باشد پاك و طاهر؟

شمر ـ بود رأس حبیب ابن مظاهر

یزید ـ دو سر بینم بگو یك یك ز نامش

شمر ـ یکی عابس دگر شوذب غلامش

یزید ـ سر مرد سیاهی پیش عین است

شمر ـ غلام ترك شاه دین حسین است

Yazid: I see two heads here, like a pair of stars.

Šemr: They are the heads of Zeynab's sons.

Yazid: I see a head whose face is like the Houris.[20]

Šemr: This is 'Abbās, standard-bearer to Huseyn.

Yazid: Tell me about the swordsmanship of that skillful man.

Šemr: He cut, killed, bound or felled many.

Yazid: Bravo, well done, to that strength and that arm.

Šemr: Yes, he had the strength of Heydar.

Yazid: Tell me, whose is this shining head?

Šemr: That is the head of Prince Akbar.

Yazid: I heard that his heart had been cheered by marriage.

Šemr: He was not the groom, Qāsem was the groom.

Yazid: How was the candle of Qāsem's soul blown out?

Šemr: He married, but he died young.

Yazid: Šemr, you scoundrel, whose is this head?

Šemr: It is 'Ali Asġar, who did not drink milk.

Yazid: I do not see the head that I am looking for.

Šemr: The head that you cannot see, that you say is not here, is this.
You say it is not on his enemy's lance, but it is.
[To himself] O Huseyn! I'm like a blind man, who has fallen in a well,

یزید ـ دو سر بینم در این جا چون دو کوکب

شمر ـ بوند آنها سر طفلان زینب

شمر ـ سر عباس علمدار حسین است

یزید ـ بگو از ضرب دست آن هنرمند

شمر ـ بسی بدرید و کشت و بست و افکند

یزید ـ زهی احسنت بر آن زور و بازو

شمر ـ بلی بودی به حیدر هم ترازو

یزید ـ بگو از کیست این رأس منور؟

شمر ـ بود آن سر سر شهزاده اکبر

یزید ـ شنیدم شد ز دامادی دلش شاد

شمر ـ نشد داماد قاسم گشت داماد

یزید ـ چگونه شمع جان قاسم افسرد؟

شمر ـ کرد اما نوجوان مرد

یزید ـ همین سر از که ای شمر شریر است؟

شمر ـ علی اصغر ناخورده شیر است

یزید ـ عروسی سری کو هست منظورم نه پیداست؟

شمر ـ آن سری کز دیده ناپیداست گویی نیست هست
بر فراز نیزه اعداست گویی نیست هست
کورکورانه فتادم یا حسین در چاه من

A blind man is aware of what he has done: you may say he is not, but he is.
O bloody head, Yazid demanded you from me.
This court will surely pass away; one may think not, but it is so.
[To the head] Yazid, Henda's son, is coming; receive him.
Honouring the king is a good deed; you may say it is not, but it is.
[Holding it up] This is Huseyn, this is Huseyn, this is Huseyn's [head].

Yazid: Bring him before me, he who has two houris beneath him.[21]
O adornment on the Prophet's shoulder! You are welcome
O successor of Heydar-e Safdar! You are welcome
You did not want to come alone to our presence?
You are welcome, with 'Awn, Qāsem and 'Ali Akbar.

Yazid: O Šemr! Know that I have several questions.

Šemr: Tell me, so that I may cheer your soul.

Yazid: Was this head severed with a cleaver?

Šemr: O Commander, what do you mean by asking this question?

Yazid: Why are the bones of his neck broken in pieces?

Šemr: If I say it, the [hearts of] friends and enemies will burn.

Yazid: Say it, to ease the fire in my heart.
May Muslims never hear it, and the infidel never see it.
Did you cut through it, or strike it off from a distance?

Šemr: As butchers do, I cut it off with a cleaver.

Yazid: How many blows did you take to cut off his head?

Šemr: I cut off his head with ten blows, in my enmity.

کور اندر کار خود بیناست گوِیی نیست هست
ای سر پر خون، یزید از من طلبکار تو شد
رفتن آن بارگه بر جاست گوِیی نیست هست
زاده هنده یزید آمد تو استقبال کن
حرمت شه داشتن زیباست گویی نیست هست
حسین است این حسین است این حسین است

یزید ـ حضور آور که در پایش دو عین است
ای زیب دوش پیمبر خوش آمدی
ای جانشین حیدر و صفدر خوش آمدی
تنها نخواستی که بیایی حضور ما
با عون و قاسم و علی اکبر خوش آمدی

یزید ـ بدان ای شمر دارم مطلبی چند

شمر ـ بفرما تا کنم جان تو خرسند

یزید ـ مگر این سر جداگشته به ساطور؟

شمر ـ امیرا زین سؤالت چیست منظور؟

یزید ـ چرا خرد استخوان گردن اوست؟

شمر ـ اگر گویم بسوزد دشمن و دوست

یزید ـ بگو تا آتش از جانم نشیند
مسلمان نشنود کافر نبیند
بریدی یا زدی ضربت تو از دور؟

شمر ـ چو قصابان زدم با ضرب ساطور

یزید ـ جدا کردی سرش با چند ضربت؟

شمر ـ به ده ضربت بریدم از عداوت

Yazid: What did he say when you struck the first blow?

Šemr: He cried, 'O Muhammad! O Muhammad!'

Yazid: What did he say in his helplessness, when you struck the second blow?

Šemr: He said, 'O Mother Fatima! Where are you?'

Yazid: And what did that solitary king say when you struck the third blow?

Šemr: He said, 'O Ali! Come to my aid!'

Yazid: What did he say when you struck the fourth blow?

Šemr: He said, 'O Hasan! Look to Huseyn!'

Yazid: By God, tell me what he said at the fifth blow?

Šemr: He said, 'Alas Zeynab, alas Zeynab.'

Yazid: What did that peerless man say when you struck the sixth blow?

Šemr: He said, 'O Sakina, my daughter you have lost your father.'

Yazid: May I know what he said at the seventh blow?

Šemr: He said, 'I am the intercessor for the Shiites.'

Yazid: What did he say when you struck the eighth blow, O Šemr?

Šemr: He said, 'Where is faithfulness, where is chivalry, O Šemr?'

Yazid: My soul burns! What did he say when you struck the ninth blow?

Šemr: He said, 'Alas for my wives!'

یزید ـ چه گفت اول که بر او ضربت آمد؟

شمر ـ بگفتا وا محمد! وا محمد!

یزید ـ دوم ضربت چه گفت از بینوایی؟

شمر ـ بگفتا فاطمه مادر کجایی؟

یزید ـ سوم ضربت چه گفت آن شاه بی کس؟

شمر ـ بگفتا یا علی فریاد من رس!

یزید ـ چه حرفی گفت ضرب چارمین را؟

شمر ـ بگفتا ای حسن بنگر حسین را

یزید ـ چه گفتا پنجمین ضربت به یارب؟

شمر ـ بگفتا وای زینب! وای زینب!

یزید ـ ششم ضربت چه گفت آن بی قرینه؟

شمر ـ بگفتا بی پدر بابا سکینه

یزید ـ چه گفتا هفتمین ضربت ندانم؟

شمر ـ بگفتا من شفیع شیعیانم

یزید ـ چه گفتا او به هشتم ضربت ای شمر؟

بگفتا کو وفا! کو غیرت ای شمر!

یزید ـ نهم ضربت چه گفتا سوخت جانم!

شمر ـ بگفتا وای بر حال زنانم

Yazid: What did he say when you struck the tenth blow, O disciple of cruelty?

Šemr: He said one word that struck fire in my soul!

Yazid: What did he say, you scoundrel? Answer me!

Šemr: He said, 'I thirst for one drop of water.'

Yazid: Did you pour any water on the fire in his soul?

Šemr: I kicked his mouth with my booted foot.

Yazid: What did he say when you kicked him?

Šemr: At that, he fainted, and surrendered his soul with his lips still dry.

Yazid: What happened after his death?

Šemr: Both the earth and the sky were shaken.

Yazid: O Cupbearer, pour the sun-like wine
Quickly, the movement of the sphere knows no delay,
O Cupbearer! Remove the veil from the face of that lady, the wine jar,
Pour blood in the spirit of the lineage of Bū Turāb[22]
O thirsting King! Taste this, the day of our pleasure
Wet your dry lips with wine.
O King! Come, so that I may pour wine on your face
O noble Seyed! Abstain from wine.
O Yazid! Alas what a sin this was, what an act this was?
Be ashamed before the beauty of He who is the intercessor on the Day of Judgment,
Where is the Qur'ān? Where is the wine? Dust be on my head!
You there! Fill the cup with wine.
Although you cannot sleep, come,
put your head on Yazid's lap and sleep a while.

Zeynab: O hand of the heavens, set to work!

یزید ـ دهم ضربت چه گفتا ای جفا کیش؟

شمر ـ کلامی گفت بر جانم زد آتیش

یزید ـ چه گفتا رو سیه برگو جوابم

شمر ـ بگفتا تشنه یك جرعه آبم

یزید ـ بگو، آبی زدی بر نار جانش؟

شمر ـ زدم با پای چکمه بر دهانش

یزید ـ چه گفتا او ز تو چون یك لگد خورد؟

شمر ـ بدان غش کرد و جان لب تشنه بسپرد

یزید ـ ز بعد قتل او برگو چه رو داد؟

شمر ـ زمین و آسمان در لرزه افتاد

یزید ـ ساقی به جام باده چون آفتاب کن
دور فلك درنگ ندارد شتاب کن
ساقی نقاب از رخ خاتون خم بگیر
خون در روان سلسله بو تراب کن
ای شاه تشنه کام بود روز عیش ما
لب‌های خشك خویش تو تر با شراب کن
شاها بیا شراب بریزم به صورتت
ای سید نجیب ز می اجتناب کن
آه ای یزید این چه خطا و چه کار بود؟
شرم از جمال شافع یوم الحساب کن
قرآن کجا، شراب کجا، خاك بر سرم
هان ای بشر تو مشربه را پرگلاب کن
خواب ارچه نایدت به دو چشمان، ولی بیا
بر دامن یزید زمانی تو خواب کن

زینب ـ ای دست کردگار تو پا در رکاب کن

Zeynab's veil is gone to the winds,
Lay hands on the ring on Damascus' gates,
Destroy them, as Kheybar's tower and wall were destroyed.

Yazid: Alas, I have remembered the battle of Nahravān.
[To Huseyn's head] Sit in the golden bowl, and parry questions with me.
How does it feel to be beaten with a stick, O son of Bū Torāb?
Now complain about me to your grandfather and father.

Imam 'Ebād: You oppressor! You beat one whom the Prophet has kissed.
May your hand be cut off! Hammer away, do your worst.
O Shameless One! The friend of God is present,
you are beating the beloved in the presence of the lover.
He is Jacob and I am Joseph, under the oppression of Egypt.
I am Joseph and you are beating Jacob in my presence.

Yazid: Who are you, poor suffering soul,
burning with fever and bound in chains?
With such dignity, glory and finery,
perhaps you are 'Ali Ibn Huseyn.

Imam 'Ebād: May you be struck blind, if you do not know me!
I will tell you my name, that you may know me,
The highest throne is the carpet in our portico,
all who breathe are our guests.
North South East and West are like the ball to our polo stick.
The wind, rain and clouds obey our commands.
I am heir to the king through whom the Faith has flourished,
O Infidel! I am the enemy of your soul,
Do I have to say my name more clearly than this?
I am Seyed-e Sajjād, Zeyn al-'Ābedin.

Yazid: O 'Ali! Have you seen the justice of God?
How justice has been placed at the centre?
Though Huseyn's heart was turned away from us,
You see, in the end, he was killed with a dagger.

Imam 'Ebād: O shame of the Arabs, uncouth fellow,
Do you boast without reason, in the presence of this head?

بر باد رفته معجر زینب شتاب کن
دستی بزن به حلقه دروازه‌های شام
مانند برج و باروی خیبر خراب کن

یزید ـ آوخ که یادم آمد از جنگ نهروان
بر تشت زر نشین و سوال و جواب کن
چون نی به زیر چوب ایا سبط بوتراب؟!
اکنون شکایتم به بر جد و باب کن

امام عباد ـ ظالم به بوسه گاه نبی چوب می‌زنی
دستت بریده باد بزن خوب می‌زنی
ای بی حیا حبیب خدا حاضر است و تو
پیش حبیب چوب به محبوب می‌زنی
یعقوب اوست یوسف مصر ستم منم
یوسف منم تو چوب به یعقوب می‌زنی

یزید ـ کیستی ای مستمند دردمند
با تن تبدار و با زنجیر و بند
با چنین قدر و جلال و زیب زین
بلکه می‌باشی علی ابن الحسین

امام عباد ـ کور شو ای دشمن ار نشناسی‌ام
گویمت من نام تا بشناسی‌ام
عرش اعلا فرش در ایوان ماست
هر که روزی می‌خورد مهمان ماست
شش جهت چون گوی در چوگان ماست
باد، باران، ابر در فرمان ماست
وارث سلطان دین پرور منم
دشمن جان تو ای کافر منم
گویمت من نام واضح تر از این
سید سجاد زین‌العابدین

یزید ـ یا علی دیدی تو عدل کردگار
حق چه سان بگرفت بر مرکز قرار
گر حسین قلبش زما برگشته شد
عاقبت دیدی ز خنجر کشته شد

امام عباد ـ در حضور این سر، ای ننگ عرب
فخر بی جا می‌کنی ای بی ادب

His father's rank is higher than the sphere,
His mother is the Prophet's daughter.

Yazid: You, who have survived the storm of Karbalā,
You victim of injustice, honourable Zeyn al-'Ebā,
Listen to me! Break with your practice,
confirm my leadership.

Imam 'Ebād: You imagine that you have merely killed Huseyn,
You have only drowned one body in blood.
But you have killed both Muhammad and 'Ali.
You have killed both the Prophet and his vicegerent.
You have killed three sisters and six brothers.
You have killed seven fathers and eight mothers.
O oppressor! You killed the essence of the world beyond.
O Shameless one! You have killed the blood of God.
If you wish to consult with me,
Tell me about your grandfather, your father and your mother.
You adulterer, son of an adulterer, son of an adulteress.
Both your father and your mother were criminals.

Yazid: Ho! Executioner! Ho! Executioner!
You apostate, deceitful executioner! I am talking to you!
Cut off the head of Zeyn al-'Ebād, ill as he is.

Šemr: I obey you, I obey you.
Confess the oneness of God, because I am going to cut off your head.
I am going to separate your soul from your body.

Imam 'Ebād: Farewell, my homeless aunts,
Farwell, my broken-hearted sisters.

Zeynab: Alas, 'Ābedin, your aunt is dying for you.
You look at me each moment,
my dear, but I have no remedy.
What can I do? [Confess that] there is no God but God.

Sakina and Now 'arūs together (to the audience):
O you who are present! If you are Muslim,
say something in intercession.

قدر بابش از فلك بالاتر است
مادر او دختر پیغمبر است

یزید ـ ای ز طوفان کربلا بر جا
ای ستمکش جناب زین العبا
بشنو از من تو ترك عادت کن
بر من اقرار بر امامت کن

امام عباد ـ تو گمان کردی حسینی گشته‌ای
مختصر جسمی به خون آغشته‌ای
هم محمد هم علی را کشته‌ای
هم نبی و هم ولی را کشته‌ای
تو سه خواهر، شش برادر کشته‌ای
هفت بابا هشت مادر کشته‌ای
ظالم عین ماسوا را کشته‌ای
بی حیا خون خدا را کشته‌ای
گر تو می‌خواهی سخن در مشورت
گو سخن کو جد و باب و مادرت
زانی ابن زانی ابن زانیه
باب تو جانی و مادر جانیه

یزید ـ جلاد! جلاد!
خطاب من به تو جلاد مرتد غدار
بزن تو گردن زین العباد تن بیمار

شمر ـ لبیك لبیك
بگو شهادت که سر از تنت جدا سازم
میان جان و تنت طرح دوری اندازم

امام العباد ـ الوداع ای عمه‌های در به در
الوداع ای خواهران خون جگر

زینب ـ عابدین عمه‌ات بمیرد آه
دم به دم می‌کنی به من تو نگاه
چاره‌ای من ندارم ای عمه
چه کنم لا اله الا الله

سکینه و نوعروس با هم ـ
ایا جماعت حضار اگر مسلمانید
شما برای شفاعت لبی بجنبانید

Is there no Muslim among you?
Is there no firm believer in Damascus?
Now I beat my head with a stone for the [lack of] manliness [here].
I will go to the European ambassadors to entreat them.
O Europeans! We are so cowed by the tyranny of Šemr and Yazid
That now we entreat you.

European: O God! What do I see?
The eye of the sphere has never seen its like!
I am amazed at the Muslim sovereign,
why is he the enemy of the faithful?
No one has done the like to the people of his own religion,
for as long as the heavens have been turning.
O Muslims present in this meeting,
someone should intercede for these prisoners.
It is not acceptable, to our way of thinking,
for a Christian to intercede for Muslims.
But where there is immeasurable oppression,
intercession for the innocents will be rewarded [in the hereafter].
Come, executioner, that I may kiss your hand and foot,
Do not kill him, may my soul be a sacrifice for you.

Šemr: No Muslim in the court of Yazid
intercedes on behalf of this person who must give up all hope of life.
Leave me, because I will not release him.
[To Imam 'Ebād] Confess the oneness of God, my blade is on your throat.

Sakina: O European! We are strangers in this city.
Here, we are foreigners, who have no portion.

European: Executioner, stay your hand.
Do not torment a person who is ill, like this.
I am going to meet Yazid the Unchivalrous.
I will intercede on their behalf,
I will have no regard for my own dignity, in his presence,
so that he may refrain from execution.
O Yazid, show mercy to these children,
or may I be a sacrifice in their path.
Do not kill a youth who is ill,
who is ailing, and weeping and pitiful.

مگر میان شما یك نفر مسلمان نیست
به شهر شام مگر هیچ اهل ایمان نیست؟!
زنم به فرق خود این لحظه از حمیت سنگ
به التماس روم پیش ایلچیان فرنگ
ز ظلم شمر و یزید آن قدر ذلیل شدیم
فرنگیان! که شما را کنون دخیل شدیم

فرنگی ـ خداوندا چه می‌آید به دیده
که چشم چرخ مانندش ندیده
عجب دارم ز سلطان مسلمان
چرا دشمن شده با اهل ایمان
کسی با اهل دین خود چنین جور
نکرده تا که گردون می‌زند دور
ایا حضار مجلس از مسلمان
یکی گردد شفیع این اسیران
نباشد این به زعم ما گوارا
شفیع مسلمین گردد نصارا
ولی جایی که ظلم بی حساب است
شفاعت بهر مظلومان ثواب است
بیا جلاد بوسم دست و پایت
مکش او را شود جانم فدایت

شمر ـ مگر نبود مسلمان به بارگاه یزید
که تا شفیع شود بهر این ز جان نومید
برو که از سر او دست برنمی‌دارم
بگو شهاده به حلق تو تیغ بگذارم

سکینه ـ در این شهر ای فرنگی ما غریبیم
در این جا ماغریب و بی نصیبیم

فرنگی ـ پس ای جلاد دست اکنون نگه دار
مده این خسته را این گونه آزار
روم پیش یزید بی مروت
کنم از بهر ایشان من شفاعت
بریزم پیش او من آبرو را
که سازم منصرف از کشتن او را
ای یزید رحم بر این طفلان کن
یا مرا در رهشان قربان کن
بگذر از قتل جوان بیمار
که علیل است و چنین زار و نزار

Have mercy on these strangers,
These people whose portion is grief are innocent.
It is obvious that this despised group
Have no [male] relative, except this helpless one.
What is the benefit of killing an ill person?
Is there even any blood in his veins, for you to spill?
Have mercy on him, leave him alone, he has no-one.
Otherwise, I offer my head to your dagger.

Yazid: Come European; sit on the throne [beside me].
You have distressed us to no effect.
Intervention is not acceptable here.
Order is necessary.
Ho, Executioner! Ho, Executioner!

Zeynab: Withdraw your hand from the family of the Prophet.
Otherwise I will untie my hair in this court.
I will wail in God's court of law,
I will plead with the Almighty for vengeance.
I will go to Najaf without veil or footwear.
I will hold fast to the grillwork around the tomb of the king of Najaf, to arouse the zeal of the lion of God [Imām 'Ali].
I will lament so bitterly that the earth and heavens roar.
O 'Ali, my dear father! O 'Ali, my dear father!

Amir-e ġāyeb (Imām 'Ali): Do not kill him, do not kill him, lest the heavens be turned upside down.
Do not kill him, do not kill him, lest the hearts of the Prophet's family turn to blood.
Do not kill him; do not kill him, because the daughters of Huseyn have been dishonored.
Do not kill him, do not kill him, because the sisters of Huseyn are prisoners.

Imam 'Ebād: O my grandfather! Look at my broken head.
O my grandfather! Look at my hands that they are bound in chains.

Amir-e ġāyeb: I wanted your head to be broken, so that,
I may faithfully intercede for my people on the Day of Judgement.

بیا رحمی نما بر این غریبان
گناهی نیست با این غم نصیبان
بود معلوم این جمعی که خوارند
بجز این بینوا محرم ندارند
ز قتل شخص بیماری چه خیزد
ندارد خون به تن برگو چه ریزد
ترحم کن از این بی کس تو بگذر
وگرنه از من این سر از تو خنجر

یزید ـ بنشین فرنگی، بر روی اورنگ
بیهوده کردی، ما را تو دلتنگ
اینجا وساطت جایز نباشد
باید نظامی در کار باشد
جلاد! جلاد!

زینب ـ بدار دست تو از عترت رسول الله
وگر نه موی پریشان کنم در این درگاه
فغان به محکمه حضرت اله برم
شکایتت بر جبار دادخواه برم
کنون روم سر و پای برهنه سوی نجف
ضریح شاه نجف را بگیرم اندر کف
که غیرت اسداللهی‌اش به جوش آرم
ز گریه ارض و سما را به جنب و جوش آرم
ای بابا جان یا علی ای بابا جان یا علی

امیر غایب ـ مکش مکش که سماوات سرنگون گردد
مکش مکش که دل اهل بیت خون گرد
مکش مکش که حقیرند دختران حسین
مکش مکش که اسیرند خواهران حسین

امام عباد ـ سر شکسته من را نظر کن ای جدّا
دو دست بسته من را نظر کن ای جدّا

امیر غایب ـ سر شکسته تو خواستم به روز جزا
کنم شفاعت این امتان ز راه وفا

Šemr: O ill-fated Yazid! I am speaking to you.
Listen, I will explain the condition of this distressed soul.
When I was about to cut off his head in my rancour,
Someone in a black veil came, from the direction of the kiblah.
The masked one terrified me so that,
my whole body was trembling for fear.
A sudden terror so petrified me
that the dagger fell from my hand at once.

Yazid: Apostate, deceitful Šemr: go to one side.
Do not repeat what you have said to anyone.

European: O God, who is this shining moon?
He is covered in blood, as if he were rolled in it.
It seems that I have seen him in some city.
He looks familiar to me.
O head, tell me the circumstances.
You are like the sun passing over the contingent world.[23]
If you are Adam, where is Ceylon?[24]
If you are Noah, where are the sea and the storm?
If you are Khalil, where is the fire of Namrūd?
If you are the Ishmael, where is the Ram?
If you are Jacob, separated from Joseph,
this is neither Egypt, nor Canaan.
From [the sight of] these demons and beasts,
I am sure that you are Solomon among them.
I am certain that you are Muhammad,
reciting the verses of the Qur'ān like this.
It seems that Ahmad said, 'O Huseyn,
your head will be cut off with a sharp blade.'
It seems that you are a stranger here and have no mother,
that she cries for your sake like a cloud giving rain.
Do not be sorrowful, because Christians will cry,
in sympathy with you.

Yazid: Tell me European, what nonsense is this?

شمر ـ خطاب من به تو باد ای یزید بد اختر
بدار گوش تو بر شرح حال این مضطر
چو خواستم سر او را کنم ز کینه جدا
ز سمت قبله بیامد نقابدار سیاه
نهیب کرد به من آن نقابدار چنان
که گشت جمله وجودم ز ترس آن لرزان
نهیب ناگه او کرد آنچنان پستم
که اوفتاد در آن لحظه خنجر از دستم

یزید ـ برو به یك طرف ای شمر مرتد غدار
به نزد خلق مکن این سخن دگر تکرار

فرنگی ـ یا رب که باشد، این ماه تابان
گردیده در خون، غلتان بدین سان
گویا که او را دیدم به شهری
آید به چشمم از آشنایان
ای صاحب سر احوال بر گو
هستی چو خورشید در برج امکان
گر آدمی تو پس کو سراندیب؟
ور نوح هستی کو بحر و توفان؟
گر تو خلیلی کو نار نمرود؟
ور تو ذبیحی پس کوت قربان؟
یعقوبی ار تو در هجر یوسف
اینجا نه مصر و اینجا نه کنعان
زین دیو و زین دد گشته یقینم
در بین آنها هستی سلیمان
باشد یقینم باشی محمد
این گونه خوانی آیات قرآن
گویا حسینی، می‌گفت احمد
برّند رأست با تیغ برّان
گویا غریبی مادر نداری
گرید ز بهرت چون ابر باران
اما مخور غم چون در غم تو
باشد نصارا از دیده گریان

یزید ـ برگو فرنگی داری چه غوغا

What are you telling that head, here?
What are these tears amidst our festivity?
All the time you are debating with yourself!

European: The infidel Zoroastrian, are you questioning me?
See the result of your own behaviour.
By God! The injustice you have done to Islam,
I have never seen from one infidel to another.
What I have seen, is beyond words.
The Lord, whose head this is, amazes me:
how honoured he is in the eyes of God,
how honoured he is in the eyes of the Prophet.
I see angels standing wing to wing.
From the heavens to the earth's surface.
Now explain to me in detail, the circumstances of this head
So that I can recount these things day and night,
in Europe, from the top of the pulpit.

Yazid: You are asking me about the circumstances? Listen then,
I cut off his head as one kills a sheep.
His name is Huseyn the son of Heydar.
His grandfather is Muhammad, his mother is Zahra.

European: May your tongue be cut out
by a bolt of lightening.
In the end, you killed Huseyn out of enmity.
May your line die out!
You chained his wives in a line,
despised and bareheaded.
God is great, God is great.

Yazid: Did you see Huseyn in some city?
Did you touch your head to his foot?

European: Listen, I will tell one secret about this head.
Remember my gem-like words.
I was King John's ambassador

با سر چه گویی اکنون در اینجا
در عین شادی این گریه‌ها چیست
با خویش داری هر لحظه غوغا

فرنگی ـ پرسیدی از من ای گبر کافر
از کرده خویش بر خویش بنگر
ظلمی که دیدم از تو به اسلام
بالله نکرده کافر به کافر
اینها که دیدم از خاطرم رفت
در حیرتم من از صاحب سر
دارد چه قربی نزد خداوند
دارد چه قدری نزد پیمبر
کز آسمان‌ها تا سطح غُبرا
بینم ملائك پر بسته بر پر
باری به تفصیل اکنون بیان کن
احوال این سر با من سراسر
کاندر فرنگ این، قصه بخوانم
هر صبح و هر شام بالای منبر

یزید ـ پرسیدی از من احوال بشنو
چون گوسفندی ببریدمش سر
نامش حسین است فرزند حیدر
جدش محمد، زهراش مادر

فرنگی ـ امیدوارم از تیغ آذر
گردد زبانت قطع ای ستمگر
از کینه آخر کشتی حسین را
نسلت ور افتد گردی تو ابتر
بستی به زنجیر یك سر زنانش
در عین خواری، عاری ز چادر
الله اکبر، الله اکبر

یزید ـ آیا حسین را دیدی به شهری
آیا به پایش ساییده‌ای سر؟

فرنگی ـ بشنو بگویم سری از این سر
در گوش درکش حرفم چو گوهر
از یوحنا شاه ایلچی بدم من

to Medina, to the Prophet.
At once, I saw the face of this lord coming in.
like a shining moon.
Muhammad rose immediately,
He took him to his bosom like his own dear soul.
Zahra the Pure
put a vest on him.
The fastening was so tight around his pure throat,
you could see a circular line.
Muhammad kissed him constantly
and shed tears like pearl.
I asked him: 'Why you are crying?'
He said: 'This line will be cut with a dagger.'
I asked him where this event would be seen.
That glorious king said: 'At Karbalā.'
I asked: 'What is his worthy name?'
He said: 'His name is Huseyn. It is a pure name.'
I asked: 'Who will his killer be?'
He said: 'Yazid, an infidel.'

Yazid: If you have anything else to narrate, do it.
Tell me about the condition of this man.

Bahr-e tavil[25]

European: O Yazid, do you not know that this pure shining head, lying despised in the golden bowl, is a portion of Zahra's heart? You will not know and will not understand, unless I tell you this story: there was once a young gazelle, it was beautiful, elegant and delicate. In the open plains, it fell in a trap, and a hunter brought it before the Lord of 'But for Thee.'[26] He presented it to the lord of the spheres.

اندر مدینه نزد پیامبر
ناگه بدیدم از در درآمد
چون ماه تابان این صاحب سر
برخاست از جا آن دم محمد
چون جان شیرین بگرفت در بر
پیراهنی را پوشانده بودی
بر قامت او زهرای اطهر
از سختی بند بر حلق پاکش
بودی نمایان خطی مدور
بوسید او را هر دم محمد
می‌ریخت اشکش مانند گوهر
پرسیدم از وی این گریه از چیست؟
گفتا که برّند این خط به خنجر
گفتم کجا این، رخ می‌نماید؟
در کربلا گفت آن شاه با فر
گفتم چه باشد نام شریفش؟
گفتا حسین است، نامی مطهر
گفتم که او را قاتل که باشد؟
گفتا یزید است، یك مرد کافر

یزید- گر باز هم تو تعریف داری
برگو برایم از حال این سر

بحر طویل

فرنگی ـ ای یزید این سر پاکیزه پر نور که در طشت طلا خوار نظرهاست، ندانی که جگر گوشه زهراست؟ ندانی تو و نشناسی اگر، با تو من این قصه بگویم که یکی بره آهوی قشنگی و لطیفی و ظریفی به بیابان به یکی دام در افتاد و صیاد بیاورد بَرِ سید لولاك دهد تحفه به آن سرور افلاك.

That King of Religion, that companion and friend of the trustworthy Gabriel, took the fawn and gave it to Hasan. He was his little darling, his grandchild, the son of her Holiness, Zahra.

When Huseyn, another grandson [of the Prophet], saw Hasan's fawn, he jumped up and went directly to the *al-Aqsā* mosque.[27] He asked his grandfather, 'Where is my gazelle?' The Prophet said, 'Another gazelle will arrive at any moment. It is for Huseyn, the light of my eyes'.

At once a voice cried out from the throne [of God] to a mother gazelle, saying 'You are the ornament of the gazelles of the world, take your fawn quickly to the mosque of *al-Aqsā*, to the Ornament of the Prophets. He is going to give your fawn to Huseyn, the light of his eyes, so that the heart of that darling child should not be saddened'.

I will tell you another story. Once, the one whose head lies here, along with his grandfather who is the ornament of mankind, was on the way to the noble and pure house, as a guest.[28] At once a cloud appeared. It rained fire, and water. As Huseyn was passing through to go to his mother, the Prophet, who is the master and chief [of both worlds], turned his face to implore the heavens, saying, 'O Powerful Creator, stop the rain from this cloud for a while, so that it does not rain on the head of one who is the light of Zahra's heart and eyes'.

O Yazid! Son of the adulterous sinner Henda, the tyrant. You cut at the roots of Islam by killing one whom the Prophet loved and honoured. On top of that, why are you now beating his pure lips and teeth with a stick? May God cut off your hands, you wicked scoundrel! May God strike you dumb and cut off both your hands [*sic*] for killing the son of the Lion of God, Imām 'Ali.

گرفت آن شه دین، همدم و هم صحبت جبرئیل امین آن بره آهو به حسن داد، که فرزند عزیزش بُد و دلبند عزیزش، نوه‌اش، آن پسر حضرت زهرا.

چون دید حسین،آن پسر دیگر او برّه آهو بود از آنِ حسن، زود ز جا خاست، بشد راست سوی مسجد اقصی به بر جدّ کبارش که مگر آهوی من هست کجا؟ گفت نبی آهوی دیگر که بود مال حسین نور دوعین، می‌رسد از راه هم السّاعه، همین جا.

ناگه از عرش ندا آمد بر مادر آهو که تو ای فخر غزالان جهان بره خود را بدوان زود ببر مسجد اقصی به همان جا که بود فخر رسولان بدهد بره آهو به حسین نور دو عینش که نرنجد دل آن کودك دلبند دلارا.

بازگویم به تو یك قصه دیگر که همانا مگر این صاحب سر همره آن جدّ کبارش که بود فخر بشر داشت گذر تا که به بیت‌الشرف طاهره مهمان بشود، لیك عیان گشت به ناگاه سحابی، چه سحابی که فرو ریخت از آن آتش و آبی، چو حسین بود روان تا که رود در بر مادر، نبی آن سرور و سالار برآورد رخ عجز سوی گنبد دوّار که ای خالق جبّار، دمی بارش این ابر نگه دار، نریزد به سر آن که بود نور دل و دیده زهرا.

ای یزید، ای پسر هند زناکار خطاکار جفاپیشه زدی تیشه تو بر ریشه اسلام که کشتی تو کسی را که نبی داشت عزیزش، دگر اکنون تو چرا چوب زنی بر لب و دندان تمیزش، قَطَع الله یدیك، مردك بدکار، الهی که شوی لال و شود قطع دو دست تو

Yazid: Be silent, you Zoroastrian infidel!
I will order them to cut your head from your body.
Ho, executioner! Ho, executioner!
O Executioner you are a master of tyranny,
Cut off the head of this idol worshipper, for injustice's sake.

Šemr: Confess the Oneness of God, because I am going to cut your head from your body.
I am going to separate your soul from your body.

European: Stop it, you cursed, merciless, oppressor, Yazid.
I am a Christian, but I have not martyred the family of the Prophet.
You thirst for my blood: very well: give me some water.
Give a sip of water for my sorrowing, restless heart.

Yazid: O Šemr, give water to the European, for fidelity's sake,
then cut his head from his body.

Šemr: Yazid, we did not give water to Huseyn.
We martyred him while his lips were dry.
Why should I give water to the European?
It is not a sign of fairness and fidelity.
[To the European]: Take this crystal cup full of water,
Now, quench the fire in your heart with water.

European: [To Imām Huseyn] O thirsty one, you had no power over the dagger.
It seems you were a stranger and lost your mother.
[To Šemr]: I am a European, and you give me water.
You killed Huseyn while he was thirsty and distressed.
I will not drink this water, God forbid!
while Zahra's children are thirsty.
[To Imam 'Ebād]: O Memento of the King of the Virtuous,
make me a Muslim now.

که کُشتی پسر شیر خدا را.

یزید ـ لب را فرو بند ای گبر کافر
گویم ببرّند از پیکرت سر
جلاد! جلاد!
خطاب من به تو جلاد در جفا استاد
بزن تو گردن این بت پرست از بیداد

شمر ـ بگو شهاده که از سر تنت جدا سازم
میان جان و تنت طرح دوری اندازم

فرنگی ـ بس کن ای ملعون بی رحم ستمگر ای یزید
من نصارایم نکردم سبط پیغمبر شهید
باری ای تشنه به خونم تشنه‌ام آبم بده
جرعه آبی به قلب زار بی‌تابم بده

یزید ـ ای شمر آب ده به فرنگی تو از وفا
وانگاه رأس او بنما از بدن جدا

شمر ـ به حسین آب ندادیم، یزید
با لب تشنه نمودیم شهید
به فرنگی بدهم آب چرا
نبود شرط ز انصاف و وفا
جام بلوری، پر آب دریاب
بر آتش دل اکنون بزن آب

فرنگی ـ ای تشنه لب تو طاقت خنجر نداشتی
گویا غریب بودی و مادر نداشتی
ز اهل فرنگم، بر من دهی آب
کشتی حسین را بی آب و بیتاب
آبت ننوشم حاشا و کلاّ
لب تشنه باشد اولاد زهرا
ای یادگاری از شاه خوبان
اکنون بفرما من را مسلمان

Imam ʻEbād: You have been favoured, O devout European
that you confess the religion of Muhammad.
Say: ʻthere is no God but God,
Muhammad is the Messenger and ʻAli is the Vicegerent of God.'

European: O Master, on the Day of Resurrection, bear witness
that I said, ʻthere is no God but God
Muhammad is the Messenger and ʻAli is the Vicegerent of God.'

Šemr: Get out of here, European, because I am going to cut off your head.
I am going to separate your body from your soul.

European: I am delighted to go now, to the Messenger of God,
Saying, ʻthere is no God but God.
Muhammad is the Messenger and ʻAli is the Vicegerent of God.'

Yazid: Put the head of Huseyn Ibn ʻAli in a golden bowl,
Take it to his sorrowing daughter in the ruins.

Šemr: I place the head of Huseyn Ibn ʻAli in a golden bowl.
I take it to his sorrowing daughter in the ruins.

Zaynab: This scent is like the flowering path to Huseyn's door.
I am amazed! From whom can the scent of Huseyn be coming?
O Women! Huseyn has come, with honour and glory.
Offer all your souls at his feet.

Šemr: O group of prisoners! Huseyn's head is coming.
O army of mourning![29] The General of the two worlds is coming.

Zeynab: O head! My heart is crushed on seeing your face, brother, brother.

امام عباد ـ خوشا به حال تو باد ای فرنگی دین‌دار
که می‌کنی تو به دین محمدی اقرار
بگو که اشهد ان لا اله الا الله
محمد است رسول و علی ولی الله

فرنگی ـ گواه باش به روز قیامت ای آقا
که گفتم اشهد ان لا اله الا الله
محمد است رسول و علی ولی الله

شمر ـ برون برو تو فرنگی سرت جدا سازم
میان جان و تنت طرح دوری اندازم

فرنگی ـ روم ز شوق کنون جانب رسول الله
اقول اشهد ان لا اله الا الله
محمد است رسول و علی ولی الله

یزید ـ سر حسین علی را به طشت زر بنهید
برای دختر زارش سوی خرابه برید

شمر ـ سر حسین علی را به طشت زر بنهم
برای دختر زارش سوی خرابه برم

زینب ـ شمیم گلشن کوی حسین می‌آید
به حیرتم ز که بوی حسین می‌آید
مخدّرات، حسین آمده به عزّت و ناز
به پای او همه جان‌ها کنید پا انداز

شمر ـ ایا گروه اسیران سر حسین آمد
سپاه تعزیه، سردار عالمین آمد

زینب ـ ز دیدن رخت ای سر دلم به تنگ آمد برادر برادر

How strange, how strange, that you have remembered those who have no-one, brother, brother.
You are not on the road now; why do you have your face covered, brother, brother?
I am the one who came on foot, why are you tired, brother, brother?
You have come to this ruin without roof, without door, brother, brother,
Did you have no feet that you come with a head, brother, brother?

Zeynab: How black your lip is, O pearl on the exalted throne, my dear brother Huseyn.
If I am not mistaken, it is the sign of Yazid's stick, my dear brother Huseyn.
When they took your head to the monastery and church, my dear brother Huseyn,
They took me to the cities as a spectacle, my dear brother Huseyn.
I smelled the food in all the houses, my dear brother Huseyn,
But for three days and nights I went to sleep hungry, my dear Huseyn.
Drink no water, although you desire it, my brother, my brother,
No-one gave us water, not for forty stations,[30] my dear brother Huseyn.
Enough salt is poured on the wound in my heart, my brother, my brother,
To see your killer standing before me, dear brother Huseyn.
O Ruqiya! This is life for your lifeless body.
Good news, good news! Your father is our guest.

Ruqiya: O dear father, have you heard any news about me?
My hands are tied with rope, did you know that?
A yellow-haired [European] asked me from Yazid, to be his slave girl.
Did you know how despised I am?
Šemr slapped my face and said: 'you are orphaned'.
Alas, did you have any news of this pain and sorrow?

عجب عجب که تو را یاد بی کسان آمد برادر برادر
ز ره رسیده چرا روی بسته شدی برادر برادر
پیاده آمده‌ام من چرا تو خسته شدی برادر برادر
در این خرابه بی سقف و بی در آمده‌ای برادر برادر
مگر که پای نبودت که با سر آمده‌ای برادر برادر

زینب ـ کبودی لبت ای گوشوار عرش مجید برادر حسین جان
اگر غلط نکنم هست جای چوب یزید برادر حسین جان
سر تو را که به دیر و کلیسیا بردند برادر حسین جان
مرا برای تماشا به شهرها بردند برادر حسین جان
ز خانه همه بوی طعام بشنیدم برادر حسین جان
ولی سه روز و سه شب من گرسنه خوابیدم برادر حسین جان
نخوردی آب برادر، اگر به خواهش دل برادر برادر
به ما نداد کسی آب تا چهل منزل برادر حسین جان
نمک بس است بر جراحت دل من برادر برادر
همین که قاتلت استاده در برابر من برادر حسین جان
ای رقیه تن بی جان تو را جان آمد
مژده ده مژده که بابای تو مهمان آمد

رقیه ـ جان بابام ز من هیچ خبر داری تو؟
بسته دستم به رسن هیچ خبر داری تو؟
زردمویی ز یزیدم به کنیزی طلبید
از چنین خوار شدن هیچ خبر داری تو؟
شمر سیلی به رخم می‌زد و می‌گفت یتیم
وای از این رنج و محن هیچ خبر داری تو؟

The women gave me bread and dates, as alms.
Nothing passed my lips, did you hear any news of that?
The pillow for my head was gold brocade.
Now, a brick is my pillow, did you hear any news of that?
O Father, I have used an old worn rug,
to cover my body, did you hear any news of that?
[Soliloquy] I am so happy on seeing my father's beautiful face
that I am freed from the pain of the world.
O Aunt, come beside me for a moment.
Listen to this, my Will.
Take Akbar's curl,
when you go to Medina, give it to Suġrā.
O noble one! By the truth of the Qur'ān,
by the dignity of exalted 'Ali,
send me quickly to my father.
I am freed from the pain of the world.
O Father! The pain of separation from you takes me to the grave.
I say, I bear witness that there is no God but God.

Zeynab: O Muslims! Reason and wisdom have left me,
I do not hear the voice of my child.
O my nightingale, why are you silent?
O my dove, why have you swooned?
O my dear, why are you lifeless, having surrendered your life
like a rose petal, in a corner of this ruin.
Come my dear, that I may close your eyes,
I will stretch out your arms and legs towards the Kiblah.
Come, I will lay a brick under your head.
I am a sacrifice for your sorrow-filled heart.
O my dear ones, this is the ancient custom of the world.
Ruqiya's covering is a worn out rug.
O my master Huseyn, Zeynab's support,
Where are you, light of my eyes?
Why you do not enter these ruins?
Why are you separated from we prisoners?
O enfeebled 'Abedin, may I be your sacrifice!

نان و خرماست که زن‌ها به تصدق دادند
نگذارم به دهن هیچ خبر داری تو؟
متکّای سر من سُندَس و استبرق بود
خشت شد بالش من هیچ خبر داری تو؟
این گلیمی که شده مندرس و کهنه، پدر
کرده‌ام پوشش تن هیچ خبر داری تو؟
ز شوق روی جمال بابا
خلاص گشتم ز رنج دنیا
بیا به نزدم زمانی عمه
بده تو گوشی به این وصایا
بگیر از من تو زلف اکبر
مدینه رفتی بده به صغرا
بزرگوارا به حق قرآن
به حق جاه علی اعلا
رسان به زودی مرا به بابم
خلاص گشتم ز رنج دنیا
غم فراق تو بابا به گور بردم آه
اقول اشهد ان لا اله الا الله

زینب ـ مسلمانان ز سر شد عقل و هوشم
صدای طفل من ناید به گوشم
چرا ای بلبلم گشتی تو خاموش
چرا ای قمری‌ام گشتی تو مدهوش
چرا عمه چو برگ گل فسردی
در این کُنج خرابه جان سپردی
بیا عمه ببندم چشم‌هایت
گذارم سوی قبله دست و پایت
بیا خشتی نهم زیر سر تو
به قربان دل غم‌پرور تو
عزیزان رسم دنیا از قدیم است
رقیه پوششش کهنه گلیم است
ای یار زینب آقا حسینم
اندر کجایی ای نور عینم
در این خرابه از چه نیایی
از ما اسیران از چه جدایی
شوم فدای تو ای عابدین افسرده

May you live long, now that your sister is dead.

Imam 'Ebād: Come my sister that I may close your eyes.
I will stretch out your arms and legs towards the Kiblah.
O my sister! Why are you lifeless, having surrendered your life
like a rose petal, in this roofless ruin?
O God, O God! I am sorrowful and alone in the corner of this ruin.
O God, O God! To whom can I turn my face, in Damascus?

Zeynab: There is no candle, no lantern, no assistance or companion
There is no light in my dark night. O God, O God!

Imam 'Ebād: O my sister! I sacrifice myself for the chain on your neck.
I weep for your condition, O God, O God!

Zeynab: Yesterday this afflicted one [Ruqiya] said one word to me,
That burnt my wounded soul, O God, O God!

Imam 'Ebād: Tell me, what my afflicted sister said to you?
I am sorrowful and lamenting for her.

Zeynab: She said 'There is no one in Damascus as hungry as I am.'
I have no more strength or energy, O God, O God!

Yazid: One of you, go to the ruins,
Bring me some news quickly.

Šemr: I will go to the ruins again.
I will bring news for you, O ill-fated one.
O Yazid the unchivalrous, how long will you oppress?
O Yazid the unbridled, how long will you oppress?
The storm of tyranny has taken a rose.
O Yazid! A child has died in these ruins.
What a beautiful and well-spoken child she was.

سر تو باد سلامت که خواهرت مرده

امام عباد ـ بیا خواهر ببندم چشم‌هایت
گذارم سوی قبله دست و پایت
چرا خواهر چو برگ گل فسردی
در این ویرانه بی سقف مُردی
کنج خرابه بی کس و زارم خدا خدا
در شهر شام رو به که آرم خدا خدا

زینب ـ نه شمع و نه چراغ و نه یاری، نه همدمی
نوری نمانده در شب تارم خدا خدا

امام عباد ـ خواهر فدای دانه زنجیر گردنت
از بهر تو سرشك ببارم خدا خدا

زینب ـ دیروز این حزینه به من یك سخن بگفت
که آتش زده به جان فگارم خدا خدا

امام عباد ـ برگو چه گفت خواهر محزون من تو را؟
از بهر او غمینم و زارم خدا خدا

زینب ـ گفتا چو من گرسنه نباشد کسی به شام
دیگر توان و تاب ندارم خدا خدا

یزید ـ یکی اندر خرابه پا گذارد
خبر زودی برای من بیارد

شمر ـ روم اندر خرابه بار دیگر
خبر آرم برایت ای بد اختر
یزید ای بی مروت ظلم تا کی
یزید ای بی حمیّت ظلم تا کی
گلی را تندباد ظلم برده
یزید طفلی در این ویرانه مرده
چه طفل نیك روی خوش بیانی

She told her secret grief to me.
She told me, 'My father is dead,
I am an orphan, so people do not honour me.'
My heart burnt for her when they slapped her face.
Your slave girls pulled her hair from her head.

Šemr: O Yazid! Be manly, bridle your desires, you will be rewarded.
O Yazid! Zeynab's heart is burning tonight.

Yazid: Alas, that there is no cure for my pain.
On the Day of Judgment, Murtezā [Imam 'Ali] will be my enemy.
Go and tell the woman who washes the dead [the Ġassāla],
To wash Huseyn's pitiful child, with wailing and lamenting.

Šemr: Ho! Ġassāla, go and wash Huseyn's pitiful child,
with wailing and lamenting.

Ġassāla: O my dears, I am going to the ruins,
to wash the body of this dead child.
Greeting, you who are alone in the trap of affliction.
I wish you all well.
O my dears! Go to one side,
that I may wash the body of this dead child.
Why is the mouth of this child so dry?
Why is her pillow made of raw brick?
I am sure that she has no mother.
She is an orphan, she has no protector.
Why is the chin bound to her arm?
Why is her body afflicted and broken?
What was her sin in this life?
Who has bound her arm in this way?

Ġassāla: O Lady, may I ask you a question?

Zeynab: Ask your question, I have no heart [for this] any more.

به من می‌گفت غم‌های نهانی
به من می گفت من بابا ندارم
یتیمم پیش مردم جا ندارم
دلم سوزد زدند سیلی به رویش
کنیزانت ز سر کندند مویش

شمر ـ مروّت کن حمیّت کن صواب است
یزید امشب دل زینب کباب است

یزید ـ وای بر حالم که دردم بی دواست
دشمنم در روز محشر مرتضاست
رو بگو غسّاله با صد شور و شین
تا بشوید طفل افگار حسین

شمر ـ آی آی غسّاله با صد شور و شین
رو بشوی این طفل افگار حسین

غسّاله ـ روم اندر خرابه، ای عزیزان
بشویم پیکر این طفل بی جان
سلام ای بِی کسان در دام محنت
بگویم جملگی را سر سلامت
روید اندر کناری ای عزیزان
بشویم من تن این طفل بی جان
چرا این طفل این سان خشك کام است
چرا بالین او از خشت خام است
یقینم شد که او مادر ندارد
یتیم است و کسی بر سر ندارد
چرا زنجیر بر بازوش بسته
چرا جسمش شده رنجور و خسته
چه بوده جرم او در روزگاران
که بسته بازوی او را بدین سان؟

غسّاله ـ الا ای زن سؤالی از تو دارم

زینب ـ سؤالت را بگو من دل ندارم

Ġassāla: It seems that you are the first among these women.

Zeynab: Why do you pour salt on my wounds?

Ġassāla: Why is her neck as black as tar?

Zeynab: Know that this sign shows that she was chained.

Ġassāla: Why has a thorn pricked her foot?

Zeynab: She was running in the desert so much.

Ġassāla: I am sure that she has no mother.
She is an orphan and has no protector.
I am not going to wash her body right now.
They have killed this child with sticks and stones.

The family of the Prophet (in unison): Where are you Fātima?
O mother! Where are you?
In the corner of these ruins?
Why you do not visit your children
in the corner of these ruins?
O Sphere! Was it fair, that in Karb-o balā,
you inflicted such injustice on Huseyn?
See what you have done to those whose hearts burned!
O Sphere, may your house prosper!

غسّاله ـ بزرگ این زنان گویا تو باشی

زینب ـ نمك بر زخم من بهر چه پاشی؟

غسّاله ـ چرا پس گردنش قیر است ای زن؟

بدان این جای زنجیر است ای زن

چرا خاری به پای او خلیده؟

زینب ـ ز بس اندر بیابان‌ها دویده

غسّاله ـ یقینم شد که او مادر ندارد
یتیم است و کسی بر سر ندارد
من نمی‌شویم تن او بی درنگ
کشته‌اند این طفل را با چوب و سنگ

اهل بیت با هم ـ کجایی فاطمه مادر کجایی
در این کنج خرابه
چرا سر وقت طفلانت نیایی
در این کنج خرابه
کی روا بود که در کرب و بلا
به حسین این همه بیداد فلك!
آنچه کردی به جگر سوختگان
خانمانت همه آباد فلك!

Notes

1 Q. 4:145.
2 Q. 26:227.
3 گر توانی بکش حلالش کن: the meaning is obscure: 'release him from his misery' may be meant.
4 Q. 114/4-5.
5 I.e., Without armour.
6 The heads are carried in on lances.
7 In mystic poetry and love poetry, the lover is 'drawn to the bazaar': he wanders in public showing how love has maddened him.
8 *Fate, destiny.*
9 '*eyd-e qurbān*', the last day of the pilgrimage to Mecca, when sheep are sacrificed.
10 *dār al-Nazām.*
11 Literally 'Aunt', an affectionate name for her maid, who appears below.
12 Zaynab and her sister 'Umm-e Kulṯūm.
13 Nonsense words, to show that the speaker is a foreigner.
14 In Steingass's Persian dictionary (1892), *dūr-bin* is a telescope and the players would presumably have had two telescopes as props. Nowadays the word refers to a camera.
15 Ahmad is a name of the Prophet Muhammad.
16 Fātima, the daughter of Imām Huseyn, is called *Now 'arūs* throughout the text, perhaps to avoid confusion with Fātima, the daughter of the Prophet Muhammad.
17 Zahrā is a title of Fātima, the Prophet's daughter.
18 There is a play on two meanings of *'aziz* here: grandeur and beloved.
19 Seven and four allude to the seven planets: the moon, Mercury, Venus, the Sun, Mars, Jupiter and Saturn; and the four elements: air, wind, fire and water. See A.A. Seyed-Gohrab, *The Mirror of Meanings*, p. 2.
20 Hūr-e 'eyn, referring to the Qur'ān 44/55.
21 Reading *'eyn* as the plural of *a'yān,* the word has different meanings; the name of a letter 'eyn, eye; source; essence; and appearance. With respect to the meanings the line may be translated in different ways. See A.A. Seyed-Gohrab, *The Mirror of Meanings*, p. 22.
22 Bū Turāb is a title of Imām 'Ali.
23 Lit: 'in the tower of the contingent world,' but 'tower' here refers to a sign of the zodiac.
24 In the Islamic tradition, the story of Adam and Eve is located in Ceylon.
25 This refers to the metre of the section that follows: 'long' metre.
26 A title of the Prophet, referring to a tradition in which God says: 'But for thee, I would not have created the heavens.'

27 *Sic.* When this *ta'ziya* text was composed, this could only refer to the *al-Aqsa* mosque in Jerusalem.

28 This could be a particular house known by this title, but the term is not in common use today. The meaning may simply be that the Prophet has been invited to a noble, pure house.

29 *Sepah-e ta'ziya*, referring both to the defeated remnants of Huseyn's army, and the audience of the *ta'ziya*.

30 Meaning stations on the road, where travellers stop.

Bibliography

Afra, H., *Encyclopaedia Britannica*, under Reza Shah Pahlavi.

Aghaie, K.S., *Martyrs of Karbalā: Shi'i Symbols and Rituals in Modern Iran*, Seattle: The University of Washington Press, 2004.

___., 'The Gender Dynamics of Moharram Symbols and Rituals in the Latter Years of Qajar Rule,' in *The Women of Karbalā: Ritual Performance and Symbolic Discourses in Modern Shi'i Islam* ed. K.S. Aghaie, Austin: The University of Texas Press, 2005.

Andrzej, W., 'Semiological Aspects of Ta'ziyeh,' in *Ta'ziyeh: Ritual and Drama in Iran,* ed. P.J. Chelkowski, New York: New York University Press & Soroush Press, 1979.

Ansary, P.R., 'The Ta'ziyeh of the Martyrdom of Hussein,' in *The Drama Review*, vol. 49, no. 4 (T118), Winter 2005.

Ayati, I., *A Probe into the History of Ashura*, Karachi: Islamic Seminary Publications, [n.d.].

Ayoub, M., in *Encyclopaedia Iranica,* under 'Arba'in.

___., in *Encyclopaedia Iranica,* under 'Āšūrā.

___., *Redemptive Suffering in Islām: A Study of the Devotional Aspects of 'Āshūrā in Twelver Shi'ism*, The Hague: Mouton Publishers, 1978.

Baktash, M., 'Ta'ziyeh and its Philosophy,' in *Ta'ziyeh: Ritual and Drama in Iran,* ed. P.J. Chelkowski, New York: New York University Press & Soroush Press, 1979.

Bar-Asher, M.M., *Scripture and Exegesis in Early Imāmī Shiism*, Jerusalem: The Magnes Press, 1999.

Bassett, J., *Persia the Land of the Imams: a Narration of Travel and Residence 1871-1885*, London: Black & Son, 1887.

Beeman, W.O. & Ghaffari, M.B., 'Acting Styles and Actor Training in Ta'ziyeh,' in *The Drama Review,* vol. 49, no. 4 (T118), Winter 2005.

Beeman, W.O., *Iranian Performance Tradition*, California: Mazda Publications, 2011.

___., 'Cultural Dimensions of Performance Conventions in Iranian Ta'ziyeh,' in *Ta'ziyeh: Ritual and Drama in Iran,* ed. P.J. Chelkowski, New York: New York University Press & Soroush Press, 1979.

Bilgrami, M.H., *The Victory of Truth: The Life of Zeynab bint 'Ali,* Karachi: Zahra Publications, 1986.

Bulūkbāši, A., *Ta'ziya-khāni, hadiṭ-e qudsi-ye maṣā'eb dar namāyeš-e ā'ini*, Tehran: entešārāt-e Amir Kabir, 1383/2004.

Bosworth, C.E., in *The Encyclopaedia of Islam* (second edition), under Qisma (a.), Qismet (t.).

Boyce, M., *Zoroastrians Their Religious Beliefs and Practices*, London: Routledge & Kegan Paul Ltd, 1979.

Browne, E.G., *A Literary History of Persia (1500-1924)*, vol. iv, Cambridge: The University Press, 1924.

Bruijn, J.T.P. de, in *Encyclopaedia Iranica*, under Elegy.

___., in *Encyclopedia of Islam* (second edition) Muḥtas̲h̲am Kās̲h̲āni.

Burney Abbas, Sh., 'Sakineh, The Narrator of Karbalā: An Ethnographic Description of a Women's *Majles* Rituals in Pakistan,' in *The Women of Karbalā: Ritual Performance and Symbolic Discourses in Modern Shi'i Islam,* ed. K.S. Aghaie, Austin: The University of Texas Press, 2005.

Calmard, J., in *Encyclopaedia Iranica*, under 'Abbas B. 'Ali.

___., in *Encyclopaedia Iranica*, under 'Ali Akbar.

___., in *Encyclopaedia Iranica*, under 'Alam va 'Alamat.

___., in *Encyclopaedia Iranica*, under 'Ali Asġar.

___., in *Encyclopaedia Iranica*, under 'Azādārī.

Chelkowski, P.J., 'Ta'ziyeh: Indigenous Avant-Garde Theater of Iran,' in *Ta'ziyeh Ritual and Drama in Iran*, ed. P.J. Chelkowski, New York: New York University Press & Soroush Press, 1979.

___., in *Encyclopaedia Iranica*, under Dasta.

___., in *The Encyclopaedia of Islam* (second edition), under Hosayn Ibn 'Ali.

___., 'From Maqātil Literatrue to Drama,' in *al-Serāt*, vol. xii, Paper from Imam Huseyn Conference, London: Routledge & Kegan Paul ltd, 1986.

___., 'Dramatic and Literary Aspects of Ta'zieh-khani – Iranian Passion Play,' *Review of National Literature*, ed. Anne Paolucci & Javad Haidari, vol. ii, no. 1, spring 1971.

___., 'From the Sun-Scorched Desert of Iran to the Beaches of Trinidad: Ta'zieh's Journey from Asia to the Caribbean,' in *The Drama Review*, vol. 49, no. 4 (T118), Winter 2005.

___., 'Iconography of the Women of Karbalā: Tiles, Murals, Stamps, and Posters,' in *The Women of Karbalā: Ritual Performance and Symbolic Discourses in Modern Shi'i Islam,* ed. K.S. Aghaie, Austin: The University of Texas Press, 2005.

___., 'Art for Twenty-Four Hours,' in *Islamic Art in the 19th Century: Tradition, Innovation, and Eclecticicism*, eds. D. Behrens-Abouseif & S. Vernoit, Leiden: Brill, 2006.

___., 'Islam in Modern Drama and Theater,' in *Die Welt des Islams*, New Series, Bd., 23/24 (1984).

___., 'Popular Shī'ī Mourning Ritual,' in *al-Serāt*, vol. xii, Paper from Imam Huseyn Conference, London: Routledge & Kegan Paul ltd, 1986.

____., 'Shia Muslim Performance,' in *The Drama Review*, vol. 29, no. 3, Processional Performance (Autumn, 1985).

Cohlberg, E., in *The Encyclopaedia of Islam* (second edition), under Shahīd.

Daniel, E.L. & A.A. Mahdi, *Culture and Customs of Iran*, Westport, CT: Greenwood Press, 2006.

Deeb, L.Z., 'From Mourning to Activism: Seyyedeh Zaynab, Lebanese Shiʻi Woman, and the Transformation of Ashura,' in *The Women of Karbalā: Ritual Performance and Symbolic Discourses in Modern Shiʻi Islam,* ed. K.S. Aghaie, Austin: The University of Texas Press, 2005.

El-Awa, S.M.S., in *Encyclopaedia of the Qurʾān*, under Zaqqūm.

Fahd. T., in *The Encyclopaedia of Islam* (second edition), under Sakina.

Finnegan, R., *Literacy and Orality Studies in the Technology of Communication*, Oxford: Opus, 1988.

Fischer, M.M.J., *Iran: From Religious Dispute to Revolution*, Cambridge & Mass, London: Harvard University Press, 1980.

Flaskerud, I., 'Oh, My Heart is Sad. It is Moharram, the Month of Zeynab: The Role of Aesthetics and Women's Mourning in Ceremonies in Shiraz,' in *The Women of Karbalā: Ritual Performance and Symbolic Discourses in Modern Shiʻi Islam*, ed. K.S. Aghaie, Austin: The University of Texas Press, 2005.

Gardet, L., in *The Encyclopaedia of Islam* (second edition), under Ikhtīyār.

____., in *The Encyclopaedia of Islam* (second edition), under Ḳiyāma.

Garsoian, N., 'Bizantium and the Sasanian,' in *The Cambridge History of Iran, the Seleucid, Partian and Sasanian Periods*, vol. 3(1) ed. E. Yarshater, Cambridge: Cambridge University Press, 1983.

Ghadially, R., 'Gender and Moharram Rituals in an Ismaʻili Sect of South Asian Muslims,' in *The Women of Karbalā: Ritual Performance and Symbolic Discourses in Modern Shiʻi Islam,* ed. K.S. Aghaie, Austin: The University of Texas Press, 2005.

Gimaret, D., in *The Encyclopaedia of Islam* (second edition), under Shahāda.

Graf, F., in *The Encyclopaediaof Islam* (second edition), under Predestination, the Theory of.

Haar, J.G.J. ter, 'Taʻziye: Ritual Theater from Shiite Iran,' in *Theatre Intercontinental: Forms, Functions, Correspondences*, eds. C.C. Barfoot & C. Bordewijk, Amsterdam: Rodopi, 1993.

Hanaway, Jr. & William, L., 'Stereotyped Imagery in Taʻziyeh,' in *Taʻziyeh: Ritual and Drama in Iran,* ed. P.J. Chelkowski, New York: New York University Press & Soroush Press, 1979.

Hasson, I., in *Encyclopaedia of the Qurʾān*, under Left hand and right hand.

Hawting, G.R., in *The Encyclopaedia of Islam* (second edition), under Al-Mukhtār b. Abī 'Ubayd al-Thaqafī.

Hegland, M.E, 'Two Images of Huseyn: Accommodation and Revolution in an Iranian Village,' in *Religion and Politics in Iran: Shiʻism from Quietism to Revolution*, ed. N.R. Keddie, New Haven & London: Yale University Press, 1983.

___, 'Women of Karbalā Moving to America: Shi'i Rituals in Iran, Pakistan, and California,' in *The Women of Karbalā: Ritual Performance and Symbolic Discourses in Modern Shi'i Islam,* ed. K.S. Aghaie, Austin: The University of Texas Press, 2005.

Herzfeld, M., 'In Defiance of Destiny: The Management of Time and Gender at a Cretan Funeral,' *American Ethnologist*, vol. 20, no. 2 (May, 1993).

Heyder, S.A., 'Sayyedeh Zaynab: The Conqueror of Damascus and Beyond,' in *The Women of Karbalā: Ritual Performance and Symbolic Discourses in Modern Shi'i Islam,* ed. by K.S. Aghaie, Austin: The University of Texas Press, 2005.

Humāyūni, Ṣ., *Shirāz khāstgāh-e ta'ziya,* [Shiraz]: Bonyād-e Fārsšenāsi, 1377/1998.

___., *Ta'ziya va ta'ziya khāni*, [Tehran]: čāpkhana bist-o panjom-e šahrivar, [1354/1975].

___., 'A View from the Inside, the Anatomy of the Persian Ta'ziyeh Plays,' in *The Drama Review*, vol. 49, no. 4 (T118), Winter 2005.

___., *Ta'ziya dar Iran,* Tehran: Navid, 1368/1989.

Jafri, M.S.H., *The Origins and Early Development of Shi'a Islam*, Qum: Ansariyan Publications, 1989.

Kāšefi, Ḥuseyn Wā'ez, *Rawżat al-Šuhadā*, ed. Ḥ. Ṣirāni, Tehran: Eslāmmiya, 1371/1982.

Káldy, N.G., in *The Encyclopaedia of Islam* (second edition), under Ḳadā.

Kohlberg, E., in *Encyclopaedia Iranica*, under 'Ali B. Abī Ṭāleb.

Kohlberg, E. & I.K. Poonawala, in *The Encyclopaedia of Islam* (second edition), under Muslim b. Aqīl B. Abī Ṭālib.

Kohlberg, E., in *The Encyclopaedia of Islam* (second edition), under Shahīd.

___., *Medieval Muslim Views on Martrydom*, Amsterdam, KNAW Press, 1997.

Kruk, R., 'The Bold and the Beautiful: Women and 'Fitna' in the Sirat Dhat al-Himma: the Story of Nūra,' in *Women in the Medieval Islamic World, Power, Patronage, and Piety,* ed. G.R.G. Hambly, New York: St. Martin's press, 1998.

Leemhuis, F., in *Encyclopaedia of the Qur'ān,* under Apocalypse.

Losensky, P., in *Encyclopaedia Iranica,* under Muḥtašam Kāšānī, Šams-al-šo'arā Kamāl al-Dīn.

Losensky, P.E., in *The Encyclopaedia of Islam* (second edition), under Waqār.

Madigan, D., in *Encyclopaedia of the Qur'ān*, under Preserved Tablet.

Mahjub, M.J., 'The Effect of European Theater and the Influence of its Theatrical Methods upon Ta'ziyeh,' in *Ta'ziyeh: Ritual and Drama in Iran*, ed. P.J. Chelkowski, New York: New York University Press & Soroush Press, 1979.

Mamnoun, P., 'Ta'zieh from the View Point of the Eastern Theatre,' in *Ta'ziyeh: Ritual and Drama in Iran*, ed. P.J. Chelkowski, New York: New York University Press & Soroush Press, 1979.

Moomen, M., *An Introduction to Shi'i Islam, the History of Doctrines of Twelver Shi'ism*, Oxford: George Ronald, 1985.

Morabia, A., in *The Encyclopaedia of Islam* (second edition), under Lawn.

Morier, J., *Second Journey through Persia, Armenia, and Asia Minor between the Years 1810-1816*, London: Longman & *et al.*, 1818.

Mostofi, A., *The Administrative and Social History of the Qajar Period: The Story of My Life*, vol. I, From Agha Muḥammad khan to Naṣer al-Din Shah (1794-1896), trans. by Nayer Mostofi Glenn, Costa Messa Californa: Mazda Publishers, 1997.

Mottahedeh, N., 'Karbalā Drag Kings and Queens,' in *The Drama Review*, vol. 49, no. 4 (T118), Winter 2005.

___., '*Ta'ziyeh*: A Twist of History in Everyday Life,' in *The Women of Karbalā: Ritual Performance and Symbolic Discourses in Modern Shi'i Islam*, ed. K.S. Aghaie, Austin: The University of Texas Press, 2005.

Murata S., *The Tao of Islam: A Sourcebook on Gender Relationships in Islamic Thought*, Albany, N.Y.: State University of New York Press, 1992.

Narasimahan, R., 'Literacy: Its Characterization and Implications,' in *Literacy and Orality*, ed. D.R. Olson & N. Torrance, New York: Cambridge University Press, 1991.

Nasr, S.H., Dabashi, H. & Nasr, S.V.R., *Expectation of the Millennium Shi'isim in History*, Albany, N.Y.: State University of New York Press, 1989.

Pelly, L., *The Miracle Play: Hasan and Husain*, vol. I & II, London: W.M.H. Allen & Co., 1879.

Pinault, D., 'Zaynab bint 'Ali and the Place of the Women of the Households of the First Imāms in Shiite Devotional Literature,' in *Women in the Medieval Islamic World Power, Patronage and Piety*, ed. G.R.G. Hambly, New York: St. Martin's Press, 1998.

___., *The Shiites: Ritual and Popular Piety in a Muslim Community*, London: I.B. Tauris & Co Ltd Publishers, 1992.

Ponafidine, P., *Life in the Moslem East*, trans. by E.C. Ponafidine, London: Hodder and Stoughton, 1911.

Radtke, B., *et al.*, in *The Encyclopaedia of Islam* (second edition), under Walī (A., Pl. Awlīyā).

Rosiny, S., 'The tragedy of Fāṭima al-Zahrā, in the Debate of two Shiite Theologians in Lebanon,' in *The Twelver Shia in Modern Times, Religious, Cultures and Political History*, eds. R. Brunner & W. Ende, Leiden: Brill, 2001.

Ruffle, K.G., *Gender, Sainthood, & Everyday Practice in South Asian Shi'ism*, North Carolina: The University of North Carolina Press, 2011.

Ṣafā, Dh.A., & EIr, in *Encyclopaedia Iranica*, under Hātef, Sayyed, Aḥmad Eṣfahānī.

Sāleḥi, N. Najafābādi, *Šahid-e jāvid* (The Eternal Martyr), Tehran: mu'assesa-ye khadamāt-e farhangi-ye Rasā, 1361/1982.

Sāleḥi Rād Darbandsari, H., *Majālis-e ta'ziya*, vol. 2, Tehran: Soroush, 1380/2001.

Savory, R.M. & C.E. Bosworth, in *The Encyclopaedia of Islam* (second edition), under Tahmāsp (Tahmasb).

Schimmel, A., in *The Encyclopaedia of Islam* (second edition), under Color.

___., *Mystical Dimensions of Islam*, Chapel Hill: University of North Carolina Press, 1975.

Schmidt, H.P., in *Encyclopaedia Iranica*, under Mithra, I. Mitra in Old Indian and Mithra in Old Iranian.

Seyed-Gohrab, A.A., 'The Symbolism of Veiling and the Poetics of Unveiling in Early Modern Persian Poetry,' in *Khil'a: Journal of Dress and Textiles in the Islamic World*, no. 1, Leuven: Peeters, 2005, pp. 107-121.

___., *The Mirror of Meanings*, Costa Mesa, California: Mazda Publishers, 2002.

___., *Layli and Majnūn, Love Madness and Mystic Longing in Nizāmī's Epic Romance*, Leiden & Boston: Brill, 2003.

___., *Van Mystieke Weg tot Oorlogspad*, Amsterdam: KNAW Press, 2009.

Shaham, R., in *The Encyclopaedia of Islam* (second edition), under Yatīm.

Shahidi, A., 'Literary and Musical Developments in the Ta'ziyeh,' in *Ta'ziyeh: Ritual and Drama in Iran*, ed. P.J. Chelkowski, New York: New York University Press & Soroush Press, 1979.

Shaki, M., in *The Encyclopaedia of Islam* (second edition), under Ḳā'ānī.

Sharma, S., *Persian Poetry at Indian Frontier, Mas'ud Sa'd Salman of Lahore*, Oxford: Permanent Black, 2000.

Shirazi, F., 'The Daughters of Karbalā: Images of Women in Popular Shi'i Culture in Iran,' in *The Women of Karbalā: Ritual Performance and Symbolic Discourses in Modern Shi'i Islam*, ed. K.S. Aghaie, Austin: The University of Texas Press, 2005.

Smith, J.I., *Encyclopaedia of the Qur'ān*, under Eschatology, The Reckoning (al-ḥisāb).

___., *Encyclopaedia of the Qur'ān*, under Eschatology, The Bliss of the Gardens.

___., in *Encyclopaedia of the Qur'ān*, under Eschatology, the Crossing the Bridge (*ṣirāt*), the Possibility of Intercession (*shefā'a*) and Preparation for the Final Consignment.

___., in *Encyclopaedia of the Qur'ān*, under Eschatology, Human Life and Death.

___., in *Encyclopaedia of the Qur'ān*, under Eschatology, the Torment of the Fire (*al-nār*).

Solomon, R.C., & Kathleen, M.H., *From Africa to Zen: An Invitation to World Philosophy*, Rowman & Littlefield, 2003.

Sundermann, W., in *Encyclopaedia Iranica*, under Mithra, III. in Manicheism.

Al-Tabari, Abū Ja'far Muhammad Ibn Jarīr, *The History of al-Tabari*, vol. xix, The Caliphate of Yazid Ibn Mu'āwiyah, trans. I.K.A. Howard, New York: State University of New York Press, 1990.

Taqiyān, L., *Dar bāra-ye ta'ziya va te'ātr dar Iran*, Tehran: Našr-e markaz, 1374/1995.

Tešna dar miqātgah, matn va matnšenāsi-ye ta'ziya, tasḥiḥ va taḥlil az Ḥuseyn Ismā'ili, Tehran: Našr-e mo'in, 1389/2010.

The Glory of the Shia World: The Tale of a Pilgrimage, trans. by P.M. Sykes, London: Macmillan & Co., 1910.

The Koran Interpreted, trans. A. Arberry, London: Allen & Unwin, 1955.

Toolan, M.J., *Narrative, a Critical Linguistic Introduction*, London & New York: Routledge, 1988.

Tucker, J.E., 'Women in the Middle East and North Africa: The Nineteenth and Twentieth Centuries,' in *Women in the Middle East and North Africa*, ed. G. Neshat and J.E. Tucker, Indiana: Indiana University Press, 1999.

Turner, C., *Islam without Allah? The Rise of Religion Externalism in Safavid Iran*, Richmond: Curzon, 2002.

Vaglieri, L.V., in *The Encyclopaedia of Islam* (second edition) under Khaybar.

___., in *The Encyclopaedia of Islam* (second edition) under (al-)Ḥasan b. 'Alī b. Abī Ṭālib.

___., in *The Encyclopaedia of Islam* (second edition), under Ghadīr Khumm.

Walter J.O., *Orality and Literacy the Technologizing of the World*, London & New York: Methuen, 1982.

Warnock Fernea, E., & B.Q. Bezirgan, 'Women's Religious Rituals in Iraq,' in *The Women of Karbalā: Ritual Performance and Symbolic Discourses in Modern Shi'i Islam*, ed. K.S. Aghaie, Austin: The University of Texas Press, 2005.

Yarshater, E., 'Ta'ziyeh and Pre-Islamic Mourning Rites in Iran,' in *Ta'ziyeh: Ritual and Drama in Iran*, ed. P.J. Chelkowski, New York: New York University Press & Soroush Press, 1979.

___., 'Iranian National History,' in *The Cambridge History of Iran, the Seleucid, Parthian and Sasanian Periods*, vol. 3 (1), ed. E. Yarshater, Cambridge: Cambridge University Press, 1983.

Zarrinkūb, A.H., 'The Arab Conquest of Iran and its Aftermath,' in *The Cambridge History of Iran*, vol. 4, ed. R.N. Frye, Cambridge: Cambridge University Press, 1975.

Index

Backlist IRANIAN STUDIES SERIES

J.C. Bürgel & C. van Ruymbeke (eds.)
A Key to the Treasure of the Hakīm. Artistic and Humanistic Aspects of Nizami Ganjavi's Khamsa
ISBN 978 90 8728 097 0

J. Coumans
The Rubáiyát of Omar Khayyám. An Updated Bibliography
ISBN 978 90 8728 096 3

F. Lewis & S. Sharma (eds.)
The Necklace of the Pleiades. 24 Essays on Persian Literature, Culture and Religion
ISBN 978 90 8728 091 8

C. Pérez González
Local Portraiture. Through the Lens of the 19th-Century Iranian Photographers
ISBN 978 90 8728 156 4

A. Sedighi
Agreement Restrictions in Persian
ISBN 978 90 8728 093 2

A.A. Seyed-Gohrab
Courtly Riddles. Enigmatic Embellishments in Early Persian Poetry
ISBN 978 90 8728 087 1

A.A. Seyed-Gohrab (ed.)
The Great 'Umar Khayyam A Global Reception of the Rubáiyát
ISBN 978 90 8728 157 1

A.A. Seyed-Gohrab & S.R.M. McGlinn (eds.)
One Word – Yak Kaleme. 19th-Century Persian Treatise Introducing Western Codified Law
ISBN 978 90 8728 089 5

A.A. Seyed-Gohrab & S.R.M. McGlinn (eds.)
Safina Revealed. A Compendium of Persian Literature in 14th-Century Tabriz
ISBN 978 90 8728 088 8

A.A. Seyed-Gohrab, F. Doufikar-Aerts & S. McGlinn (eds.)
Embodiments of Evil: Gog and Magog. Interdisciplinary Studies of the 'Other' in Literature & Internet Texts
ISBN 978 90 8728 090 1

S. Tabatabai
Father of Persian Verse. Rudaki and his Poetry
ISBN 978 90 8728 092 5

K. Talattof & A.A. Seyed-Gohrab (eds.)
Conflict and Development in Iranian Film
ISBN 978 90 8728 169 4

R. Rahmoni & G. van den Berg (eds.)
The Story of Barzu. As told by two storytellers from Boysun, Uzbekistan
ISBN 978 90 8728 116 8

Forthcoming titles in the IRANIAN STUDIES SERIES

J.T.P. de Bruijn, *The Journey of the Faithful to the Place of Return. A Persian Allegory on the Development of the Human Soul by Sanâ'i of Ghazna, Founding Father of Persian Sufism*

J.T.L. Cheung, *The Nartic Epic Tradition. Remnants of Iranian Lore from the Caucasus*

S.R.M. McGlinn, *Abdul-Baha's Sermon on the Art of Governance*

Bahman Solati, *The Reception of Hafiz. Sweet Poetic Language of Hafiz in Nineteenth and Twentieth Century Persia*